$30.00

D0086491

# British Sieges
## of the
# Peninsular War

SPELLMOUNT

**Staplehurst**

# British Sieges
## of the
# Peninsular War

by
**Frederick Myatt**

*For Liz*

British Library Cataloguing in Publication Data:
A catalogue record for this book is available from the British Library

Copyright © 1987 Frederick Myatt

ISBN 0–946771–59–6

This printing published in the UK in 1995 by
SPELLMOUNT LIMITED
The Old Rectory
Staplehurst
Kent TN12 0AZ

1 3 5 7 9 8 6 4 2

The right of Frederick Myatt to be identified
as the author of this work has been asserted by him in
accordance with the Copyright, Designs and Patents act 1985

All rights reserved. No part of this publication may be reproduced,
stored in a retrieval system or transmitted in any form or by any
means, electronic, mechanical, photocopying, recording or otherwise,
without prior permission in writing from Spellmount Limited, Publishers.

Printed and bound in Great Britain by
Butler & Tanner Ltd, Frome and London

# British Sieges of the Peninsular War

# INTRODUCTION

The Peninsular War is a subject of perennial interest to students of British military history, and so much has been written about it in the last hundred and seventy years or so that few aspects remain uncovered. There does however appear to be a place for a fairly specialized study of the various sieges conducted by the British and their allies in the period 1811-1813; the major historians of the war, Napier, Fortescue, and Oman, all naturally give good general accounts of them, and Maj-Gen Jones's highly technical three-volume work is almost entirely devoted to them, but apart from the fact that few of these works are easily available to the general reader, there also seems to be a need for something in between. This being so it is hoped that this book will go some way towards filling the gap.

The Peninsular Army is perhaps best remembered for its mobility—an army in the words of the Duke of Wellington could 'go anywhere and do anything'. Yet from time to time it was essential for the furtherance of his broad plans that some strong place should pass firmly into British hands before any further progress could be made. These resulting sieges were often strange affairs, conducted on both sides by skilled engineers carrying out a series of more of less stylised moves, made all the more incomprehensible to the outsider by being described in a highly technical jargon, mainly French in origin. When these preliminaries had reached a certain stage however, brute force then took over in the hopes of finally bringing the operation to a successful, if often bloody, conclusion, this in its turn being frequently succeeded by conduct so hideous on the part of the assaulting troops as to defy description. It is perhaps one of the strange paradoxes of human nature that orderly, well-disciplined soldiers would behave with supreme gallantry until success had been achieved, when, in a flash, they abandoned all pretext of discipline, decency, or human feelings, until exhaustion (allied to the fear of the rope or lash) brought them back to their duty. This said, it may be as well to add that this book is mainly a study of military affairs, and is only incidentally concerned with human depravity.

In order to make the book comprehensible to the non-technical reader the first chapter consists of a general dissertation on siege-craft, (supported by a glossary at the end of the book), together with a broad outline of the role and capacity of siege artillery. A brief precis of connecting events is also included in each chapter so that the sieges themselves can be seen in their proper context. Although good maps are essential for a work of this kind it is desirable that they should be clear and simple, since nothing is more frustrating than having them so cluttered with symbols, lines, and arrows that they are unintelligible. This is all the more important because it is no longer possible to provide the large folding maps so often found in earlier works. The maps used here are based broadly on those of General Jones's work (second edition) although much simplified for the reasons given. I started collecting books on the Peninsular War in 1946 and now have a sufficiently good library to be largely independent of other sources. Inevitably there were some gaps to be filled and I am grateful to the Librarian and Staff of the Ministry of Defence Library (army and central) for their untiring efforts in this direction, and I must thank Maj-Gen B P Hughes CB, CBE for his patience in answering endless questions on the subject of 19th century artillery, on which he is an authority. I must also pay tribute to my old war-time friend Colonel D G Dickson OBE, MC, TD, now alas dead. We shared a common interest in the Peninsular War and spent many interesting days walking Spanish and Portuguese battlefields together.

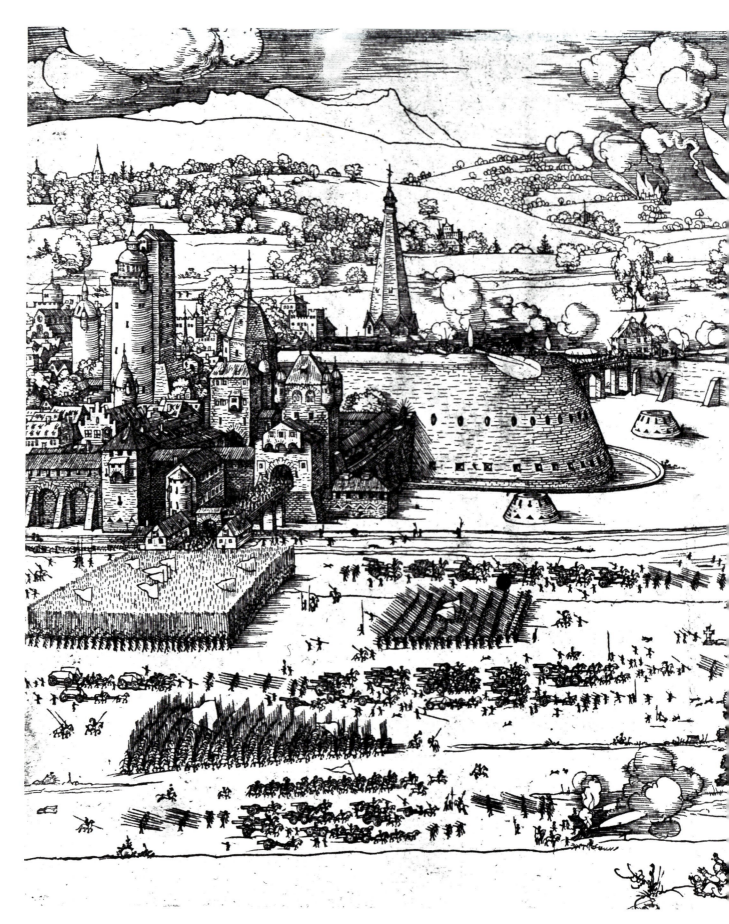

# CHAPTER ONE
## Siege Craft

Before the invention of gunpowder the main requirement for any fortified place was height. It was very difficult to breach a well-built wall with a battering ram in the face of a resolute defence, and although mining beneath the foundations might cause it to collapse this was at best a slow and tedious operation even in suitable soil. When the wall was based on rock, which was often the case, it was impossible. This being so, the only method of entry was over the wall, and sometimes movable towers could be used for this purpose. Often however attackers had to resort to using heavy, clumsy, locally-improvised scaling ladders, a form of attack easily repelled by even a few determined men.

The steady development of the gun changed all this, for the hitherto impregnable wall was extremely vulnerable to cannon. Progress was of course slow, but by the early 16th century it was probable that a practicable breach could eventually be made. Fortresses constructed in the modern, *ie* post-gunpowder, styles were thus planned completely differently, and as far as possible adopted a low profile, height of rampart being achieved by the use of deep ditches. Ideally all that should be visible to an attacker from the foot of the wide field of fire surrounding the place, were the embrasures along the top of the wall.

Practically all fortresses were built for some strategic purpose and by the period in question this was usually to defend the country concerned against external aggression. Those still in active use therefore were usually situated on, or very close to, the frontier in order to cover communication centres, bridges, navigable rivers offering likely supply lines, mountain passes and

*'Siege of a Fortress' in 1527 by Durer. The recent improvement in artillery has obviously influenced the rounded and less-angular design of the place.*

other points which it was desirable to deny to an aggressor, and as land frontiers always had a country on either side of them, this pattern tended to be duplicated on both sides. Bearing in mind that the effective range of fortress artillery at the beginning of the 19th century was no more than a thousand yards, it is therefore very evident that the individual planning of the fortress had very little scope for varying its location if it was to be effective, and was thus dependant on a degree of good fortune to overcome the vagaries of the ground. Lucky indeed was the engineer who found an ideal site in exactly the right place. Usually it was a matter of finding a compromise solution to minimise disadvantages. Often, for example, an otherwise good site was commanded by some other feature within gunshot, which naturally caused problems. In more modern times it would not be insurmountably difficult to move such a feature, but in the days of pick and shovel that was not possible. Sometimes the fortress could be constructed with a slope away from the offending feature, and invariably it was

necessary to have very strong defences on that side, including perhaps an outwork on the commanding height itself.

Fortunately there were often compensating advantages; one front might be on a steep cliff, or on the banks of a wide river, and so virtually unassailable, which allowed resources to be diverted to the more threatened fronts. In the nature of things, most fortresses had been there for many years and had stood sieges before, so that their strengths and weaknesses were well known to all educated military engineers.

Not all fortresses defended land frontiers. Many were sited on the coast to protect harbours, but these usually had a land front as well, which had to be defended. Wooden navies were understandably reluctant to attack permanent fortifications and where possible much

*Surrender following a siege in 1575. Such places, built before cannon became widely used, were particularly vulnerable to gunfire. Here, gabions protect the cannon of the defenders as well as those of the attackers.*

preferred to support the landing of troops to tackle the land front.

In the Peninsula there was yet a further category of strong place, the numerous temporary places of refuge which were essential to the French, an army of occupation in the midst of an implacably hostile population. Some had been built from scratch, others ingeniously converted from convents and similar buildings, and they existed in hundreds for only by such means could stores, installations and vital routes be guarded economically, while leaving a sufficient number of troops available for field operations. Many of these little places could never have withstood a siege in form, but this was not their function. Their enemies were the guerrillas, fierce and numerous but usually lacking artillery and thus helpless in the face of quite simple

*The beautiful, asymmetric science of Vauban-style fortifications direct maximum firepower against attackers, while providing cunning killing-grounds between the layered lines of defence.*

walls, provided only that they were resolutely defended (which was almost invariably the case) and adequately supplied with stores and munitions.

None of the fortresses dealt with in this book were modern in the sense of being post-gunpowder, but they had all been modernised, sometimes to a considerable extent, and as traditional techniques had naturally been used it may be as well to consider the fundamental principles of fortress construction so that the process can be understood.

A standard purpose-built modern fortress usually consisted of a polygonal trace with a minimum of five straight sides, usually referred to as 'curtain walls'. These consisted of solid earth ramparts, forty or fifty feet thick at the top, and faced with masonry. The level top, the *terreplein*, was the platform on which the guns were located, being protected by a parapet pierced with embrasures. At each angle between the curtain walls there was a bastion, a protruding work which allowed flanking fire to be brought onto the adjacent curtains and the faces and fronts of the neighbouring bastions,

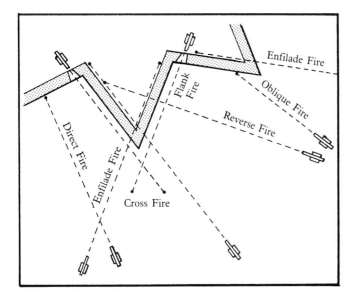

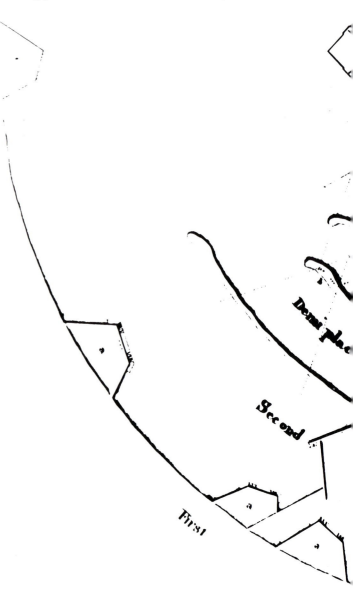

the whole fortress being surrounded by a ditch. Within this ditch there were triangular, detached works known as ravelins, whose object was to protect the curtain from direct fire, and usually other earthworks too, designed to fill any gaps between the ravelins. Along the outer side of the ditch, known as the counterscarp, was a ledge with a parapet. This was the covered way and was primarily intended to allow musket fire to be brought to bear on the glacis.

Any outworks intended for serious resistance were strongly built on the front and flanks, but the rear was

**Above:** *Angles of artillery (and musketry) fire used by the attackers and defenders during a siege. Direct and oblique fire were used directly against the walls. This could be augmented by enfilade or reverse fire to sweep the defenders' positions. In reply, the defenders could apply flank- and cross-fire to sweep the face of the walls themselves, during an assault.*

**Right:** *The classic progress of a siege to the point of assault. Just forward of the 1st parallel are the supporting bombardment batteries. Each parallel and support trench is connected by a series of zig zag communication trenches, none of which can receive enfilading fire from any point of the defence works.*

**Below:** *A simplified plan of complex defences. The main curtain wall of the fortress, with its corner bastions, is protected by a **tenaille** with, further forward, a **ravelin** with ditches and traverses.*

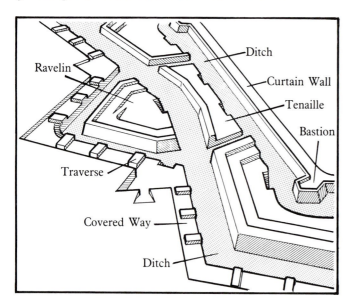

usually only protected by palisades and a ditch, so that when the work finally fell to the besiegers it could be made untenable by fire from the main body of the place.

Siege techniques against fortresses built or modernised in the artillery era were largely developed by French and Dutch engineers, in the 17th century, probably the best known amongst them being Vauban. As neither fortresses nor guns had changed very much in the interim these same techniques were used in the Peninsula. As, in general, the fortresses there were not of the first class, and as the tempo of warfare had speeded up considerably, methods of construction sometimes tended to be less elaborate, and short cuts were sometimes taken to save time, although these often meant correspondingly higher casualties. When the proper scientific combination of gun and spade was used, the fall of a fortress could be predicted with considerable accuracy. Napier, the first of the great historians of the Peninsular War wrote:

'There is no operation in war more certain than a modern siege if the rules of art are strictly followed; and unlike the ancient sieges it is also

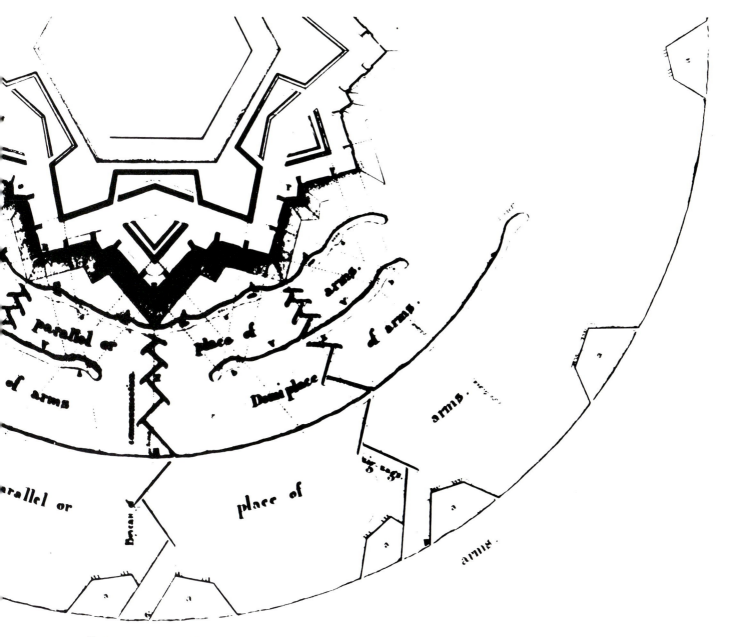

different in this, that no operation is less open to irregular daring because the course of the engineer can neither be hurried nor delayed without danger.'

The ideal preliminary to a siege was the complete isolation of the stronghold by a close blockade. Simultaneously a part of the army was posted as a covering force to prevent, or at least delay, any outside intervention. This part usually included a high proportion of cavalry, whose value in a siege was otherwise limited.

The commander then made a detailed reconnaissance with his artillery and engineer advisers. If the place had been besieged before, it was to be hoped that his engineer knew about it, although he might not necessarily advise the same plan because of different circumstances. It was also advisable at this stage to consider diversionary attacks, to keep the garrison guessing as to the selected breaching point for as long as possible. Once the defenders were certain of it, they would construct secondary defences behind it, and the less time they had to do this the better.

The next thing to decide was the position of the first parallel, a trench to be dug parallel to the face to be attacked and as close as possible to it. If the fortress was well situated this parallel could be 700yds or more away, but a lucky accident of ground might make it possible to site it much closer. It was marked out with pegs and tape at last light and dug by a strong working party, with a covering force lying out in front. If care was taken and weather conditions were right, the defenders might not be aware that the work was in progress until first light, when its presence would of course be obvious. Given a good working party (and most did work hard in the certain knowledge of what awaited them at dawn) and suitable soil, they could be

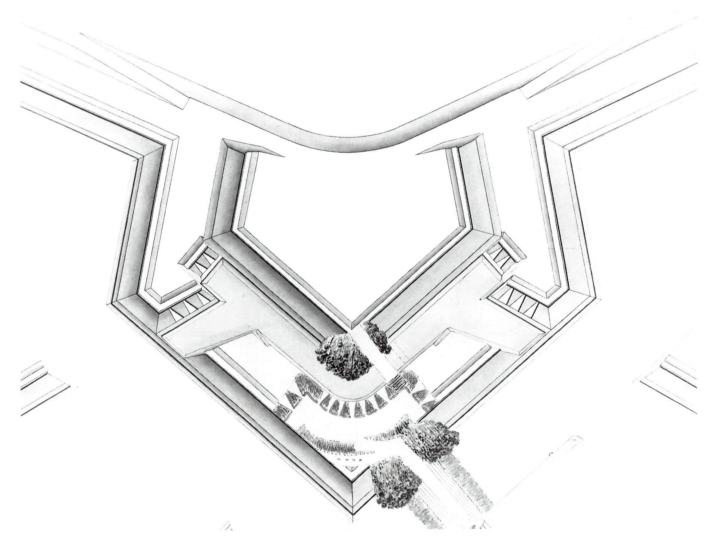

under good cover by the time the besiegers opened fire. When the situation demanded it, parapets could be raised quickly by the use of gabions, rough wicker baskets two or three feet high and a couple of feet in diameter, into which earth could be shovelled. They were not of course artillery proof and a well-handled gun could knock them about, but unless the situation was desperate the garrison might not care to waste valuable ammunition unnecessarily. Communications trenches also had to be dug back to dead ground so as to allow free movement backwards and forwards.

Zig-zag trenches, so aligned that the branches could not be enfiladed by the garrison, were then dug forward and a second parallel started. Batteries were also constructed and armed so as to keep down the fire of the defenders. Only a limited number of the guns in the fortress could be brought to bear on any one section of the perimeter, whereas with luck and hard work a considerable superiority of fire could be concentrated on them by the attackers. A third parallel might be necessary depending on ground, and from there the engineers would sap forward and blow in the counterscarp so as to allow easy access to the breach.

Meanwhile the breach would be established by the artillery pounding away at the curtain wall until it came down, bringing with it a mass of soil to provide a ramp up onto the *terreplein*. It was desirable that the batteries be placed to batter the base of the wall over, or around, any earthworks designed to prevent this, and even in modernised fortresses it was often possible to find some suitable site from which this could be done. By night an active garrison would clear away as much rubble as possible so as to make the ascent slow and difficult. They would also cut trenches across the *terreplein* on either side of the breach, construct breast-works behind it, block the breach with *chevaux-de-frise*, (beams of wood inset with hundreds of sword blades), old carts, and similar obstacles. The besiegers could hamper this work by laying guns and howitzers to fire onto the breach by night, although with only very primitive methods of laying, these weapons soon lost range and direction.

When it was clear that an assault was imminent the garrison manned its positions. The defenders would have grenades, shells, rocks, beams and other missiles

*Static defences usually lack adaptability. Here the defenders have cut through the walls of both their own cavalier and bastion to provide egress to the outer works. A surprise counter-attack is covered by the clever entrenchments within the ditch.*

ready to hurl down and would probably have also sited mines to be fired by quick match at their attackers. The troops to defend breaches were always carefully selected, and each man often had two or three muskets available so that the first fire would be heavy. The attack which was usually by night would be preceded by a forlorn-hope, a party of a dozen or twenty men under an officer, whose hazardous task was to draw the first fire and induce the defenders to blow their mines. They were followed by a storming party of a couple of hundred men, and then by the main body. Once the breach was entered in force the place usually fell. In theory it was possible for the garrison to withdraw to some central keep and continue to resist, but in practice it was rarely possible in the wild confusion of the assault.

In the more leisurely warfare of the 17th and 18th centuries the custom had been for the governor of a fortress to ask for terms when a practicable breach had been made. Napoleon however, a more ruthless general and one moreover very conscious of the value of time in war, had made it clear to his army that any governor who surrendered a fortress without standing an assault would be court-martialled. By the rules of war this entitled the besieging general to put the survivors of the garrison to the sword, but in practice this was never done. The main problem was that once an assault had succeeded the troops, wild with excitement, inevitably dispersed to plunder and could rarely be restrained until daylight, and not always then. There was a tradition that a place which stood an assault could be sacked by the attackers, but although this was perhaps acceptable in an enemy country, it was bad luck on the Spaniards who inhabited the various fortresses taken by the British in Spain.

Although the general theory of siege operations was known to the British engineers, none of them had any practical experience of the business. Great Britain had no land frontiers, and the British Army's experience of siege work was almost entirely confined to the occasional reduction of native hill forts, where the lack of skill of the defenders made it possible to use rough and ready methods far removed from those of Vauban. The only European land campaign in which Britain had taken part in living memory was in 1793-4, but although they had been nominally involved in the siege of Valenciennes the technical part of the operation had been kept firmly in the hands of their Austrian allies, whose army, like most of those in Western Europe included a full establishment of engineers with a proper proportion of sappers, miners, pioneers and skilled tradesmen to support them.

## Siege Artillery

Cannon of a sort were in use by the middle of the 14th century, but inevitably their development was slow at a time when technical knowledge was limited, so it is probable that they did not become a serious threat to the old pre-gunpowder medieval castles until the end of the 15th century.

By that time a new race of gun-makers, probably basing their experience on that of bell founding, had begun to cast guns in molten metal, the mould being placed vertically, muzzle uppermost, with a central core which could later be removed to form the bore. This method, although an improvement on earlier ones, was never wholly satisfactory, due mainly to the problems of getting the bore absolutely central, and by the third quarter of the 18th century new and improved machinery had made it possible to cast the pieces solid and drill them out later, power being provided either by horse or water. This method enabled the guns to be bored more accurately and thus considerably improved their capability.

Although there had been some earlier experiments with iron, most of the early cast guns were made of various brass compounds whose exact formulae are now not known. By the mid-18th century however brass had given way to bronze, a mixture of tin and copper often known as gun-metal which was a tougher compound than brass. Somewhat confusingly such guns were still described as 'brass' guns, so that the only rough guide to the exact mixture is to go by the date.

By the beginning of the 19th century, greatly improved techniques had made it possible to cast iron guns. These, calibre for calibre, were heavier than brass pieces but they were also very much harder and less susceptible to wear caused by the iron roundshot used in them. They also had the added advantage that they cooled much more quickly than the earlier types which made them suitable for siege guns (or battering guns as they were often called), where sustained fire was necessary and weight not a serious disadvantage. The lighter and more mobile field guns continued to be made of 'brass'.

All these guns were loaded from the muzzle end with

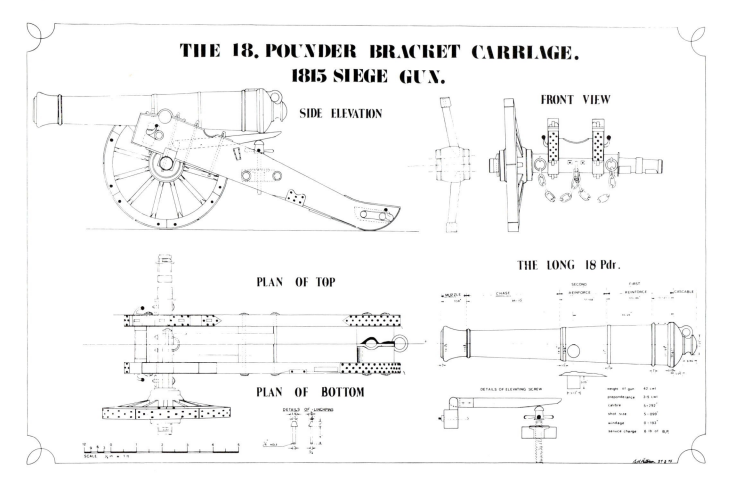

a charge of powder in a flannel bag, together with a roundshot or other projectile, so that it was necessary for the roundshot to be of lesser diameter than the actual bore, partly to facilitate loading, and partly to allow for the occasional slightly over-sized shot. The usual difference, known as windage, was up to 0.3in depending on calibre, although as shot-casting techniques improved this was progressively reduced to about 0.2in. The powder charge was normally one third of the weight of the projectile.

Muzzle-loaded guns were discharged by the direct application of fire to the priming in the vent, which was a hole of about 0.2in diameter drilled on the top surface of the breach end so as to communicate with the charge. At first, priming was done with loose powder, but eventually priming tubes were used. These often consisted of goose quills packed with a special explosive composition, designed to give a powerful flash, and were inserted into the vent, the flannel of the main cartridge having been pierced previously with a priming wire so as not to obstruct the passage of the flame into the charge. When the gun was fired there was a considerable rush of burning gases up through the vent, which eventually enlarged it. This was a particular problem with brass guns, so the usual practice was to drill a threaded hole of about 1in diameter and screw into it a plug of pure copper with a standard vent drilled through it, copper being considerably more resistant to heat than its various compounds. These plugs were usually known as *bouches*, or the anglicised form, bushes.

*Typical muzzle loading gun-drill of British 19th century artillery. While the piece is sponged-out, the crew's No4 holds his thumb over the vent to prevent re-ignition of residual glowing fragments caused by the forced draught caused by the rammer, prior to loading and ramming home the charge and shot, and priming the touch-hole.*

Iron guns, being of harder metal, were at first thought to be proof against this problem, but it was soon found that sustained fire did wear away the vent, although the process was much slower. Before a fresh charge was rammed into a gun the bore was naturally sponged out to extinguish glowing fragments from the earlier charge. However, as the action of ramming the fresh charge caused a forced draught through the vent (which naturally increased the risk of a premature discharge through lingering sparks which might have survived the sponge) there was a drill known as 'serving the vent' in which one of the detachment placed his thumb, suitably encased in a stout leather stall, over the vent to prevent the rush of air through it as the charge went down. At the siege of San Sebastian in 1813 the vents of some guns had become so large by protracted firing that the only way to serve the vent was to place a filled sandbag over it. When the gun had reached this stage it was usual to pass the priming tube through a piece of paper so as to prevent its slipping too far down the vent into the charge.

The standard British siege gun in the Peninsular War

was the iron 24 pounder of 7.12in calibre. The barrel lengths varied from seven to nine feet and varied accordingly from forty to fifty hundredweight. The longer ones were generally preferred for siege work. These pieces threw a cast-iron roundshot with an initial velocity of about 1600ft per second. This was more than halved in the first hundred yards and had halved again at 1500yds, at which range however, the gun was still both powerful and reasonably accurate. There were also 18 pounders of 5.29in calibre, nine feet long, and weighing some forty hundredweight. Their initial velocities were similar to the heavier pieces and they too were formidable weapons, although must less so for breaching purposes than the 24 pounders. These guns were all cast with trunnions, blunt cylindrical projections, on either side of the piece immediately in front of the point of balance, which fitted into semi-circular recesses on the tops of the two-wheeled carriages, of a type sufficiently familiar to the general reader to make a more detailed description unnecessary. They had to be very strong to withstand the very considerable strains to which they were subjected when fired, and the usual practice was to protect them as much as possible by moving the guns on what were known as block carriages, even heavier and more robust than the normal ones but well suited to transporting two and a half tons of metal over very bad roads.

Modern British guns were well made to close tolerances, so that although they were not rifled they were nevertheless remarkably accurate when used with roundshot of the same quality and good powder.

Sighting arrangements were basic, and consisted of no more than a notch on top of the base ring and a simple foresight at the muzzle end. As the metal was thicker at the breach than at the muzzle the pieces naturally tapered, so that the line of sight did not coincide with the line of bore. This was compensated for by using a 'dispart' sight, ie a higher foresight to eliminate the discrepancy. Elevation and depression were achieved by raising or lowering the breach end by means of wedges or quoins, but lateral correction could only be made by moving the whole piece. By the early 19th century the introduction of elevating screws and tangent sights had greatly speeded up the process of laying.

When these guns were employed against strong works their best ranges were a hundred yards or less, but it was frequently necessary to have them much further back; three or four hundred yards was very satisfactory although breaches could be made at twice that range. All that was needed was more time and more ammunition, which sounds easy in theory but which was often very difficult in practice.

There was always the risk that an active enemy might send out infantry detachments to immobilise guns, which could be done quickly and simply by hammering an iron spike into the vent. When guns were particularly

*A British 10in howitzer of Peninsular War design found preserved at Quetta. The massive barrel is, of necessity, supported on a very substantial carriage. The spike, extending from the trail, enables the heavy piece to be traversed more easily.*

exposed, as at San Sebastian, it was considered advisable to prevent any risk of this by chaining iron plates over the vents when the guns were not in use.

A secondary, but still very useful, weapon was the howitzer, a short-barrelled piece designed mainly to lob shells at a high angle. The shell, being explosive, carried its own force of destruction with it, and was thus not dependant on velocity for effect. Quite small charges, as little as one twelfth the weight of the projectile, were thus possible, so that the strain on the piece was less and it could be made a good deal lighter than a gun of similar calibre. The brass 10in howitzers fired shells of 92lb weight but weighed only twenty-six hundredweight. There were also lighter iron howitzers of 5.5in calibre and firing a 24lb shell. These were apparently produced specially for the Peninsula, but were of little use against masonry, although when fired with long fuzes they did considerable damage to earthworks. Their main role however, was as anti-personnel pieces, and they were particularly useful for keeping a partly-made breach under fire at night time so as to prevent the garrison from obstructing it.

Shrapnel shells, ie iron spheres filled with musket balls and fitted with small burster charges, were often used with these pieces, and it was also possible to use them with roundshot with reduced charges. It is perhaps worth avoiding possible confusion by noting that in some contemporary accounts the 5.5in iron howitzers are occasionally referred to as 'carronades'.

A weapon of similar capacity to the howitzer was the mortar, which is almost certainly the oldest type of weapon ever to have been used for throwing a projectile by means of gunpowder. It consisted of a short, stout barrel on a low, non-mobile bed and it fired heavy shells at a high angle. It was not very portable, but was easy to conceal since it could be fired from behind high cover by means of simple but reasonably effective indirect fire

*The technique of laying a British 13in mortar was virtually the same throughout the 19th century. No1, holding a plumb line on the target, aligns the piece, while the crew, using handspikes, adjust the base of the weapon on its level bed. Range is varied by movement of the wedge-shaped quoin below the barrel of the mortar.*

devices. It was, like the howitzer, essentially an area, anti-personnel weapon.

Guns used in fortresses were very similar to those used against them, although they were usually mounted on low, four-wheeled garrison carriages, which were not very mobile but had a suitably low profile. Most fortresses also had some light guns of field type which could be man-handled to any threatened point. The besiegers also made occasional use of such weapons, although in their case all they had to do was call up field guns from their covering force.

Apart from roundshot, guns also fired two other types of anti-personnel projectile. The first was grape, which consisted of nine iron balls, either confined in three tiers of three between their metal plates or held together by canvas and cord, the total weight usually being somewhat less than that of the corresponding roundshot.

*An example of British case shot. The discharge of 100 iron shot from a single cannon wreaked havoc on both infantry in the open and poorly-protected defenders.*

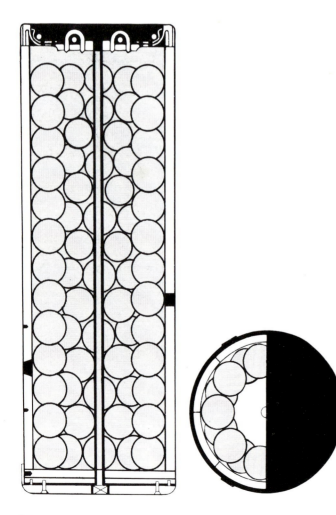

This was not a standard issue in the Peninsula, but was sometimes improvised. The second was cannister, in which balls varying in weight from one to two ounces were packed into a cylindrical container of thin metal. Both these types threw their projectiles in a pattern on much the same principle as a shotgun, although after about three hundred yards they had spread so much as to be ineffective. Like common and shrapnell shell they were considered excellent for keeping a breach under intermittent fire in the hours of darkness. Grape was not normally fired from brass guns because of its adverse effect on the bore of the piece.

One useful expedient often employed in sieges was the use of hot shot, since 24 pounder balls at red heat would readily set fire to roof beams and similar combustible items. They retained a very great deal of heat, even after repeated dousing with water and were a constant threat to buildings of all kinds. They were heated on special furnaces and loaded in the usual way, a thick wet wad having first been placed over the powder, and gunners did not much like them because of the risk of premature discharge. There were no anti-recoil devices in those days, and when fired, heavy guns came back with great force, to the detriment of anyone in their path.

Although this section is primarily concerned with artillery it may be as well to refer briefly to small arms. Many fortresses had stocks of wall, or rampart, guns, large-scale muskets firing a lead ball of 1.5in to 2in diameter. They were equipped with iron rests which fitted into sockets on the walls, and were fired from the shoulder; they were useful against small parties of men which would hardly have justified the use of a proper artillery piece. Usually small arms were also used in some numbers. The standard infantry musket, when used in haste for mechanical volleys, was not a particularly accurate arm, but when carefully loaded with a good fitting ball and a measured charge of powder it was reasonably effective up to 100yds or so, especially when the firer was ensconced behind good cover and could take his time. The British Army also had rifle regiments whose weapon, the Baker rifle, was surprisingly accurate to 250yds. Detachments of skilled riflemen, snugly hidden in trenches, could put their bullets through gun embrasures on a rampart with some consistency, and often made things so unpleasant that the gunners were driven from their pieces. The French Army had no official rifles, but from the exploits of some of their marksmen at sieges one is driven to conclude that some privately-owned weapons of this type may have been brought into use.

## The Peninsular War Up To The First British Siege of Badajos

The Peninsular War had its origins in Napoleon's plan to strangle Britain's overseas trade (on which her capacity to continue the war against him depended) by closing the ports of Europe to her. Portugal, an old ally and trading partner, was reluctant to comply with his orders regarding this and was promptly occupied by a French army with the connivance of Spain, then an ally of France, although perhaps not an enthusiastic one. Napoleon, not content with his seizure of Portugal, then occupied Spain, deposed its King, and placed his brother Joseph on the throne, where-upon the Spaniards rose in revolt.

Although technically still at war with Britain, the local provisional governments, usually known as *juntas,* at once asked for her help which was soon forthcoming in the shape of troops, ships, and *matériel* of all kind. Sir Arthur Wellesley, now of course better remembered as Wellington, fought a brief but successful campaign in Portugal before being removed for political reasons. Sir John Moore then assumed command, but having placed far too much trust in his Spanish allies, was forced out of Spain early in 1809, he himself being killed in the final successful battle to cover the re-embarkation of his army. Wellesley was then sent back with orders to confine his efforts strictly to the defences of Portugal, and very soon cleared the French out of the country.

He then essayed (with Government authority) a foray into Spain where he won a battle at Talavera but was then compelled to retreat, due mainly to the inability of the Spaniards to cover his flank and rear. The Spaniards then advanced on Madrid but were heavily defeated, after which a French army under Soult occupied Andalusia, with the single exception of the well-fortified naval base of Cadiz.

It is easy, but unfair, to blame the Spaniards. Their army had been neglected for years, and Napoleon had sent their best units off to remote garrisons in the Baltic, so that some confusion and inefficiency was inevitable. They later showed great resilience and made a considerable contribution to the defeat of the French. Apart from its regular troops, the country swarmed with guerrilla bands who harried the French unceasingly.

After Talavera Wellington (who had received a peerage for that battle) withdrew his army to Portugal where he took advantage of a lull in operations to train it and also to raise a new Portuguese army.

*Below: General Sir John Moore is carried from the field before Corunna during the evacuation of the British army from the Peninsular in early 1809. The scene, though realistic, incorrectly depicts the British infantry in the 1812 pattern shako.*
*Following pages: The return of British forces to Portugal and Wellington's short break-out into Spain culminates in the victory at the Battle of Talavera.*

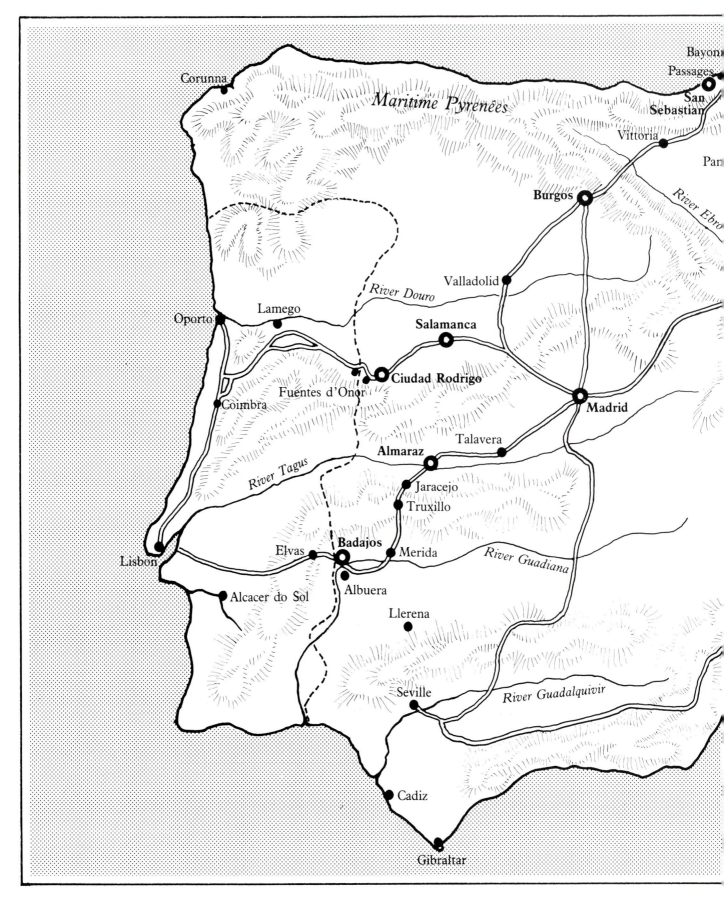

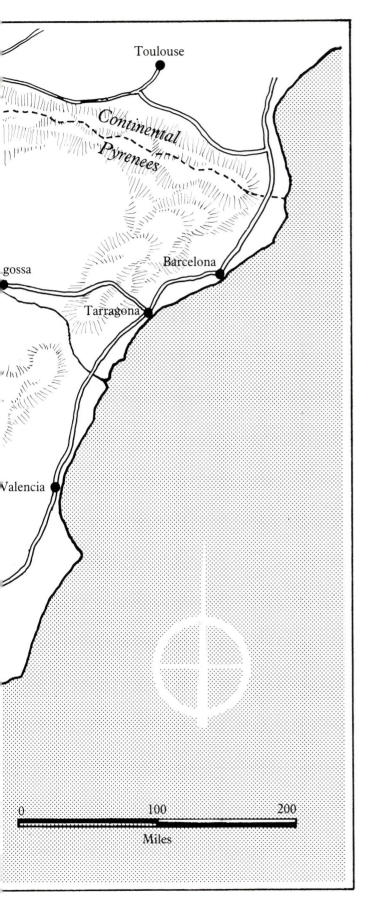

By the early months of 1810 it was clear that the French were preparing a major offensive into Portugal under the command of Massena, and by the end of August they had captured the Spanish frontier fortress of Ciudad Rodrigo and its Portuguese equivalent Almeida, and were driving southwards on Lisbon. The British, heavily outnumbered were forced to retreat, and although they fought a successful defensive action at Bussaco there was great apprehension, both in the British Government and the Army, that this was a prelude to yet another hasty re-embarkation.

Wellington however had other ideas. Since the autumn of 1809 he had been building a series of strong defences across the Lisbon Peninsula, the actual work being done by thousands of Portuguese labourers under the supervision of British engineers. In spite of the scale of the operation no rumour of it had reached the French, so that in October 1810 Massena's victorious advance came to an abrupt halt. There was then a stalemate, but as most of their route down had been laid waste, the French were soon in difficulties. Unlike the British they had no supply organisation and when they were compelled to go further afield for supplies the guerrillas and Portuguese irregulars harried them constantly.

Massena held on grimly; he knew that a regency had just been declared in Great Britain, and it was thought that the new Regent, the Prince of Wales, would oust the Tories and sent for the Whigs who were pledged to end the war. By March 1811 however his situation finally became intolerable and he was forced to withdraw into Spain with the British in pursuit.

Early in 1811 Marshal Soult, who was commanding in Andalusia, had finally decided to comply with Napoleon's instructions to relieve the pressure on Massena, and marching north with his army he captured the Spanish fortress of Badajos, which covered the southern route into Portugal, just as Massena was beginning his retreat. Wellington detached Beresford with two divisions to drive the French away. As it happened Soult had already gone, being deeply apprehensive of the activities of an Anglo-Spanish force which had sailed from Cadiz and landed further down the coast, where it beat a French force at Barossa. After some preliminary operations, Beresford was ready to lay siege to Badajos, and an account of his operations is given in the next chapter.

*The Peninsula, 1811. The strategic importance of the fortresses commanding access into Spain, and beyond into France, required that they should be neutralised, resulting in the series of sieges that were to follow.*

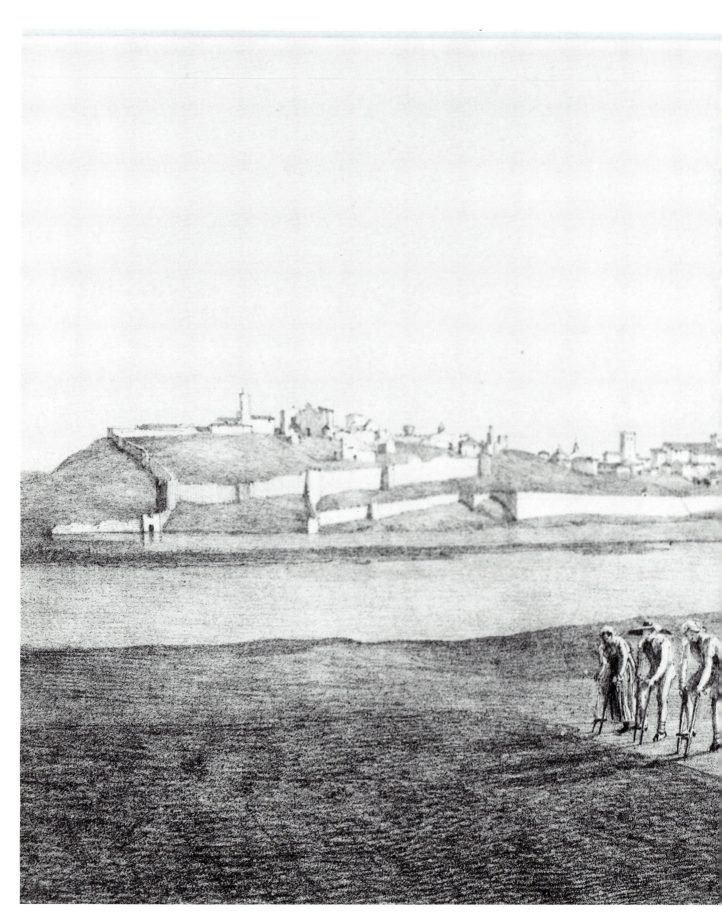

# CHAPTER TWO

## The First and Second Sieges of Badajos

Badajos stands on the south bank of the river Guadiana which in spring is a deep, fast flowing stream, nowhere less than three hundred yards wide, and subject to sudden rapid rises in level. At its highest point, in the north-east angle of the place and some 130ft above river level, stands an ancient Moorish castle with a tower and a high turretted wall. Outside this wall the ground drops steeply away to the north and east, the land on the north side going down to the river and that on the east dropping equally steeply to the Rivillas, a boggy stream which covers the eastern front of the place before running into the main river just north of the castle. The town had originally been surrounded by a medieval wall, but had been modernised in the mid-18th century by a proper front of eight bastions some thirty feet high and having a good ditch with a counter-scarp averaging twenty-five feet in height. The curtain wall was covered by ravelins, which although unrevetted and otherwise incomplete, still afforded it a considerable degree of protection. These new additions to the defences had been done cheaply, and the general quality of the stonework was believed to be poor. These works did not cover the north-western face of the perimeter, which being adequately protected by the river still depended on the old curtain wall.

The place was further covered by four out-posts: a crown-work, Fort Pardeleras, some 200yds to the south; a lunette, Fort Picurina, about 400yds to the east across the Rivillas; a smaller lunette, that of San Roque, a few hundred yards north of it, and Fort Cristoval. The last was a strong, enclosed work, standing on a rocky cliff on the north bank of the Guadiana, and dominating the

*Badajos as viewed from the north bank of the River Guadiana, close to Fort Cristoval. To the left is the Castle and, to the right, the bridge across the river.*

castle at a range of almost five hundred yards. There was a bridge across the river, entering the stronghold in the centre of the north-west face and covered by a fortified bridge-head on the north bank. It may be of interest to note that although some of the wall on the southern face has been demolished, a great deal of the original defences remain intact and can be found without much difficulty.

On 16 April Wellington having driven Massena over the frontier into Spain, arrived at Elvas to see the situation for himself, and after making a series of detailed reconnaissances with his Chief Engineer, Lt-Col Sir R Fletcher, decided that the main attack should be against San Cristoval, with diversionary attacks against Pardaleras and Picurina, a plan which was later to be the subject of a good deal of criticism.

The main point in its favour was that it offered the prospect of a quick result, and as Wellington calculated that he had at most only sixteen days before Soult arrived back to relieve the fortress, this was a vital consideration. The broad idea was that once San Cristoval was taken, a breach could soon be knocked in the ancient and exposed masonry of the castle and the place stormed, which, it was considered, would inevitably lead to the surrender of the town. As soon as the main project was well advanced it was proposed to abandon the diversionary attacks; this would of course reveal the final plan to the defenders, but by then

it would be too late for them to take any significant steps to strengthen the castle.

Having settled this plan, Wellington rode off back to the main army on 25 April, leaving with Beresford a set of comprehensive instructions to cover his actions in the event of every conceivable move on the part of the French.

The engineer support available to Beresford was perhaps as good as could be expected considering the shortages of troops of this type in the army as a whole. It consisted of Lt-Col Fletcher with nineteen other more junior officers and twenty-seven rank and file of their corps. There were also twelve officers of the Line who had volunteered their services as assistant engineers, together with forty-eight carpenters, thirty-six miners and a hundred non-tradesmen to act as sappers, all these, like the assistant engineers, being volunteers from the various Line regiments involved. Siege stores of all kinds were in short supply, due mainly to lack of transport, and consisted of no more then 500 picks and shovels, 2000 sandbags, 200 gabions, 250 fascines (tightly bound bundles of sticks for revetting) 7 gun platforms, 43 splinter-proof timbers, and some other odds and ends of wood. It did not seem a very liberal amount with which to undertake a major siege, nor were things helped by the fact that the tools were not only of poor quality but also far too heavy for the small Portuguese soldiers. A limited number of *enxadas*, small local hoes, were also requisitioned. Although the engineers' resources may have been poor, they were nevertheless vastly superior to those of the artillery. The whole question of the British siege train is discussed in the next chapter, so that all it is necessary to say here is that although excellent heavy guns were almost certainly available on ordnance store ships in the Tagus, they might just as well have been on the moon, this of course being entirely due to the very tight time limits imposed by the military situation. It was thus necessary to improvise from local resources, and on 6 April Wellington had written to Beresford ordering him to investigate the Portuguese fortress of Elvas to see what was available. As this place was only some ten miles away time was not a problem, and it was perhaps reasonable to suppose, or at least hope, that it could furnish all that was necessary.

*Left: General William Carr Beresford, entrusted by Wellington to take Badajos before Marshal Soult's relief force could arrive.*
*Right: The defences of Badajos, with the important outworks of San Cristoval, San Roque and Picurina.*

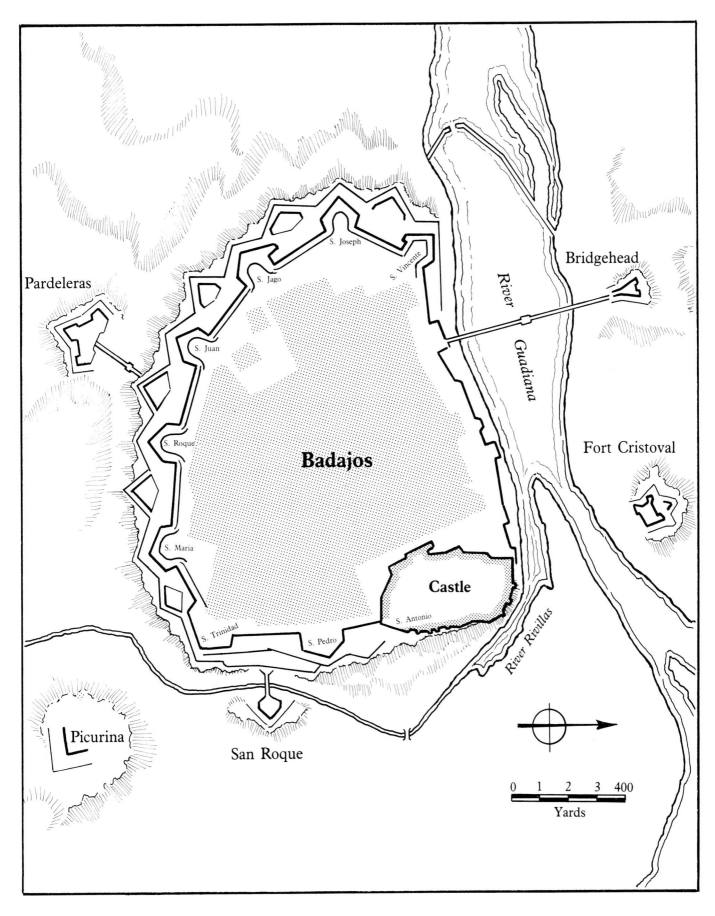

Pardeleras

S. Joseph

S. Jago

S. Vincente

River

S. Juan

Bridgehead

Guadiana

**Badajos**

Fort Cristoval

S. Roque

S. Maria

**Castle**

S. Antonio

S. Trinidad

S. Pedro

River Rivillas

Picurina

San Roque

0 1 2 3 400

Yards

The actual task fell to a young officer of the Royal Artillery, and as he will appear frequently in these pages hereafter it may be as well at this stage to give a brief pen-picture of him. Alexander Dickson, a regimental captain in his own corps and a temporary major in the Portuguese service, was at the time nearly thirty-four years old and had seen much service in the Peninsula and elsewhere. He was clearly an officer of exceptional capacity, who although a sound disciplinarian was nevertheless also thoroughly well liked by all who came into contact with him. Wellington, whose relations with his senior artillery officers were not always of the happiest, came to depend on him more and more for professional advice and assistance, so that within a couple of years he was to be placed in effective command of all the artillery in the field in the Peninsula. Apart from his other qualities, he was also a hoarder of papers and documents of all kinds, for which posterity has to thank him, for when they were finally edited almost a century later they provided a unique insight into all the affairs of the Royal Artillery. It is perhaps unnecessary to add that Dickson became a general in due course.

When Dickson actually went to investigate Elvas he was surprised and dismayed to find that the guns there were better suited to a museum than a modern frontier fortress. The newest amongst them were of early 18th century manufacture, but many were much older, so that some of the pieces actually used in siege had been manufactured very nearly two hundred years before, at a time when Portugal had been a mere appendage of the Hapsburg dominions. They were all made of soft brass, and had been cast round central cores, with all the defects and inaccuracies of boring which that ancient method entailed. They were inordinately long and heavy by modern standards and their carriages were clumsy and shaken by long years in store. Apart from roughness and corrosion, their bores all varied more or less widely from their nominal calibres, and as all the available roundshot suffered from the same defects a great deal of careful culling and gauging was also necessary to match projectiles to bores as closely as possible.

*Left: Alexander Dickson, the true hero of British siege warfare in Spain. Though painted some twenty years later, and holding one of the basic tools of an artilleryman, his face still reflects his tenacity to search out and obtain the limited ordnance and equipment so often denied him.*
*Right: Maj-Gen Charles William Stewart, whose forces invested Badajos prior to the first siege.*

Dickson persisted however, and finally managed to select sixteen 24 pounders, eight 16 pounders, two 10in howitzers, and eight 8in howitzers, not all of which were to be used in the first operations. The gunners consisted of five companies of Portuguese artillery, two from Elvas and three from Lisbon. Although brave and willing they were mainly recruits and none of them had any previous experience of siege work.

It is perhaps arguable that Dickson was somewhat over-confident regarding the capacity of this strange and archaic collection of pieces. Wellington had in fact told Beresford earlier that if Elvas could not produce the necessary equipment it would have to be obtained elsewhere, adding that 'this will take time, but that cannot be avoided', so that both the Marshal and his artillery adviser had an escape clause. It was however very clear that Wellington was anxious to get on with the business, and it is thus understandable that neither of his two subordinates should have wished to delay proceedings unnecessarily.

By the early hours of 4 May Maj-Gen Stewart had invested the main fortress on the south bank, and a bridge had been established some miles downstream, and on that same night Lt Forster of the Engineers went out to inspect the fords across the Rivillas and the slopes leading up to the castle, since it was necessary for the

success of the operation that they should be unimpeded (which turned out to be the case). As there was no Allied troops on the north bank, the French had freedom of movement there, and on 5 May they sent a strong patrol downstream to the site of the bridge. This caused some alarm and the bridge was drawn over to the south bank, a Portuguese garrison also being established in a farm near the site. The northern side was eventually sealed off by Maj-Gen Lumley. In the course of this operation a French cavalry squadron skirmished with great effect under the covering fire of the garrison of San Cristoval, and inflicted a good many casualties before it was finally driven off.

On 8 May the false attacks on the two southern outworks were started, primarily by opening the old French trenches from their siege of a couple of months earlier, and work was also started on the first parallel against San Cristoval, about 450yds north-west of the place at a point where the ground drops away quite sharply and thus allows good cover behind the crest. The plan was to establish a battery, No1, at the eastern end of the parallel at a point where the curtain wall on the east face of Cristoval could be seen to its base, although the shot would strike at an oblique angle. Considerable problems arose immediately, due mainly

to the nature of the ground, which consisted of almost solid rock with a bare foot of topsoil above it. Considerable use was made of the gabions to raise adequate cover, but the garrison shot so well that progress was slow.

Early on the morning of 10 May the French launched a sortie from the fort and entered the battery. Due to the problems of protection, the trench guard had been posted behind the crest but they at once counter-attacked with great dash and drove the French back. Unfortunately in their enthusiasm they pursued them almost to the ditch of Cristoval, thus exposing themselves to heavy artillery fire which caused the losses of some 400 killed and wounded, the bulk of the casualties falling to the 40th Regt, so that Charles Boutflower, their surgeon, noted in his diary that it was 'the most painful day of my life'. As the attackers had clearly come from the main fortress by way of the bridge, another battery, No4, was started at the western end of the parallel at a point where fire could be directed

*Three batteries and a parallel were raised against the northern defences of Badajos. An additional battery was sited to bombard the Castle and to prevent reinforcement via the Bridgehead to San Cristoval.*

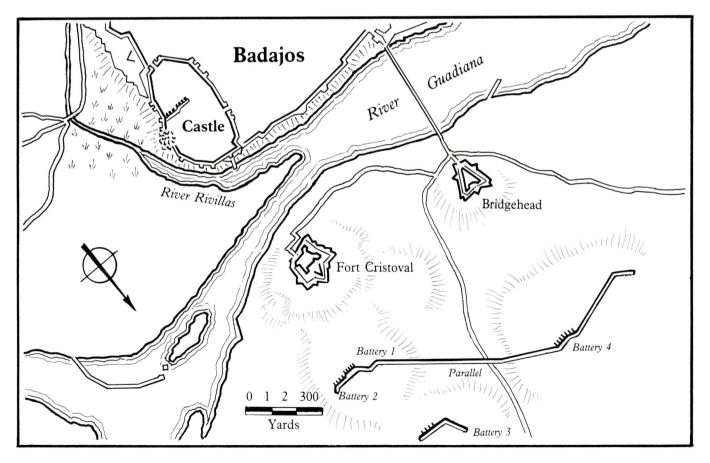

straight along the bridge and at a range of almost 700yds from it. Three 12 pounder field guns were to be brought from Elvas to arm it. In spite of all the problems, breaching battery No1 was completed on the night of

10 May, and armed with three 24 pounders and two 8in howitzers. There does not appear to have been any question of testing or zeroing these venerable pieces, for if there had been Dickson would have mentioned it.

Fire was opened at first light on 11 May, but the combination of ancient guns and inexperienced gunners meant that the shooting was poor. It was very much otherwise with the garrison, who shot so well, both from Cristoval and a flanking battery in the castle, that all the guns and one of the howitzers were soon disabled and the battery silenced. It was not an auspicious start.

By the night of 11 May the bridge battery was almost complete. Col Jones noted tersely that Capt Dickinson (of the Engineers) had his head carried off by a cannon shot, which probably sums up the dangers of siege work in a single short sentence. On that same night a new breaching battery No2 was started on the immediate left of the silenced one; four guns were brought over the river to arm it, the damaged ones being withdrawn. The battery to sweep the bridge was armed with three 12 pounders and a howitzer borrowed from a field brigade. By 12 May the inevitable wastage of trench work had reduced the troops besieging San Cristoval so much that they could not find enough men both to guard the trenches and labour on them, so virtually all work had to be suspended.

While the main attack was grinding to a halt, diversionary operations still continued against Pardeleras and Picurina, and work began on the night of 13 May on a new parallel from which the castle might be breached. By then however it was abundantly clear that a French relieving force under Soult was getting dangerously close, so in the course of that night the guns were all withdrawn and their platforms and other timber worth salvaging were taken up. On 14 May the guns and stores were sent to the rear for safety and all other stocks of fascines and gabions were burnt, so that by the 15th the siege was finally over, and the troops were moving off southwards to face the new threat. As the rearguard moved off the French launched a sortie in some force and roughly handled a Portuguese light battalion, these being the final shots fired in this notably sterile operation.

Siege warfare was of course a complete novelty to both

*Left: Marshal Nicholas Jean-de-Dieu Soult, who was expected to raise the first siege of Badajos within sixteen days.*
*Following pages: British forces, withdrawn temporarily from the siege works at Badajos, defeat Marshal Soult at the Battle of Albuera.*

officers and men of the British Army and they appear to have regarded their first abortive attempt at it with very mixed feelings. Possibly Capt Moyle Sherer of the 34th Regt summed it up when he wrote:

'I regard the operations of a siege as highly interesting; the daily progress of the labours; the trenches filled with men who lie secure within range of the garrison; the fire of the batteries; the beautiful appearance of the shells and fireballs by night; the challenges of the enemy's sentries; the sound of their drums and trumpets; all give a continued charm and animation to the service. But the duties of a besieging force are both harassing and severe; and, I know not how it is, death in the trenches never carries with it that stamp of glory which seals the memory of those who perish in a well-fought field. The daily exploits of the northern Army under Lord Wellington and Graham's victory at Barossa, made us restless and mortified at our comparative ill-fortune'.

It is of interest to note that this officer soon had his well-fought field (which happily he survived) at the murderous battle of Albuera.

In the north Massena, having reorganised and re-equipped his army after its long and costly retreat, and re-enforced it with some additional troops borrowed from the Army of the North, advanced to relieve Almeida, the last French foothold in Portugal. He and Wellington met at Fuentes d'Onor, and after a wearing two day battle fought on the 3 May and 5 May, the French were defeated and withdrew, upon which the garrison of Almeida blew the place up, and by some blunder on the part of the British troops, who were encircling the place in anticipation of that very event, the bulk of them escaped. This was to be Massena's swansong, for soon after the battle he was relieved by Marshal Marmont.

On 16 May, the day after the siege of Badajos was raised, Beresford met Soult at Albuera, some fourteen miles further south, and there fought the bloodiest battle of the war, after which Soult retreated to Seville leaving Beresford the victor (if a somewhat shaken one). The French marshal had not apparently been able to communicate with the garrison, who were therefore in complete ignorance of what was going on outside, although the somewhat precipitate raising of the siege must have given them hope that relief was at hand.

On 19 May Badajos was reinvested by a Portuguese brigade, presumably in accordance with Wellington's earlier detailed orders to Beresford, and on the same day Wellington himself arrived at Elvas, with two more infantry divisions close behind him. The French armies of Portugal and Andalusia had both been very roughly handled indeed and he calculated that if he moved fast he might yet take Badajos before the two French marshals could reorganise their forces and combine against him.

The resources available for the new attempt were in some ways much superior to those which had been allotted to Beresford. The bulk of the army was present,

*Elvas, Dickson's source of artillery. The defences of Badajos were observable twelve miles away, by using a telescope on the tower of Fort La Lippe (far right).*

and a considerable convoy of siege stores had just reached Elvas from Lisbon. There were twenty-one Engineer officers available, together with twenty-five rank and file of the Royal Military Artificers, eleven officers of the Line as assistant engineers, and one hundred and sixty-nine assorted tradesmen, mostly carpenters and miners, from the same source.

By far the weakest part was the artillery, which had again to be found from Elvas by the infatigable Dickson. His problem was greatly aggravated by the poor condition of many of the carriages used in the earlier siege, for as no block carriages had been available the guns had been taken back to Elvas on their normal carriages, which had suffered considerably in the process, particularly since the circumstances of their return had made it necessary to move them as fast as possible. By diligent searching however Dickson succeeded in assembling thirty 24 pounders, four 16 pounders, four 10in howitzers, and eight 8in howitzers, many of which had of course been brought forward, although not necessarily used, in the first siege. Sir Charles Oman claims to have detected a discrepancy here between Dickson's numbers and those given by Jones, but if it exists the author of this work failed to find it after a careful comparison of the two accounts.

In view of the general incapacity of the Elvas's guns, arrangements had been made for six modern Portuguese iron ship's guns to be sent up from Lisbon, together with a company of British artillery-men so as to give a leaven of trained gunners to the inexperienced Portuguese. Wellington's new plan was based closely on his earlier one, although he proposed to use a greater number of guns in a counter-battery role in an attempt to keep down the fire from the fortress, and also planned to construct many more works to protect the besiegers against sorties. In particular he considered it essential to conduct all the various operations simultaneously and with equal vigour, so as to confuse the garrison as to his final point of attack until the last possible moment. By 27 May all was ready, with the 7th Div at Cristoval, and the 3rd Div and the Portuguese on the main front. The bridge had been replaced and the stores were all in position. Before operations started however, it was necessary to conduct a careful reconnaissance of the castle, since if it had been strongly re-trenched on the north side, any fire brought to bear on it from Cristoval would be a good deal less effective. It was in fact found that no work had been done, but in order to maintain constant surveillance a very powerful telescope was mounted on the tower of Fort La Lippe at Elvas, some twelve miles away. It was said that just before sunset,

when the light was behind the observer, it was possible to see every detail with clarity. On the night of 29 May works were opened against Pardeleras with the intention of misleading the besieged, while on the next day the last division of guns was brought into the artillery park from Elvas. A system of replenishment of ammunition had been devised, by which there were never fewer than 300 rounds per gun and 200 rounds per howitzer actually available on the spot.

The next night, work began on the castle parallel, which ran in a roughly north west – south east direction, its centre being some eight hundred yards east of the place. As there had been what amounted to a dress rehearsal in the course of the earlier siege, everything went smoothly and by first light the working party was well under cover. Only six guns were turned on it, and these caused so little trouble that work was able to go on throughout the day, with the result that by the evening the trench was six feet wide and was provided with an excellent parapet.

On the night of 30 May work also began against Cristoval, the intention being to establish four batteries: No1 against the castle, No2 to breach the flank of Cristoval previously attacked, No3 to batter the defences generally, and No4 to cover the bridge, there also being a parallel to link and support these works. However things did not go well, for no sooner had work begun than a heavy fire was opened from the fort which caused many casualties. Since the last siege the defenders had painstakingly removed every scrap of topsoil, and although a row of gabions was erected in front of the works and filled with soil brought up from the rear, these only gave cover from view and were not proof against artillery. There was no possible chance of building the batteries by the normal method of pick and shovel, since trained miners were needed to deal with the almost solid rock encountered. Much the same thing occurred the next night, although battery No4, being somewhat off to a flank, was completed, the miners having to resort to blasting to sink the guns into the rock. In view of the problem of maintaining proper line at night, much of the fire came from 16in mortars from the castle, which caused many casualties, although fireballs fired from guns would often give enough light for grape and cannister to be employed. Nevertheless work continued on the next night, that of 1 June, soil being brought forward in sandbags and baskets from wherever it was available, a slow and tiring process. Fortunately the parallel was on the lip of a fairly steep slope so that many of the shells which landed just over the work rolled downhill before exploding. The fuzes

for these had to be cut by hand, and in general it was usual to over-estimate slightly to avoid premature outbursts well short of the target. In this particular case the practice proved beneficial to the besiegers. Work on the castle parallel, being in soft soil, progressed well and did not draw a great deal of fire from the defenders.

On the next night things went better. Considerable quantities of woolpacks had been bought in Elvas, and these were used to form excellent parapets for the Cristoval attack. Work continued throughout the day, albeit under steady fire, and the construction of the batteries and magazines went so well that they were finished during the night of 2 June.

One of the most remarkable things about this attack was the great use made by the defenders of musket fire, which was apparently very effective even at ranges of over 400yds. Work on the castle parallel was, by comparison, largely undisturbed. By some miscalculation however the parallel was too short; it had been planned to approach the castle as its right end was extended, but in view of the importance of time, the decision was taken to accept that the breaching battery would have to be further away from its target.

By first light on 3 June all the batteries were completed, armed, and ready to open fire. By this time the British artillery-men had been hurried up from

| Distribution of pieces against Badajos 3 June 1811 | | |
|---|---|---|
| **Battery** | **Pieces** | **Target** |
| No1 | 5 × 24 pounders | Cristoval |
| No2 | 4 × 24 pounders | Cristoval |
| | 4 × 8in howitzers | Cristoval |
| No3 | 4 × 24 pounders | Cristoval |
| No4 | 4 × 16 pounders | Badajos Castle |
| | 2 × 10in howitzers | Badajos Castle |

Lisbon by mules and distributed amongst the various batteries, ready to open fire at 0930am. Firing was at first inaccurate, but as the gunners began to master the idiosyncracies of their particular gun, it improved noticeably, even though the range to the castle was far too long for the pieces in use. By the late afternoon the castle wall had begun to disintegrate, but it was soon clear that at that point it was no more than a stone facing to a perpendicular wall of hard clay, which fell away in flakes without showing much sign of providing a practicable slope.

The guns soon began to show their age. One of the 24 pounders in the castle battery blew out its bush, and a second became so hot from continuous firing that its metal softened to the extent that the barrel actually drooped at the muzzle. In the operation against Cristoval the French return fire was fast and accurate, and one 8in howitzer was soon knocked out. A 10in howitzer then broke its carriage; these pieces had had their wheels removed and were being used as mortars with their carriages resting on the ground. This was satisfactory provided the elevation of the barrel did not exceed 30°, but in this case it was raised to 40° and the carriage soon collapsed; yet another of the brass guns drooped and so became unserviceable, although the rate of fire was no more than one hundred rounds per day. Ammunition supply was maintained by means of one hundred and sixty mules, and one hundred and fifteen bullock carts; Pte Wheeler of the 51st Regt, on trench guard near Cristoval recounts how one of the latter came to grief:

'An old Portuguese had just arrived with a cart loaded with ammunition drawn by two oxen; he had just got his load deposited in the magazine when the enemy favoured us with a shell from Big Tom of Lincoln (the name we have given to one of their tremendous mortars). I watched its

*A Royal Engineer moves up a gabion, an essential piece of equipment for protection against defensive fire, where the rocky ground at Badajos limited the depth of trench work.*

progress and saw it burst a few feet over the oxen, they were cut to pieces with the cart. When the cloud of dust and smoke had cleared away we observed the old fellow running like a deer. He had miraculously escaped unhurt. Besides killing the oxen one of our guns in the battery was dismounted'.

On the night of 3 June the castle parallel was extended to the right to enable a new battery, No6, to be constructed closer to its target. Next morning fire continued from the original battery, but the clay remained perpendicular and the losses were high. One 24 pounder dropped, one was disabled, and one 10in howitzer damaged its carriage due to over-elevation. Fire was reduced to a maximum of eight rounds per hour in an attempt to avoid overheating. Firing also continued against Cristoval but one 24 pounder drooped and two 10in howitzers smashed their carriages, for which no replacements were available, these casualties also being due to the use of too high an elevation. That

*No5 battery and connecting parallel to the east of Badajos. The latter was subsequently extended to the north-west and batteries No6 and No7 erected closer to the town to deliver heavier fire into the Castle breach.*

night the new battery against the castle was completed and armed with the guns from No5. When fire was opened next morning the garrison of Cristoval had moved a gun to bear on the castle parallel, and solid earth traverses had to be built to protect the workmen. The 24 pounder which had blown its bush on 3 June was brought back into service having been re-bushed locally, apparently by filling the hole with molten copper and re-drilling the vent.

The fire from No6 battery continued to be very good, but the breach still remained perpendicular. The garrison had achieved so much progress in retrenching it that they were able to continue to work during daylight hours. Two more 24 pounders became unserviceable, drooping at the muzzle in spite of the reduced rate of fire.

The breach in Cristoval was also improved considerably, although two more 24 pounders failed. No3 battery, having proved ineffectual, was dismantled and its guns used to replace casualties in the other batteries. On the night of 5 June work began on a further extension of the parallel to the right and yet another battery was marked out for the iron ship's guns which were expected from Lisbon. On the same night Lt Forster of the Engineers had examined the breach

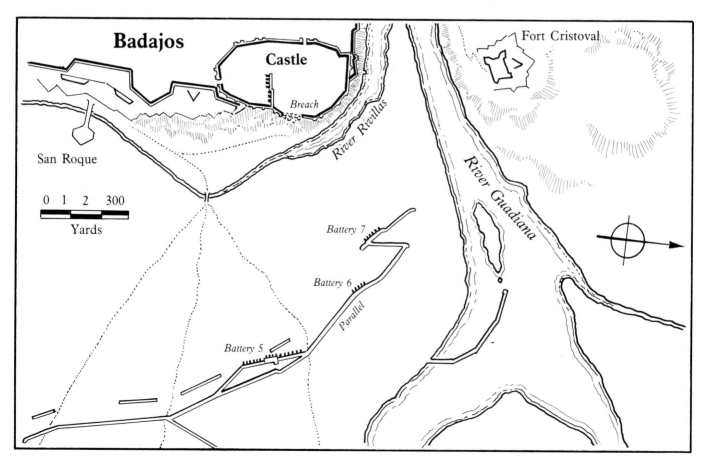

in Cristoval and decided that entry was feasible. Fire was therefore continued throughout 6 June with a view to assaulting the defences after dark that evening. The fire from the fort continued to be heavy and accurate, and one 24 pounder and one 8in howitzer were disabled in the course of the day.

It was planned that the assault should be preceded by a forlorn hope consisting of an officer and twenty-five men from the 51st Regt, guided by an engineer and carrying two ladders. Next should come a company with ten ladders, with a further company in support one hundred paces in rear. This gave a total force of about 180 men for the actual assault, and strict orders were given that it was to be conducted with the bayonet only. Other troops were also detailed to cut off the land communication between the fort and the town. The orders were that once the fort was entered it should be made proof from the fire of the castle by the digging of covered communications across it, the actual details of these necessarily being left to the engineer officer on the spot. A party of one hundred workmen with tools and gabions were to be stationed in the trenches, ready to be called forward as soon as the place had fallen. The breach was to be made passable for artillery, if possible.

The assault was launched at midnight and at first all went well. The forlorn hope, led by Ensign Dyas of the 51st Regt and guided by Lt Forster, dropped into the ditch and found the breach quite easily under a comparatively light fire, but it was here that their troubles started. The wall had been cut some seven feet above the level of the ditch, and the rubble which had come down had initially formed a perfectly practicable slope up. Due however to the long interval between last light and the actual assault, the French had been able to shovel away all the debris, and had also blocked the breach itself with old carts and other obstacles.

The ladders were therefore too short to achieve anything, and after a brief consultation Dyas and Forster came to the sensible conclusion that there was nothing else to do but withdraw. Unfortunately at this moment the main body came up with a rush under Major Mackintosh and plunged into the ditch, upon which the garrison showered shells, grenades, rocks and other missiles into the milling crowd below until over a hundred of them had been killed or wounded. These included Lt Forster who died from a musket shot in the body. The survivors of this bloody shambles then extricated themselves from the ditch and withdrew. As there was still a degree of movement between the fort and the town, it was surmised that the garrison had been temporarily reduced, otherwise casualties might well

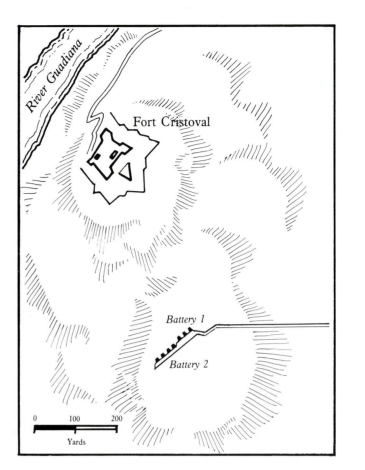

*The capture of Fort Cristoval was one of the main objectives during the first two sieges of Badajos. Though the defences were breached, the final British assault was resolutely repulsed with 70% losses.*

have been even greater.

Meanwhile, work was continuing on the castle parallel and the new battery, No7, which was completed before daylight. Fire against the breach continued at the best rate of which the ancient guns were capable, with the gun in Cristoval continuing its plunging fire upon them. Attempts were made to break up the still vertical face below the breach with shells with long fuzes, but the clay was so hard that the shells simply bounced off and exploded harmlessly far down the slope.

That night the seven iron 24 pounders from Lisbon were run into the new No7 battery and they commenced firing on the morning of the 8th. Their effect was soon apparent, for the clay finally began to crumble until it looked as if the castle breach might be accessible to a single active man. This, although encouraging was still not good enough, so fire continued steadily. At daylight on 8 June Wellington also reconnoitred the breach in Cristoval and ordered fire on it to be kept up. Inevitably the brass guns continued to become unserviceable one

after the other as firing continued, while on the castle front one of the new iron guns was also disabled by a shot from the fortress.

That night Capt Patton of the engineers went out with a small patrol to ensure that the fords across the Rivillas were still unobstructed and the approaches to the castle breach otherwise clear. They unfortunately clashed with a French *picquet* on the way back, and Capt Patton was mortally wounded. His patrol got him back to the trenches however, and he was able to report before he died that all was still well on the front.

A steady fire of grape and case was kept up on the castle breach all night, but the garrison nevertheless succeeded in clearing a great deal of the accumulated rubble. This was said to be due to the very small size of the balls in the Portuguese missiles, which lost their velocity far too quickly to be effective at 500-600yds range. Fire continued next day and by that evening so much more rubble had come down that the breach was again considered practicable. A new and more efficient form of grape was then devised by making up eight or ten 3 pounder roundshot into sandbags and firing this from the 24 pounders, which appeared to be highly effective. The breach in Cristoval was continuously bombarded to such good effect that it was decided to assault again that evening, as soon as it should be dark enough for the attackers to approach unobserved. It was noticed that the fire from the place was greatly reduced, which gave further hope that an assault might succeed.

The plan for this assault was to attack the breach with a forlorn hope of one officer and twenty-five men, followed by a further seventy-five close behind them. At the same time a similarly-constituted party would escalade the front face of the work, ladders being of course provided for each party, six for the breach and ten for the wall. Other troops were detailed to cut off communication with the town, and strong parties were detailed to keep the parapets of the place under heavy musketry fire while the assault was in progress. As in the previous assault, workmen with tools and gabions were to be available to retrench the fort and make the breach passable for guns. The assaulting force

*An infantryman of the 51st Regiment, together with a ladder party, advances during the abortive assault on Fort Cristoval.*

comprised a total of four hundred and fifty volunteers from the 51st, 85th, Chasseurs Britanniques, Brunswick Oels, and 17th Portuguese, and was under command of Major McGeechy of the Portuguese. The forlorn hope for the breach was again led by Dyas, closely followed by Lt Hunt of the Royal Engineers and a dozen assorted tradesmen with suitable tools.

The assault was met by tremendous fire from the garrison, which it was clear had been considerably reinforced in anticipation of this second attempt. Major McGeechy and Lt Hunt were both killed early on, as were many more, but in spite of this the attack went forward with spirit, greatly harassed by showers of missiles of all kinds flung down upon them from the parapets. Inevitably there was fearful confusion, made worse by the efforts of the ladder parties to manoeuvre and raise their unwieldy burdens against the wall. It is said too, that owing to the death of Lt Hunt, the attempt was made not on the breach but on the right bastion of the citadel which had been so damaged that it might well have been mistaken for it. Indeed for all we know it may have appeared to offer a better point of entry at the time. After persisting for an hour however the attackers saw that it was clearly hopeless to continue, and withdrew. So many officers had been hit that it was impossible to know who was in command from one minute to the next, which may have been the cause of the attack's continuing as long as they did. One hundred and forty men, 70 per cent of the attacking force, had been killed or wounded, and first light revealed them scattered on the glacis. The French, very sensibly, seized this opportunity to work in daylight, in the sure knowledge that the British guns would not fire on their own people.

Pte Wheeler of the 51st was cut off in the ditch by a party of French who made a sortie out of the fort, but by soaking his white haversack in the blood of a dead man he convinced them that he was badly wounded in the hip and they left him where he lay, one of them having taken his shirt, boots and stockings. He later wrote:

'... The moon rose which cast a gloomy light round the place. Situated as I was this added fresh horrors to my view, the place was covered with dead and dying, the old black walls and breach looked terrible and seemed like an evil spirit frowning on the unfortunate victims that lay prostrate at his feet. As the moon ascended it grew much lighter and I began to fear I should not be able to effect my escape, for the enemy kept a sharp look-out and if anyone endeavoured to

*Men of the Brunswick Oels Corps formed part of the force detailed to assault Fort Cristoval.*

escape they were sure to discharge a few muskets at him. I soon perceived that when our batterys fired they would hide behind the walls. I made the most of this by sliding down as often as I observed a flash from our works. By daybreak I had got to the plain below the fort. I had nothing to do but to have a run for it across the No 1 Battery. This plain, like our camp, was covered with small dry thistles. The enemy discharged two guns loaded with roundshot, and several muskets at me, and I bounded like a deer, the Devil take the thistles. I felt none of them until I was safe behind the battery'.

A Capt Douglas kindly gave him a drink out of his bottle and he made his way back to camp, where to his astonishment he saw Dyas. He noted that 'he was without cap, his sword was shot off close to the handle, the sword scabbard was gone and the laps of his frockcoat were perforated with balls'. Dyas was

*Arthur Wellesley, 1st Duke of Wellington in 1813. Following the two unsuccessful attacks on Badajos in 1811 he is said to have commented that he would be 'his own engineer' the next time.*

promoted to lieutenant in his turn on the death of Lt Westropp in the same attack, but very surprisingly received no other recognition of his very remarkable gallantry on both occasions.

At 10am that morning, 10 June, the British asked for a truce to remove their dead and wounded. A truce was granted, and although some fire continued afterwards, this may be said to have marked the end of the Second Siege of Badajos. Wellington had information that both Marmont and Soult were advancing to relieve the castle and therefore had to get himself into a good defensive position as quickly as possible. Had progress been better he might perhaps have risked a couple more days, but as it was clear that it would take longer than that, there was no object in prolonging things to a dangerous point. There was also the consideration that he could not afford to take any more ammunition from Elvas, since once he withdrew, that place would have to look after itself.

By 12 June the guns, ammunition, and other stores were well on their way, and any other material, which although not worth moving might be of use to the garrison, had been burnt. The blockade continued until 16 June, when the whole allied army concentrated at Albuera in preparation for a withdrawal, and on 19 June Marmont and Soult entered the place. The garrison was already on half-rations and in another ten days would have been compelled either to capitulate or make an attempt to destroy the place and cut its way out.

The two sieges just described did not reflect any great credit on Wellington or his professional advisers. Wellington was not of course a trained engineer, and perhaps more important, had never had any practical experience of a European siege in full form. He had in his time seen many Indian hill forts taken by rough and

*The second siege of Badajos as seen from the two left-hand batteries firing down onto Fort Cristoval with the River Guadiana beyond.*

ready methods, which may have given him a somewhat exaggerated idea of the ease with which sheer dash and courage would take British soldiers over stone walls, but no amount of dash and courage would be enough against skilful and determined defenders unless it was properly directed. The essence of the thing was time. When Sir William Napier, author of one of the early great histories of the war in which he himself had served with some distinction, wrote the passage on the rules of the art previously quoted in this book, he was stating no more than the obvious. It is however also necessary to make it clear that he was stating it in terms of the 17th and 18th centuries, when those same rules had been formulated.

Although Vauban accepted that all fortresses varied, it was still possible for him to lay down quite detailed guidelines for the time needed to take an 'average' one (which, incidentally, he calculated as forty-three days) but the nature of warfare had changed considerably by the Napoleonic era, and therefore sometimes the rules no longer applied.

The problem was that Wellington always had to reckon the time he had as being the time it would take his opponents to move superior numbers against him, and this was never really long enough to allow the rules to be complied with. Col Fletcher's plan to strike first at San Cristoval, a stoutly-built fort standing on solid rock, which virtually precluded the digging of

*An 18pdr gun from the Napoleonic War on its original carriage at Herat in Afghanistan. Such British guns suffered less from excessive wear during the sustained siege work.*

approaches in the normal way, was by no means ideal, but it did afford just a chance of success in the time available. Given normal conditions San Cristoval could be disregarded, but as we shall see later in the account of the next (successful) attack on the place in 1812, the more orthodox alternative, conducted with superior means, still took twenty-one days of open trenches. It is true that none of the engineers had had any first-hand experience of a siege, and equally true that they lacked both skilled workmen and stores, but they were competent men and would have carried the thing through had time not defeated them.

The problems with the guns have already been discussed in some detail, but it may be of interest to add that after the end of the Napoleonic wars a certain amount of consideration was given to the subject of droop. As it does not appear to have been a significant matter except with the ancient Portuguese guns, the research was to a great extent academic and the results inconclusive. Maj-Gen Hughes, a leading modern expert on muzzle-loading ordnance, is of the opinion that although a degree of actual droop may have occurred, much of the trouble was probably due to, or at least greatly increased by, excessive wear. We know that the metal used was extremely soft and the bores heavily pitted and corroded, so it is not surprising that prolonged firing with roundshot, (much of it ill-fitting) and good powder soon took its disastrous toll.

It may perhaps be said that Major Dickson was possibly optimistic in his assessment of the capacity of museum pieces to batter breaches in modernised works, but would Wellington have believed him if he had reported otherwise? His somewhat precarious relationships with a series of senior artillery officers is well known, and it is very possible that in his determination to go on he might well have decided to go ahead with the inadequate materials available, despite advice to the contrary. The decision to go ahead was his, and as he was by no means a rash general he must have calculated that success was reasonably possible with the resources available. Perhaps old General Picton, whose long ordeal in the Court of King's Bench after his Governorship of Trinidad had given him a taste for legal jargon, summed it up wittily when he commented that Wellington had 'sued Badajos in former pauperis'.

Before leaving the reasons for the failure it is but fair to say that one of the causes, not specifically stated but very clear from any account of the siege, was the devoted gallantry and professional competence of the commander of the place and his garrison, particularly those members of it which held San Cristoval.

# CHAPTER THREE

## Ciudad Rodrigo—
## The Preparatory Moves

By 17 June 1811 Wellington had his army in a strong, defensive position on the river Caia, while General Blake and his Spaniards had gone off on a wide swing southwest through Portugal so as to threaten Seville.

On 23 June the combined French armies approached Wellington's position and reconnoitred it carefully, although as it was, as usual, well concealed, and entrenched where necessary, they did not discover very much. There was a little skirmishing, but the French declined battle. Soult, although in many ways a fine commander was never at his best on the battlefield itself, and he probably knew enough of Wellington's reputation as a defensive fighter on a position of his own choosing, to be somewhat unnerved at the thought of attacking him. He was in any case apprehensive about Andalusia, which he seems to have regarded as virtually a private kingdom, since in his absence the guerrillas had been very active. At the end of June therefore, he marched off southwards, to the great fury of Marmont, who felt, not unnaturally, that he had been badly treated. There was however nothing he could do about it, so after spending the next fortnight in scraping together some provisions for Badajos he marched back to the Tagus.

As soon as Wellington was sure that the French had dispersed, he too departed. The valley of the Guadiana was notoriously bad for fever in the summer months and he was anxious to get his troops back further north to the healthy uplands along the Portuguese frontier. He was by that time sufficiently strong to begin contemplating operations in Spain, but before he could

*British artillery on the move during the Napoleonic Wars. Field guns travelled with the armies during the campaign but for attacks on fortresses and strong points special siege trains were formed.*

*Marshal August Frédéric Marmont. Though an active and capable commander, his ability to concentrate sufficient forces against the British was constantly hampered by poor supplies and communications.*

settled he moved north, and by mid-August had Ciudad Rodrigo under effective blockade.

Before describing Dickson's operation however it may be as well to consider the whole question of the British siege train, which has for many years caused acute differences between the various historians of the war. There appears to have been in the past a surprising amount of uncertainty regarding the location, and indeed the very existence, of a British siege train, before the first siege of Badajos in 1811. Napier and Oman both blame the failure of the second siege of Badajos on the neglect by the Government to supply Wellington with a proper complement of battering guns, but the general weight of evidence seems to be against them. As early as 1808 we find Wellesley (as he then was) discussing ordnance store ships in his despatches, and further mention of them is made in the proceedings of the inquiry after Cintra. None of this mentions siege guns specifically, as opposed to ordnance stores, but

do this he had to ensure a safe retreat into his base in Portugal by seizing the two great barrier fortresses, and as Badajos was not a practical proposition at that time of the year he decided to tackle Ciudad Rodrigo. It might be some time before he could start siege operations, but in the meanwhile he could blockade it so as to make its revictualling a major operation. He was not unduly worried about Marmont's presence on the Tagus because he knew that although the French marshal was an active and capable officer his shortage of food, and even worse his lack of transport to carry it, would make his future operations difficult. Wellington's experiences before Badajos had made it clear to him that he needed a proper siege train, and he therefore sent instructions for the ordnance storeships lying in the Tagus to be sent round to Oporto. There was of course always the risk of losing a siege train—Massena had come very close to losing his on his advance into Portugal in 1810—but the land route he had selected lay across wild and desolate country into which the French had hardly penetrated. On 19 July 1811 he sent for his artillery and engineer commanders, his Commissary-General, and the by then almost indispensable Dickson, and gave detailed orders for the move of the train from Oporto to Almeida, the actual move to be carried out by Dickson. Soon after this was

it is clear that considerable thought had been given to the possible future need to conduct sieges.

Fortescue is convinced that a siege train had been lying in storeships in the Tagus for two years, and quotes Wellington's letter of 20 March 1811 to Admiral Berkeley in which he states 'I propose to disembark the ordnance storeships (with the exception of the battering train)...' which if it does not state the actual time it had been available, at least makes its existence clear beyond all doubt. The author of the 'History of the British Army' also expresses surprise that Napier should not have known about this, but Napier, a confirmed Whig and ever on the lookout for a chance to denigrate the Tory government, may have preferred to be ignorant. It is true that his history appeared before the Duke's despatches, but apart from that authority there are various other references which suggest that the existence of the siege train was no secret. Burgoyne (a distinguished engineer officer whose name will appear

*A full siege train, which may have been held in store ships in the Tagus for up to two years, was available to Wellington. Its movement to Ciudad Rodrigo was to be a major undertaking.*

frequently in this book) wrote in a letter to Lord Derby from Lisbon on 29 May 1811 that 'our heavy artillery, hitherto always kept embarked here, has been ordered round to Oporto', and while this gives no indication as to the actual time it had been there, the use of the word 'always' suggests that it was not of recent arrival.

Major Dickson, when discussing the state of the carriages for the siege guns, noted that they were much shaken 'after two years on board ship' which seems to be conclusive when coming from such a source, although to be honest he does not say definitely where the ships had been in the period. Nevertheless it seems certain that heavy guns and accessories had been available for a long time but that Wellington had preferred to keep them embarked, and when it is considered that the Government (and indeed much of the Army), had at least considered the possibility of an evacuation in the autumn of 1810 this is not surprising. It must be remembered that in spite of its great value for its particular task, a siege train constituted a fearful encumbrance to an army engaged in mobile operations, especially in a country such as Portugal where the roads were rudimentary. As we shall see in more detail later, the train moved by Dickson consisted of sixty-eight

pieces, many weighing over three tons and able to fire two or three times their own weight of shot daily. Such a convoy could only move on carefully selected and improved roads and then only at ten miles or so per day, so Wellington was probably very wise to leave it on its ships until a specific need arose. The need at Badajos was of course an unexpected one, since the greatest pessimist in the army could hardly have expected the treacherous surrender of a strong and well found fortress when a force was in actual march to relieve it.

The Memorandum issued by Wellington for the move of the train is a remarkably comprehensive document and is reproduced here in full to show the sheer size and complexity of the problem:

19 July

1. The heavy ordnance and stores, and engineers' tools, now embarked in the transports in the Douro, being required at Ciudad Rodrigo, measures must be adopted to move them thither.

2. They must be removed into boats at Oporto, and carried by water to Lamego.

3. At Lamego they must be landed, and the ordnance removed at once by 384 pairs of bullocks to Trancoso, the stores, that is to say, 350 rounds for each 18 pounder and 24 pounder gun, and 160 rounds for each 10in mortar to be removed there on 892 country carts.

4. The engineers' stores to be removed to Trancoso on 200 country carts.

5. The 892 carts mentioned in No3 to be unloaded at Trancoso, and to return to Lamego to bring up to Trancoso the remainder of the stores.

6. Upon the arrival of the second quantity of stores at Trancoso the whole ordnance and stores for 350 rounds a gun and for 160 rounds a mortar, in 892 carts, and engineers' stores in 200 carts to move to Ciudad Rodrigo.

7. The ordnance stores to be unloaded at Ciudad Rodrigo and the 892 carts to return to Trancoso for the second convoy.

8. Col Framlingham to order from Lisbon to Oporto 1600 barrels of powder, to complete the quantity at that place to what will be sufficient for the shot and shells with the battering train.

9. Major Dickson is requested to proceed to Oporto, in order to superintend the removal of the ordnance and stores from thence, and Col Fletcher

will send there an officer of the engineer department.

10. These officers will act in concert with the gentlemen employed by the Commissary-General to collect the necessary boats and carts, and the matter should be arranged in such a matter as that the stores could be at Lamego at the time the carts are ready to remove them.

11. The two companies of British artillery now at Lisbon to be ordered to Oporto by sea.

12. Probably the time will take

|  | |
|---|---|
| | 12 days for Major Dickson's journey to Oporto |
| | 6 days for the removal of the ordnance and |
| 24 | stores to the boats |
| | 6 days from Oporto to Lamego (Pezo de Regoa) |
| | 8 days from the boats moving up the hill to Lamego |
| | 4 days from Lamego to Trancoso |
| | 4 days carts to return and load |
| | 4 days second trip to Trancoso |
| | 6 days to Ciudad Rodrigo |
| | 6 days to return to Trancoso |
| | 6 days to bring the second quantity of stores to Ciudad Rodrigo |

_____

62 Days

It will be seen that in order to move the train, it was necessary to assemble hundreds of boats, together with thousands of soldiers, mules, and bullocks, and a great number of country carts, all of which then had to be conducted through a primitive and largely-undeveloped area, where roads were no more than rough cart tracks and food for both man and beast was extremely difficult to find in the quantities required. When it is considered in addition that the only means of co-ordination over this vast area was by messengers mounted on horses or mules the vastness of the problems of command and administration becomes very apparent. There was also a need for secrecy, for although the great bulk of the Spanish and Portuguese peoples were rabidly anti-French, spies nevertheless existed. As it was impossible to conceal the fact that the move was taking place, it was given out that the guns were intended to re-arm the fortress of Almeida, which the French had blown up earlier in the year, and where large-scale repair work was actually in progress, as Dickson was soon to find.

His orders bade him go to Oporto via Almeida to see how many roundshot could be salvaged from the ruins,

*Oporto, at the mouth of the Douro, where Dickson supervised the transfer of the siege train from the store ships to river craft for the journey upstream.*

since every hundred so retrieved would save over a ton on the long and difficult pull from Oporto. When he reached Almeida he found a scene of considerable desolation, for the highly competent French engineers had done their work well with the resources available to them. 'Blowing up' a fortress is of course a vague term, but they had dug a series of mines, 25ft apart and 15ft deep, immediately inside the scarp wall on the south-west side, and after piling all the guns and other non-combustible stores in the ditch in front, had blown the whole thing in, completely filling the ditch and covering its contents with hundreds of tons of earth and masonry. Fortunately 24 pounder roundshot were virtually indestructible, and since ample Portuguese labour, largely unskilled but willing, was available some eight thousand of them were finally retrieved and proved of great use in the siege which eventually followed.

Dickson then went on to Oporto, following in reverse the route laid down for him, but found much of it so bad that he wrote to Wellington suggesting that certain changes should be made. By 3 August Major Dickson had begun the transfer of the train from the storeships to river boats for passage to Lamego. It is clear that the 'gentlemen employed by the Commissary-General', to whom reference is made in paragraph 10 of the

memorandum referred to earlier, had done their work well in the assembly of suitable craft, a task in which they had been greatly assisted by the highly-developed trade in port wine which had led to a well-organised system of river transport. The main problem facing Dickson and his staff was the fact that as the Douro was rather low, and so a comparatively larger number of small craft had to be used. Nevertheless the first flotilla left on 7 August with further daily departures until 14 August.

A great deal of preliminary work also had to be done at Lamego before the train was fit for service in Spain; the timbers for example, behind which the guns were drawn, were fitted with shafts for the off-side wheel horse in accordance with normal artillery custom, but as these were quite unsuitable for bullock draught they all had to be replaced by centre poles. Special traces also had to be prepared for them, while work was also started on the manufacture of several hundred open-topped wooden boxes into which the shot would be packed for transit on bullock carts.

Dickson was at this time very unwell, due presumably to the Guadiana fever, a type of malaria, which had made Wellington so anxious to get his army away from the area. Fortunately all his plans had been made and he had a most competent second-in-command, a Major May, whom he could trust to put them into execution. The actual pieces to be moved consisted of thirty-four 24 pounders, four 18 pounders, eight 10in mortars (all iron) and two 8in brass howitzers. Later twenty 5½in iron howitzers, throwing a 24 pound shell and specially developed for siege work, were also added, and when we include spare carriages, forge wagons and general stores, to say nothing of powder and shot, the total quantity was formidable. Unfortunately there were no block carriages available, so that all the pieces had to be moved over atrocious tracks on their normal operational travelling carriages, and as many of the wheels had shrunk during their long stay on shipboard, they were in need of almost constant attention and repair. The mortars, not being on wheeled carriages, presented special problems, since they could not be transported in country carts. Eventually the problem was overcome by the use of crude but effective sledges.

On 27 August the first division lumbered off, followed at regular intervals by four more, and then the reserve. They were accompanied by a strong body of Portuguese militia, partly to act as an escort, and partly to provide labour should it be required. General Bacallas, Military Governor of the province, had of cousrse been instructed to help in every way possible, and having plenty of local militia available he quickly set them to work with great success. Although they were more or less unskilled they were all countrymen, accustomed to hard work and familiar with the practical problems involved, and perhaps more importantly, imbued with a ferocious hatred of the French and thus very willing to help an ally capable of finally defeating them. The road, so called, was little more than a bullock track, but the many difficult places had been either improved or bypassed so that the first stage of thirty-two miles to the village of Villa da Ponte was covered by some divisions in three days, while none took longer than four, so that an excellent start had been made. As this early part of the route was the one laid down by Wellington, Dickson had had no need to wait for agreement to the changes he had suggested earlier.

At this stage however, Marshal Marmont took a hand and on 9/10 September Dickson wrote to a correspondent that he thought they would not move on from Villa da Ponte for some time. So it proved, and for the next ten weeks Dickson and his vast collection

*General Jean Marie François Dorsenne whose arrival from France with two fresh divisions permitted Marmont to move against Wellington before the latter could invest Ciudad Rodrigo.*

of impedimenta remained immobile in the remote mountain villages, waiting anxiously to hear the outcome of the clash of arms which was taking place some sixty miles to the south-east.

By August Marmont had heard from his spies that considerable quantities of siege stores were being prepared in the vicinity of Ciudad Rodrigo, and decided that he must move in that direction. Like every other French commander in Spain he was chronically short of both food and the means to move it, but by great efforts, helped by the fact that the new harvest was coming in, he assembled sufficient supplies and transport to allow him to undertake limited mobile operations. Although the fortress still had adequate provisions, he took the opportunity of replenishing its stocks at the same time, which might save him a similar and costly operation later on in the year.

He had been reinforced by two new divisions from France under Général Dorsenne, so that even allowing for sick and essential garrisons his disposable force was probably just over 55,000 men. Wellington at that time had no more than 46,000 men and since many of his more recent reinforcements were still suffering in some degree from fever caught on the Walcheren expedition, his sick list was long. He had heard of Dorsenne's arrival and had no wish to fight the French, but he wanted to keep them concentrated, which would not only consume their supplies but also give the ubiquitous guerrillas an excellent chance to re-infiltrate areas they had previously strongly held. His plan was to withdraw his army, if really necessary, to a strong defensive position and then trust to his reputation to deter the French marshal from attacking him. In the meanwhile he left his army widely dispersed, believing that Marmont would do no more than re-victual Ciudad Rodrigo. In this belief he was perhaps trusting a little too much in the power of his name.

On 25 September Marmont entered Ciudad Rodrigo with his convoy, but contrary to Wellington's calculations he did not withdraw at once. He was young and ambitious and since he had never actually crossed swords with Wellington it is likely that he was at that time somewhat less impressed by the latter's reputation than some of his fellow marshals. It is clear that his spies had told him that the British were not concentrated for battle, for he at once sent out two reconnaissances in force, to find out exactly what the situation was. One of these forces, which consisted of cavalry and horse

artillery only, was quickly driven back, but the other, pushing on to the south-west, soon came upon Picton's 3rd Division, widely dispersed over six or seven miles. The British infantry, who by that stage of the war were confident of their ability to deal with French cavalry, were able to make an orderly retreat, a move in which they were greatly helped by their own cavalry, and after a couple of perilous days Wellington finally got his troops concentrated in a strong position, upon which Marmont withdrew to the general area of Talavera, with Dorsenne going even further north to the Douro. The French had achieved the destruction of a quantity of siege stores, but on the debit side had had to consume two-thirds of the supplies intended for Ciudad Rodrigo.

As soon as it was clear that Marmont had retired, Wellington resumed his watch on Ciudad Rodrigo and ordered more siege stores to be prepared. Work was also restarted on the wrecked fortifications of Almeida which were already in a sufficiently advanced stage of repair to be able to withstand anything less than a siege

*The route from the Douro to Almeida. Marmont's activites compelled Dickson to wait ten weeks at Villa da Porte. The march, though only about 100 miles, was to take some 94 days to complete.*

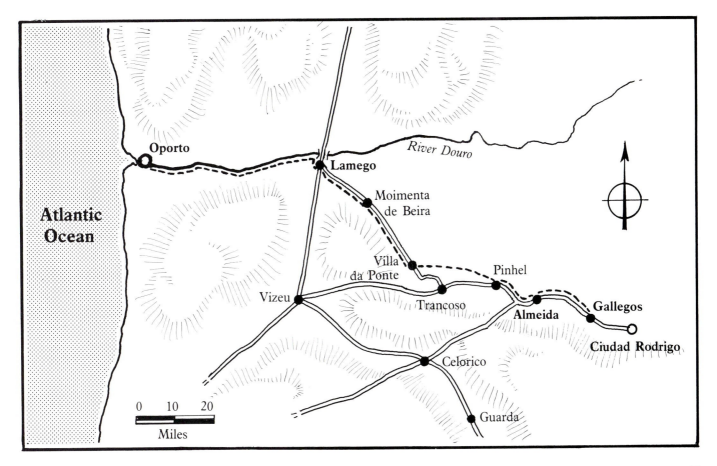

in form. Much of the actual blockade of Ciudad Rodrigo was conducted by the Spanish guerrillas, who on 15 October not only succeeded in driving off most of the garrison's beef cattle, which were grazing under guard in the near vicinity of the place, but also had the good fortune to capture the Governor who was inspecting them at the time.

On 14 November Wellington wrote to Dickson ordering him to continue on with the siege train to Almeida, a command which the latter, bored with inactivity, was more than happy to comply with as quickly as he could call in the bullocks from their grazing grounds and complete any other arrangements necessary after the long halt. Having had authority from

Wellington to vary the route as he had proposed earlier, he struck off eastwards just south of Villa da Ponte on a track which by-passed Trancoso, where the main difficulties lay, well to the north, and eventually reached Pinhel, whence a practicable road led to Almeida. It is not now absolutely clear if the alternative route to Pinhel was built from scratch by the militia, or whether they simply improved an existing track, although the latter seems to be by far the more likely. By 1 December the whole, huge convoy had reached Almeida, which was by then on the way to being completely restored to its former state, and parked in neat rows on the glacis. It had been a remarkable effort by Dickson and his officers, and much credit must also be given to the

Portuguese militia whose backbreaking work on the various tracks had made the whole thing possible. The only deficiencies were the shells for the howitzers and mortars which had been left behind due to lack of transport, but Wellington was very confident that he could settle the business with guns only.

An advanced artillery depot was then set up at Gallegos, some eleven miles west of Ciudad Rodrigo, and the bullocks sent off to recruit their strength on the best grazing available, after which the indefatigable Dickson, by then fortunately fully recovered from his earlier fever, set his technicians, mainly wheelers, to work on the gun carriages to repair the ravages of the journey. He was somewhat short of skilled tradesmen,

some of those borrowed from the arsenal at Oporto having deserted on the long march, but he borrowed replacements where he could and the work went on well. He himself then turned his personal attention to the highly technical business of restoring the guns of Almeida to enable them to fire. Almost all had been spiked by driving iron nails into their vents, and these had to be drilled out, a slow and tedious business done with hand tools and carried out by semi-skilled soldiers

*Exhausted British artillery halt during a forced march. Dickson's siege train, drawn by bullocks and escorted by Portuguese militia, who also laboured to improve the route, had a much less traumatic journey.*

with no previous experience of that type of work. In many cases it became necessary to heat the breaches of the brass guns in order to soften the metal which was to prove both difficult and potentially dangerous. All the guns had been left fully loaded with their bores jammed to the muzzle with other shot, stones and similar obstructions, and in theory these first had to be removed and the charges withdrawn. In practice this did not always prove possible, so in some cases Dickson simply had the breach end of the gun laid in a huge fire with the muzzles pointing at an earth bank. He would then retire to a safe distance, and wait for the charge to go off. Although this sounds a very rash system all apparently went well, with no casualties to guns or workmen. Some of the pieces also needed new bushes but these Dickson had made professionally in the foundry at Lisbon. As these were small items they could be carried in some numbers by a well-mounted messenger, so that there was no serious waste of time.

Wellington had a remarkably efficient intelligence service, based on agents all over the country and supplemented by numerous French despatches taken from messengers by the guerrillas who specialised in this kind of operation against small, lightly-escorted parties. The fate of the individuals concerned is probably too unpleasant to contemplate, but the despatches were usually in Wellington's hands very quickly. All this enabled him to get a remarkably clear picture of French intentions and troop movements, and by the end of the year it was clear that Marmont was sending troops eastward in considerable numbers, a proceeding which Wellington rightly deduced as being the result of orders received from Napoleon (who refused to appoint an overall commander in Spain and persisted in trying to run the campaign from Paris) to re-inforce Marshal Suchet, the commander in the eastern part of Spain. Further reports also continued to come in of extensive movements of French units back to France, and although Wellington could not know it, these were caused by Napoleon's withdrawal of troops for his Russian campaign. As the whole trend of French strength was away from Wellington's immediate objective, he finally decided to go ahead with the siege of Ciudad Rodrigo and orders were issued accordingly.

*The problems created for French commanders in the Peninsular by meagre supplies and the need to live off the land was exacerbated by continued attacks from Spanish guerrillas on their long lines of communication. Many despatches found their way into British hands, providing valuable intelligence.*

Ciudad Rodrigo stands on gently rising ground on the north bank of the Agueda, one of its earlier principal functions having been to protect the ancient Roman bridge which crosses the river at that point. The oldest part of the fortifications is almost certainly the ancient Moorish castle which still stands above the bridge, but it had later been encircled by an ancient wall, the whole perimeter being roughly oval in shape and almost eight hundred yards across on its longer axis and five hundred yards on its shorter. Apart from the original wall, the place is further protected by a *fausse-braie*, a revetted

earth bank designed to cover the base of the wall from fire, together with a number of ravelins. The soil for the *fausse-braie* had been taken from the front, so that its excavation formed a ditch. The exception to this is on the south side where the river and the original wall afforded sufficient defence. Most of the works are further protected by a long rocky glacis, so that in order to breach the wall it would be necessary to establish batteries very close to it, a proceeding which the nature of the ground rendered virtually impossible for all practical purposes.

Unfortunately (from the defenders' point of view) the place is commanded by two hills on its northern side; the little Teson, some 180yds from the ramparts and almost on the same level, and the Great Teson, some four hundred yards further north and about thirteen feet above rampart level. To make things worse the walls are separated from the little Teson by a rather steep little valley so that the northern wall of the place stands on a fairly steep down slope, with the result that the *fausse-braie*, some yards in front of it, does not afford as much protection to it as it ought. The writer has used the

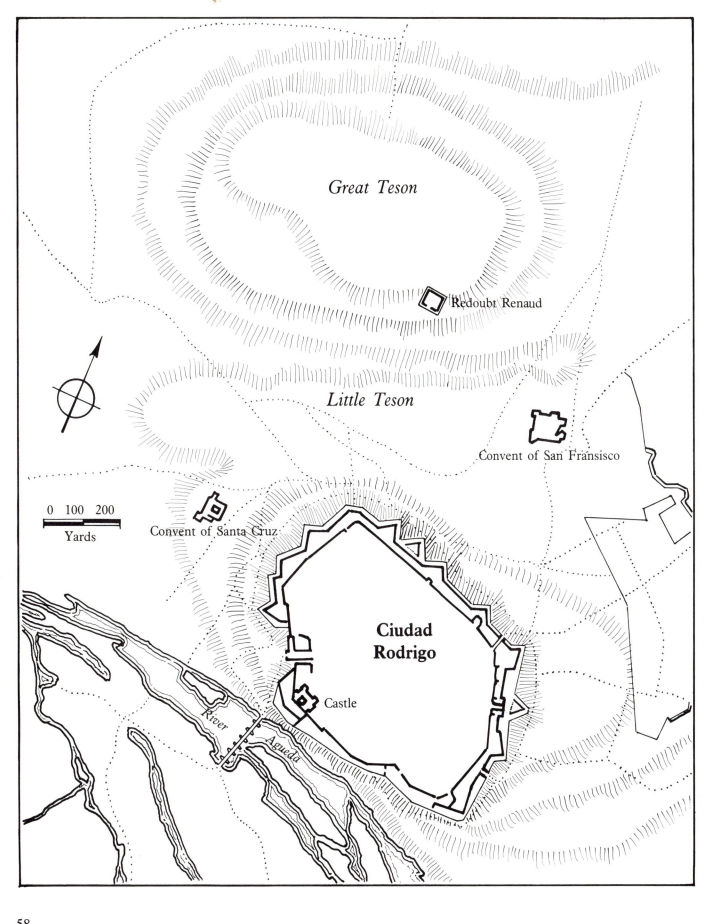

*Great Teson*

☐ Redoubt Renaud

*Little Teson*

Convent of San Fransisco

0  100  200
Yards

Convent of Santa Cruz

**Ciudad Rodrigo**

☐ Castle

*River*

*Agueda*

present tense in describing the place because the great bulk of the works appear to be very much as they were in the early 19th Century.

According to Colonel Belmas the garrison of the place consisted of 1818 of all ranks, although judging from the casualties and the returns of prisoners after the fortress had fallen, it seems that these figures are something of an under-estimate. Even if we accept, as was later claimed, that the garrison exceeded two thousand it was still not really adequate for what Captain Burgoyne, the British siege director, was later to describe as 'a very poor fortress'. The place was adequately supplied with food, since in early November General Thiebault, governor of Salamanca, had managed by a combination of skill, gallantry and daring bluff, to run a convoy in, sending with it the new governor, Brigadier General Barrié. Belmas however states that the place was short of meat, due presumably to the earlier capture of its beef cattle, so that the garrison had found it necessary to send out foraging parties to bring in what they could. As the area was sparsely populated they must have gone out for quite long distances which made them vulnerable to the lurking guerrillas, but they succeeded nevertheless in bringing in a hundred or so pigs.

Although the soil on the Tesons is stony, with water close below the surface, it was quite workable, so that the north side offered the obvious line of approach. The French, who had attacked and taken the fortress from that side in 1810, were well aware of its weakness and had done what they could to strengthen it. This they had done by building a strong redoubt, the Redoubt Renaud (named after its instigator, the unfortunate governor who had fallen into the hands of the guerrillas a few weeks earlier) and supporting it with a further crossfire of artillery from two strongly fortified convents. These were both outside the main defences the one, the convent of Santa Cruz being about 800 yards south-west of the redoubt and the other, that of San Fransisco, forming part of a suburb about 400 yards east. The whole of this suburb was further protected on the north and east by a simple earth bank of Spanish construction.

Wellington's plan for the capture of the place was essentially a simple one. He would first capture the

*The defences of Ciudad Rodrigo in 1812. The town was well defended to the south, with its curtain-wall and castle protected against siege works by the River Agueda. The two main outlying strong-points of the Convents of Santa Cruz and San Fransisco, and the lesser Redoubt Renaud, completed the defences.*

Redoubt Renaud by a surprise attack launched just after last light, and establish batteries close to it to subdue the fire of the place on that side. This was likely to be heavy because the fortress was not only well supplied with guns and munitions, but also housed the complete siege train of the Army of Portugal which Marmont had placed there so as not to be hampered by it in his earlier mobile operations.

Under cover of fire from the Great Teson the attackers would sap forward to the little Teson and there establish breaching batteries; while this was in progress they would continue to sap forward to the ditch and blow in the counterscarp so as to make a practical path forward to the breach. The breach itself would be made on the exact site of the one opened earlier by the French in the north-west corner of the works. The repairs were recent and as it was known that the mortar used had been poor, it was thought that the new masonry could soon be knocked down. As the French would undoubtedly retrench any breach made as soon as its location became apparent, it was also planned to turn all guns onto a tower further east at the last moment, the intention being to make a second point of entry by which the retrenchments of the first could be turned by a subsidiary attack.

As the fire from San Fransisco was likely to be heavy and accurate at so short a range, it was further planned to establish one battery on the east side of the Teson to make the place untenable. It was not thought that this would take long since no convent, however stoutly built, could resist for long the concentrated fire of 24 pounder iron guns only four hundred yards from it. The siege park was to be safely established in dead ground behind the great Teson, with a covered communication leading back to it.

The plan was exceptionally clear, simple and perfectly practicable with the resources available, and if nothing else its implementation would be of great interest and practical value to an Army which, as far as can be ascertained, did not include a single individual who had ever actually seen such an operation carried through to a successful conclusion.

The troops selected for the siege were the 1st, 3rd, 4th and Light Divisions who were to undertake the duty for 24 hrs each in rotation. The weather, as to be expected in central Spain in early January, was cold with frost, and as no tents were then carried for the army the troops concerned were billetted in neighbouring villages, some a considerable distance away. They were all on the wrong side of the river, which the troops had to cross by fords, and as the water was very cold and

full of large pieces of floating ice this was not a pleasant start to a day of hard and often dangerous work. Costello of the 95th (Rifles) wrote:

'One great annoyance we experienced at this time was having to cross the Agueda in going to and returning from the trenches. Pieces of ice that were constantly carried down this rapid stream bruised our men so much, that, to obviate it, the cavalry at length were ordered to form four deep across the ford, under the lee of whom we crossed comparatively unharmed, although by the time we reached the trenches our clothes were frozen into a mass of ice'.

It is perhaps as well that the comments of the cavalrymen detailed for this task do not appear to have been recorded for posterity. It is of interest to note that a trestle bridge had been built at Marialva, but as this was some eight miles west, it would have entailed an unacceptably long march to use it.

The Engineer support for the operation consisted of Lt-Col Fletcher and eighteen officers, together with eighteen rank and file of the Royal Military Artificers, together with certain other tradesmen, chiefly miners and carpenters, on loan from the regiments of the Divisions concerned. There were also twelve officer volunteers from the line as assistant engineers and one

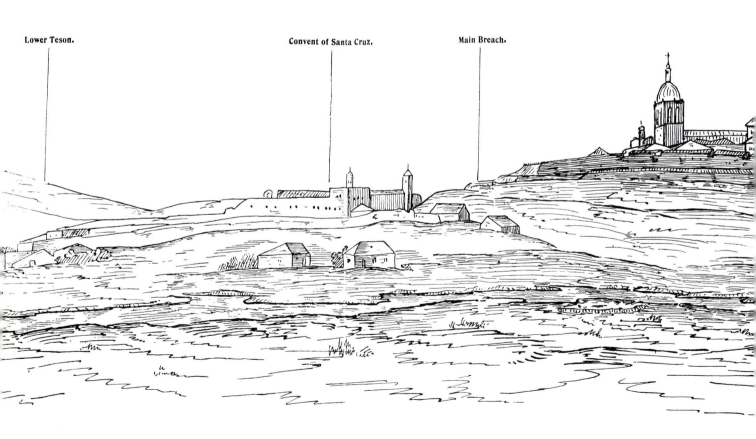

Lower Teson.  Convent of Santa Cruz.  Main Breach.

hundred and eighty men of the 3rd Division who had received some basic training as Sappers in the previous few months. The supply of tools and other siege stores was adequate, and consisted of 2,200 tools, 30,000 sandbags, 600 fascines, 1100 Gabions and the requisite quantity of timber for making batteries and magazines.

The greatest improvement was of course in the nature of the artillery available which comprised thirty-four 24 pounders of nine feet length and four 18 pounders of eight feet length, all modern iron guns, plus the necessary spare carriages and other impedimenta. Two days expenditure of ammunition was to be kept in the park and a similar amount at Gallegos, with a proportion of carts to replenish to Gallegos from Almeida and mules to carry it forward from there. The Commander Royal Artillery was Major-General Borthwick, together with Major Dickson as artillery siege director, and twelve other officers. The British gunners numbered 171, the Portuguese 370, although as the siege progressed it was found that these numbers were not enough to provide two shifts; the gunners of the field artillery batteries then came up with their division when it was on duty to help man the guns in the siege batteries.

*Panoramic drawing of Ciudad Rodrigo copied by Dickson from a sketch by Colonel May RA.*

Agueda river.

# CHAPTER FOUR
## The Siege of Ciudad Rodrigo

At noon on 8 January the Light Division forded the Agueda and invested Ciudad Rodrigo, to the no small surprise of its garrison who perhaps understandably found it incomprehensible that anyone should contemplate the siege of a major fortress in the frost and snow of midwinter. Later in the day a more conspicuous examination of the whole perimeter was made with a view to confusing the besieged as to the projected point of attack, although in the nature of things they must have had a fairly good idea as to where the blow was most likely to fall.

The attack on the Renaud redoubt, which was planned for that night, was made the responsibility of Lt-Col John Colborne who had recently transferred to the 52nd Regt from the 66th, with which regiment he had earlier greatly distinguished himself under General Hill. His force consisted, by his own account, of eight companies, two from the 43rd, four from his own 52nd, two from the 95th, and two from the Portuguese Cacadores, the selection in every case being made according to the relative seniority of their captains. At 8pm they advanced on the redoubt, and when they were fifty yards away Colborne gave the command 'Double quick', when the jangling of the equipment alerted the sentries who opened fire. The two guns and one howitzer in the place only had time to fire one round before four companies had surrounded the place and subdued the fire from the ramparts so that not a man dare lift his head to fire. The ladders were then raised under the direction of Capt Thompson of the Royal Engineers and three companies promptly mounted them

*Campbell's and M'Kinnon's brigades storm the main breach during the taking of Ciudad Rodrigo on the night of 19 January 1812. Five battalions were to pass through the gap.*

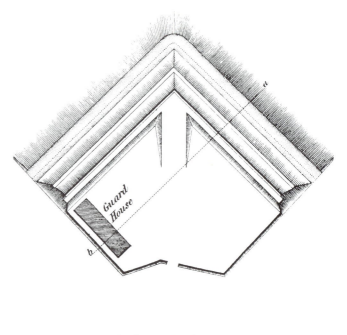

Section on the line a.b.

*Lt-Col John Colborne, in the uniform of the 52nd Regiment, led the force which took Redoubt Renaud by a coup-de-main. He narrowly missed capturing General Barrié, Ciudad Rodrigo's Governor.*

*Redoubt Renaud, with a palisaded ditch and rampart to the front but with a rear palisade only, was still expected to hold out for four days. Its lightning capture advanced British siege work considerably.*

while the fourth, moving round to the gorge of the work, forced the postern gate and rushed in. No mention is made of the Cacadores who were presumably in reserve.

The whole thing went like clockwork, so that an outpost which the French had confidently calculated would take four or five days to capture was in British hands in ten minutes, at a cost to the attackers of six killed and nineteen wounded. The garrison consisted of fifty men of whom only four succeeded in escaping back to the main fortress. According to Capt Burgoyne of the Royal Engineers this was due to the courage and presence of mind of a French artillery sergeant who flung a lighted shell amongst the attackers and then dashed through the gap caused as they scattered, followed by three soldiers. The French, confident in the belief that the redoubt would cause at least a four day delay, were clearly not as alert as they might have been, and many of their muskets were found still piled after the place had fallen. John Kincaid of the 95th, always a humourist, tells us how the French officer in

command complained bitterly of the unfairness of taking a place without first besieging it in due form, and as he had been due for relief next morning his anger was perhaps understandable. According to Colborne the Governor himself had been in the redoubt that evening and so only narrowly escaped the fate of his predecessor.

There is no doubt that the attack, which was brilliantly planned and executed, did much to set the tone for the remainder of the operation. Even the austere Craufurd, commanding the Light Division, was constrained to admit that Col Colborne seemed to be 'a very steady officer' which was possibly the highest praise he had ever bestowed on anybody in his life.

The rapid capture of the redoubt left virtually the whole of a long winter's night in which to work unseen, so that by dawn a lodgement had been made a little to the north-west of the place, and a proper communication dug back over the Teson to the engineer park on its north face. Soon after the fall of the redoubt had been confirmed to the main garrison they opened fire on it with everything they had, and as according to Col

Belmas there were no fewer than forty-eight guns on the north face of the fortification the fire was very heavy indeed. Colborne had fortunately anticipated this and had taken care to ensure that the redoubt was empty, so that no casualties were sustained.

At daylight on 9 January it was possible to obtain a good, indeed almost panoramic, view of the northern defences and the intervening ground from the lodgement, which at the stage was no more than a secure observation post, so that the chief engineer was able to decide on the location of the first parallel and the batteries. At dusk these were pegged out, and as soon as it was dark twelve hundred men were hard at work with pick and shovel, with a covering party of a further five hundred lying out in front of them. The weather was cold but dry, and a slight frost had made the soil on the Teson firm but not hard, so that work went well and by daylight the parallel was deep enough for work to continue both on the parallel and on batteries, 1, 2 and 3 each large enough to take eleven 24 pounder guns. No 1 battery, furthest to the east, was angled backwards slightly at its eastern end so that two of its guns could be brought to bear on the convent of San Fransisco. In view of the heavy concentration of French guns on the north side of the fortress, it was necessary to make the parapets of the batteries eighteen feet thick at the top. They also had to be higher than usual, otherwise the forward slope on which they were sited made it possible for the garrison to see into the back of them. All this gave rise to a need for much more soil than usual, and this was found by digging an external excavation in front of each battery. A row of filled gabions was first put into position, which at least screened the workmen from view.

At daylight on 10 January it was found that the old French redoubt screened the line of fire of five guns in battery No 1 which had been placed behind it. This was due to bad siting, an easy enough error to make in the dark, but it caused some understandable fury on the part of both engineers and workmen, who felt that they had been wasting valuable time. That part of the battery was therefore abandoned and battery No 3, further west, was enlarged to take the other guns.

Work continued the next night under very heavy shell fire from the garrison, who of course knew the range almost to the inch. They also threw fireballs which gave them enough light to correct their aim, and so deadly was their fire that external work on the batteries had to be stopped to avoid unnecessary casualties. One of the techniques used by the French was to fire very heavy mortar shells with long fuzes. These, dropping from

a considerable height, buried themselves deeply in the newly-excavated earth before exploding when, as General Jones commented ruefully, 'they blew away in an instant the work of hours'. A number of rampart guns were also successfully used by the defenders.

On the nights of 11 and 12 January the garrison of San Fransisco moved a howitzer into the garden of the convent, whence they could take the trenches in enfilade, but work nevertheless went on steadily. Unfortunately the weather had become colder and it was found impossible to expose the workmen for the whole night, so that a system of reduced shifts had to be adopted. In order to keep down the fire of the main fortress as much as possible until the guns were installed, it was decided to try the effect of riflemen instead. Kincaid of the Rifles recounts that:

'My turn of duty did not arrive until eight in the evening, when I was ordered to take thirty men with shovels to dig holes for ourselves as near as possible to the walls, for the delectable amusement of firing at the embrasures for the remainder of the night. The enemy threw fireballs among us to see where we were; but as we always lay snug until their blaze was extinguished, they were not much the wiser, except by finding, by having someone popped off from their guns every instant, that they had got some neighbours, whom they would have been glad to get rid of'.

On 13 January Wellington, having information that Marmont was preparing to move forward to the relief of the fortress, consulted his technical experts as to the practicability of making breaches from the existing batteries in the first parallel and then storming them summarily without first having sapped forward and blown in the counterscarp. In view of the fact that excellent English siege guns were to be used, this was agreed and work was continued so as to get the batteries completed and the guns into them and firing as quickly as possible. Siege work was not popular at the best of times and the constant casualties without any apparent means of reply, had begun to have an adverse effect on morale. Soldiers of all ages since the intervention of guns have always liked to feel that the enemy were not having things all their own way, and the troops before Ciudad Rodrigo were no exception. It was still proposed to continue work on the second parallel, but as the sap running to it from the west end of the first parallel could be enfiladed throughout its length by the guns in Santa Cruz that place was successfully escaladed on the night of 13 January by three hundred men of the King's German Legion and a company of the 60th Rifles.

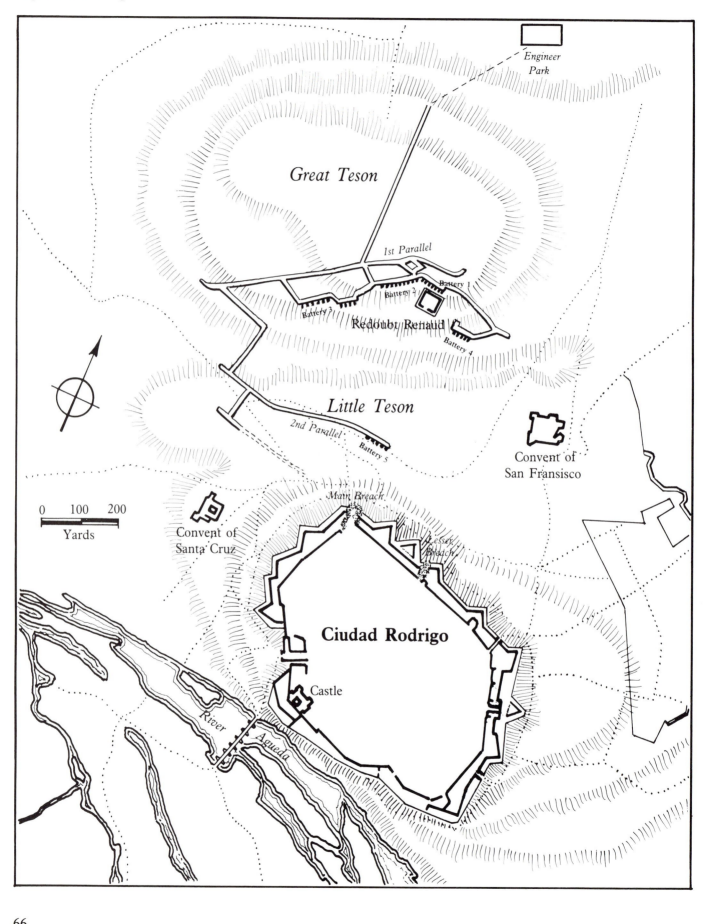

*Great Teson*

Engineer
Park

1st Parallel

Battery 1

Battery 2

Battery 3

Redoubt Renaud

Battery 4

*Little Teson*

2nd Parallel

Battery 5

Convent of
San Fransisco

Main Breach

Lesser
Breach

Convent of
Santa Cruz

0   100   200

Yards

**Ciudad Rodrigo**

Castle

*River*

*Agueda*

*The siege works against Ciudad Rodrigo. Both convents were to be captured before the main assault. No1 battery, badly sited with its fire obstructed by Redoubt Renaud, infuriated both engineers and workmen.*

That same night all the batteries were finally armed; No1 battery had two eighteen pounders only, their role being to bombard San Fransisco and if possible make it untenable, while No2 battery had two eighteen pounders and seven 24 pounders and No3 had no less than sixteen 24 pounders, the role of the latter two batteries being to breach the *fausse-braie* and the main wall. By daylight on 14 January the French must have become aware of this, for at mid morning they launched a sortie against the batteries. A somewhat casual custom had grown up in the trenches that when the relief division was seen to be approaching, usually at about 10am, the old division withdrew completely, leaving the trenches virtually empty for an appreciable period. The

*Engineers and men of the 24th and 42nd Regiments repulse the French sortie against the batteries in the 1st parallel on 14 January 1812.*

French, who probably noticed this from an observation post established in the tower of the cathedral, timed their operation accordingly. Five hundred French infantry charged out from the place, one party making for Santa Cruz while the bulk of the remainder made for the first parallel where they began overthrowing gabions. Fortunately as it happened there were still some workmen of the 24th and 42nd Regiments in the works, presumably finishing off some task under the superintendence of an officer of the Royal Engineers. These hastily lined the nearest available parapet and opened such a brisk fire of musketry that the assailants hesitated long enough for the leading elements of the new division to arrive and drive them back, so that little harm was done, although they remained for the moment in occupation of Santa Cruz. Once the situation had been restored, an operation which took a little while, the guns were able to open fire which they did in the afternoon, somewhat later than had originally been planned, their target being the site of old breach. Much to the surprise of the French the whole effort was directed at breaching and no attempt was made at counter-battery work. It was then found out that two

18 pounders in battery No1 could not see the lower part of the convent walls, due to a low rise in the ground between the battery and its intended target. Colonel Jones commented that 'a person standing upright will see an object over a small swell of ground which a gun placed on the front of a platform will not'. This is still a point to be watched by modern commanders when siting infantry slit trenches. As it happened, breaching was not the prime consideration, so the guns fired to strike the place as low as they could.

Soon after dark three companies of the 40th Regiment stormed the convent of San Fransisco, the garrison making little resistance, and as soon as this fact was confirmed the governor also evacuated his other outposts including Santa Cruz. He presumably sensed that the assault must come very soon and as the place was only weakly garrisoned he decided to concentrate on the vital point. In all the circumstances this was tactically correct, although it made life very much more comfortable for the besiegers. Nevertheless the French fire from the main fortress continued to be both heavy and accurate, although by that time the sappers had developed a drill for extinguishing light balls very rapidly with sandbags and earth, which naturally affected accuracy during the hours of darkness.

At this stage work was begun on a new battery No4, at the east end of the original lodgement and somewhat in advance, its task being to make a very rapid second breach as near as possible to the actual assault. In the meanwhile work continued on the new parallel, it being intended to form yet another battery, No5, to help with the second breach at a range of a bare three hundred yards. The engineers had a period of fog which enabled them to work outside the trenches by daylight. By this time the advanced riflemen were dug in in front of the second parallel and within easy range of the embrasures, where they made things very uncomfortable for the gunners. The latter, having ample ammunition available, showered them with grape, but single individuals well dug in were remarkably difficult to hit, and casualties were minimal. These riflemen were supported by parties of infantry in the second parallel, who kept up a heavy fire on the breach. As soon as the fog had cleared fire was re-opened by both sides. The garrison struck one 24 pounder full in the muzzle and disabled it completely, while several others had wheels smashed, and the works were also deluged by shells, one of which wounded Maj-Gen Borthwick, commanding Royal Artillery.

Before daylight on 18 January No4 battery was armed and ready, and as soon as the light was good enough

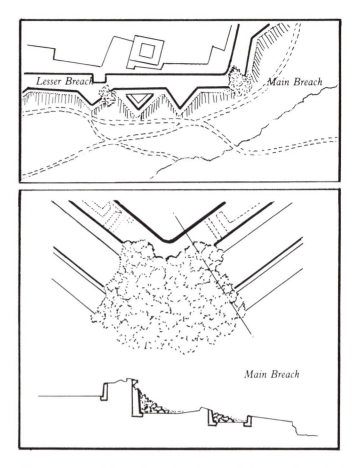

The main and lesser breaches in the defences of Ciudad Rodrigo. The rubble from the walls made a passable, if rough, ramp.

to shoot all the batteries opened together, so that twenty-three 24 pounders and two 18 pounders were battering the main breach while seven 24 pounders opened against the site of the new one. This was at a point in the wall where a tower, originally intended to flank the north wall and having a gun in it, could be seen to its base along the ditch of a ravelin, No4 battery having been sited with this object in mind. The French responded vigorously, although without great material effect. One 24 pounder burst because a ball of irregular shape jammed halfway down its bore killing two gunners and wounding five. That same night battery No5 was complete and had been armed with one 6 pounder and one 5½in howitzer from a field brigade in order to keep up a steady fire on the breach at night-time to prevent the garrison from working on interior defences.

Fire was continued on 19 January, and that afternoon the tower, which had taken a fearful battering from the guns in No4 battery, suddenly collapsed in a rush, leaving a narrow but perfectly practicable second breach. As the main one was also considered to be

*The assault by the Light Division on the lesser breach at Ciudad Rodrigo. The storming party is already up and the main assault is about to go in.*

in a satisfactory state Wellington, after a close reconnaissance, sat down in the advance trenches and wrote his orders for the attack while the breaching batteries at last turned their attention to the artillery of the defenders with very considerable success.

The attack was planned for 7pm that evening; the outline plan was for the 3rd Division to storm the great breach and the Light Division the lesser one, these main assaults being preceded by various other supporting and diversionary actions. The first of these was to be led by Lt-Col O'Toole and his battalion of cacadores, reinforced by the Light company of the 83rd Regt, who at 1850 hours were to cross the Agueda from the south bank by the Roman bridge (which being commanded from the castle had not been destroyed by the French) and attack two guns situated in an earthwork near the castle and covering the point where the *fausse-braie* rejoined the main wall of the place. The main object of this was to drive the gunners from their guns but the battalion, which was to be guided by Major Sturgeon of the Staff corps, was to carry ladders, take the place

by escalade, and destroy the guns if possible.

Once they had been dealt with, the 5th Regt was to advance from the area of Santa Cruz, force the gate into the ditch at the point which the guns had been placed to defend, mount the *fausse-braie* (on which the French had posts) and clear it to the left as far as the great breach. The 94th was to advance at the same time and clear the ditch in front of the *fausse-braie* in similar fashion; they were to carry pickaxes with ropes attached, by which they could scrabble down the counter-scarp. The 77th Regt was to remain in reserve in the vicinity of the convent.

The preliminary moves all went as planned. O'Toole and his cacadores escaladed the battery with great dash, and once it was clear that the dangerous guns were silenced the 5th and 94th began their clearing operation. The 5th soon hacked down the gate by the ditch and

*The 88th Regiment during the assault. The regiment was ordered by General Picton to carry the breach 'with the cold iron'.*

scrambled up their ladders on to the *fausse-braie*, and although a somewhat premature burst of cheering brought some fire down on them they suffered few casualties, presumably because the bulk of the garrison was being held in readiness nearer the breaches.

Well before 7pm the remainder of 3rd Division was in position, the 83rd Regt, (less its Light company with O'Toole) were lining the first parallel, their function being to open up a heavy musketry on the breaches to cover the initial part of the assault. The other two brigades of the Division were crammed into the second parallel, waiting expectantly for the signal to advance. As soon as the musketry of the cacadores attack on the battery was heard, the 83rd opened fire, and under cover of it a hundred and fifty sappers, led by Capt Thompson of the 74th Regt and Capt Mulcaster and Lt Thompson of the Royal Engineers, left their entrenchments and ran to the edge of the counterscarp. Each man carried

two large bags stuffed with hay which they flung into the ditch, reducing its depth to about eight feet and affording a soft landing for the stormers who followed them. The first of these were Maj-Gen M'Kinnon's brigade of 1/45th, 74th and 1/88th, who ran down the slope in the face of heavy musket fire from the defenders, leapt into the ditch, and floundered across the yielding hay bags, losing a good many of their number on the way. The garrison had prepared a large number of shells, powderbags and other missiles but fortunately they fired all these prematurely, so that although the whole breach appeared to explode briefly in a great rumbling explosion, very little material damage was done.

Meanwhile the 5th and 94th, moving fast, reached the breach first and found to their surprise that it was deserted. Campbell, their brigadier, who was well up with the leading files, realised at once that any delay might be fatal, and at once led them up the breach. M'Kinnon's men, checked briefly by the exploding missile, arrived at its foot at that moment and the whole of the five battalions scrambled up the slope of the hundred foot gap in an excited, yelling swarm, all order lost. On arrival on the terreplein they found a 16ft drop ahead of them into the town, the base of which was heaped with old carts, beams, and other obstructions well calculated to damage anyone bold enough to attempt the leap. One either side of the breach trenches, 10ft wide and 10ft deep, had been dug, with parapets behind them, each mounting a 24 pounder gun loaded with grape, the first discharge of which killed many of the men in the forefront of the attack. Those behind very naturally hesitated, which gave the French gunners time to reload, so that as the rush was renewed they fired again into the milling crowd. At the same time the defenders also fired a large mine which killed General M'Kinnon and many others.

The nearest and most dangerous of the guns was the one to the left, and three soldiers of the 88th, Sergeant Brasil and Private Swan and Kelly, the sergeant, presumably armed with his sword, and the privates, carrying bayonets only in order to be able to negotiate the trench, scrambled across and flung themselves on the French gunners. Swan stabbed one gunner and then had his left arm completely severed by a mighty cut from a sword and collapsed. The angry artillerymen were about to despatch him when Kelly arrived and killed two of them just as Sergeant Brasil disposed of another. Several other men of the 5th had also got across by then and they killed the last of the gallant French

gunners and thus finally silenced the gun. The fate of the second gun is less easy to determine, but as Campbell had managed to cross the right hand trench with a few men it is possible that they either killed the gunners or drove them off. Thus relieved of the terrible scourging of grape, the stormers then scrambled across the retrenchments and down into the narrow streets of the town in pursuit of the French, who were withdrawing from the breach in some disorder.

The Light Division also formed for its attack on the lesser breach near the convent of Santa Cruz. Wellington was with them and gave final orders to Major George Napier who was in command of the stormers. As they moved off behind Lt Gurwood of the 52nd Regt and his forlorn hope, one of the staff called out to Napier that he had not given the order to load, to which Napier retorted; 'If we do not do the business with the bayonet we shall not do it all' upon which according to him, Wellington said 'Let him alone; let him go his own way'. It was in fact a sensible decision, since once men stopped to fire, the impetus of the attack tended to be lost. It is interesting that Picton had made the same decision, for when he visited the 88th (the Connaught Rangers) a short while before they fell in for the operation, he announced to them that it was his intention 'to do this business with the cold iron' an announcement which greatly pleased his Irish audience who had a fearful reputation for their skill with that particular weapon.

*A private of the 52nd Regiment, the forlorn hope at Ciudad Rodrigo.*

*General Robert Craufurd had a reputation as a strict disciplinarian in the Peninsular army. He was killed, along with several senior officers, in the breach and was buried where he fell.*

The attack reached the ditch, where it was found that for some reason the cacadores whose duty it was to carry the haybags had not turned up, but this did not stop the men of the Light Division who hurled themselves recklessly into it. Here they went somewhat astray, for the forlorn hope went too far to the left and reared its ladders against a damaged earth traverse between the *fausse-braie* and the wall, with the result that the first troops actually into the breach were the stormers under Napier, although if we can believe Kincaid, who was of the party, they too had some difficulty in finding the proper route. It was, after all a bare thirty feet wide, and situated in a confused, lunar-like landscape of ditches, battered ravelins, and crumbled traverses, which must all have looked alike in the dark and the drifting powder smoke. It is also possible that the arrangements for engineer guides had gone wrong, a matter on which more will be said later.

Once the breach was located it was not difficult to gain access up it, for it was only blocked by a gun jammed across it and not retrenched. Nor were the defenders very numerous, but in spite of this casualties were very high amongst the senior officers. Napier was

hit half-way up by a grape shot which shattered his elbow; Craufurd the Divisional Commander was mortally wounded as they advanced and Vandeleur, commanding the leading brigade was hard hit, as was Colborne, one of his battalion commanders who had earlier planned and led the attack on the Redoubt Renaud. Thus in a matter of minutes command of the division had devolved on Col Barnard, normally commanding a battalion of Rifles but at that time officiating in command of the second brigade, and fortunately a most capable officer.

Once the lesser breach was gained, five companies of Rifles turned to their right along the ramparts and made for the rear of the main breach where their arrival finally completed the demoralisation of the defenders who had already received a wild rumour that the town had been escaladed from the south side. Outside the wall three more companies cleared the *fausse-braie* and ditch, also towards the great breach, while further east Pack's Portuguese brigade stormed an outwork and then attempted an escalade, but did not apparently get into the town until the fighting was over, when they at once joined the vast mob of men of the 3rd and Light Divisions who had converged on the main square, yelling and firing wildly into the air, all discipline gone. Many of their officers did what they could to restrain them, but to no avail, for they simply dispersed into the town, intent on drink, and plunder. In a short time several fires were raging and it was only due to the efforts of Col Barnard and Lt-Col McCloud of 43rd Regt, who had managed to keep a hold on some of his battalion, that disaster was averted. Many bad characters amongst the Spanish inhabitants joined in the looting, as did a number of French soldiers, against whom the British showed little animosity, but the disorders did not last long. George Simmonds, an eminently steady and reliable officer, wrote:

'My battalion formed up upon the ramparts and made fires, as the night was a clear and frosty one. Some men brought me wine, ham and eggs. I soon made a hearty meal and washed it down with some good French burgundy',

which all sounds very peaceful and orderly and far removed from drunkenness and looting—except perhaps that we may wonder where the food and drink came from. Kincaid, in the same battalion, confirms this

*A contemporary illustration of the tranquil surrender of a Spanish town during the war. Following the capture of Ciudad Rodrigo, the army ran riot for a short time.*

apparent return to normality, while Major Leach, also a Rifleman tends to dismiss the whole thing as highly exaggerated, writing that:

'When a town is stormed, it is inevitable that excesses will be, as they ever have been, committed by the assailants, more particularly if it takes place at night. It affords a favourable opportunity for the loose and dissolute characters, which are to be found in all armies, to indulge in every diabolical propensity. That this was the case to a certain extent, on the night in question, no one will deny; but, at the same time, I feel convinced that no town taken by assault did or ever will suffer less than Rodrigo. It is true that all soldiers of all Regiments got drunk, plundered, and made great noise and confusion in the streets, and houses in spite of every exertion on the part of the officers to prevent it; but bad and revolting as such scenes are, I never heard that the French garrison, when it had once surrendered, or any of the inhabitants, suffered personal indignities or cruelty from the troops'.

This may sound like special pleading, intended to present the affair as the sort of basically good tempered drunken brawl in which soldiers dearly loved to indulge, but by the standards of the early nineteenth century there may be something in what he says, particularly in the light of what happened at later sieges. It is certain that whatever the truth of the matter the whole thing was over by dawn next morning when fresh troops were marched in to take over.

It is certain that Wellington and his senior officers were taken by surprise at the disorders after the assault, and certainly little or no precautions appear to have been taken to prevent their occurrence. Indeed many officers seem to have been of the honest opinion that it was a fair reward to the troops after their dangerous exertions and regarded it as an inevitable, if very distasteful, sequel to a successful storm. In earlier times this sort of thing had largely been prevented by the civilised custom of the defenders surrendering on terms when it was clear that further resistance would be useless, which in practice usually meant when a practicable breach had been made. Napoleon however, a much more ruthless commander and one moreover very conscious of the value of time, even a few days, in military operations, had made it clear that he expected fortified places to be held as long as possible.

The overall casualties were not excessively high for a successful operation of this nature; one hundred and five men were killed and three hundred and ninety wounded, and if we can believe Capt T. Dyneley of the Royal Artillery 'more than half of these were killed by our own people', as he wrote to a friend soon afterwards, that is, killed by wild firing after the assault had succeeded.

By mid-morning 20 January the breaches had been cleared and the wounded taken care of, although in the intervening period some of these must have suffered severely. It is indicative of the sort of treatment provided for them that Major George Napier could write:

'It soon came to my turn to have my arm amputated and I then reminded my friend Walker, who was there, of his promise to me a few hours before, and begged he would be so good as to perform the operation; but he told me he could not, as there was a staff surgeon present, whose rank being higher, it was necessary he should do it, so Staff-Surgeon Guthrie cut it off. However for want of light, and from the number of amputations he had already performed, and other circumstances, his instruments were blunted, so it was a long time before the thing was finished, at least twenty minutes, and the pain was great. I then thanked him for his kindness, having sworn at him like a trooper while he was at it, to his great amusement, and I proceeded to find some place to lie down and rest, and after wandering and stumbling about the suburbs for an hour I saw a light in a house, and on entering I found it full of soldiers and a good fire blazing in the kitchen. As I went towards the fire I saw a figure wrapped in a cloak sitting in the corner of the chimney place, apparently in great pain. Upon nearer inspection I found this was my friend John Colborne, who had received a severe wound in the shoulder. Upon asking me if I was wounded I showed him the stump of my arm, which so affected him, poor fellow, that he burst into tears'.

Certain aspects of the siege inevitably gave rise to controversy, some of which continued for years. The first was the question of who had entered the town first which was to be the cause of endless argument between the 3rd and Light Division, both very fine formations with a great deal of understandable pride in themselves. It is not proposed to re-open the discussion here except to say that as some members of the leading companies of the 95th, hastening towards the great breach along the ramparts, were killed and wounded by the explosion of the mine which killed M'Kinnon (which occurred after some of the 3rd Division had been on the *terreplein* for some time) it seems likely that the latter had the better claim, although there can be no doubt that the final retreat of the French from the breach was as a direct result of the rush of the Rifles upon their right flank and rear.

The next, and more personal one, arose over the question of the surrender of the French Governor. Gurwood of 52nd, who commanded the forlorn hope of the Light Division, was no sooner in the town than he made for the castle and there received the surrender of Barrié, the Governor, who handed over his sword. Rather amusingly Lt Mackie of the 88th, who had led the forlorn hope of the 3rd Division (perhaps another ambitious young man) had the same idea and accepted what one might call a 'stand-in' surrender from the Governor's ADC who handed over *his* sword on behalf of his commander. Mackie claimed to have seen Gurwood arrive, but the latter had the governor firm by then, and hastened with him to Wellington who bade him keep the sword and mentioned him in his despatch.

*John Gurwood, who commanded the 52nd Regiment's forlorn hope, seen here in later life in the uniform of an esquire to the Duke of Wellington.*

Gurwood, whom Kincaid described tolerantly as 'a sharp fellow', subsequently rather over-played his hand by claiming to have twice mounted the breach, and twice been tumbled down, before the stormers arrived, a claim which excited a great deal of protest from even his erstwhile supporters of the Light Division. Major George Napier and Capt Ferguson, both with the stormers, hotly denied this claim and were supported by William Napier, brother of George and the historian of the War, who quotes the case as an 'instant of the great difficulties which a contemporaneous historian has to encounter in relating such exciting events as battles or assaults where these engaged in them, though men of unimpeachable honour and veracity, are afterwards found to give such contradictory accounts'. This possibly sums it up but the arguments and claims went on, particularly as regards the Governor. Maxwell, author of a standard biography of Wellington, actually stated as a fact that Mackie had accepted the surrender. Harry Smith agreed. Gurwood finally burst into print in the *RUSI Journal* thirty one years after the event, so it is likely that the controversy continued as long as

there were any survivors of the affair left alive.

The third, last, and less well-known controversy arose over the question of Engineer guides to the breaches, and had some connection with the Gurwood affair. Many years afterwards a Lt-Col Elliott, then an infantry officer, stated in conversation with a retired officer of the Light Division that he had been the Royal Engineer who guided that division to the breach. Having been in India for many years he was not aware of the Gurwood/Mackie row, but simply confirmed as a fact that no forlorn hope had preceded the stormers up the breach. Then came the curious part. Elliott and Rice had been Engineer subaltern on siege duties, and

*Two officers inspect the main and lesser breaches in the outer walls of Ciudad Rodrigo after the siege. Casualties were 105 killed and 390 wounded.*

although not detailed for anything specific in the assault itself had gone down to watch as a matter of professional interest. A Royal Engineer major, unnamed, then approached them and ordered them summarily to guide the two divisions to the breaches on the grounds that the officers detailed in orders that had not turned up, Elliott being ordered to the Light.

He protested that having been employed elsewhere he knew nothing of the location of the breach, but having been bidden to do what he could, duly went with them, found the lesser breach by the light of the fortuitous flash of a gun, and led the stormers up it. He then went off and reported to Lt-Col Fletcher, Chief Engineer, who knew nothing about it. According to William Napier, the Chief Engineer said 'what are you talking about, Sir? you did not lead the attack—you were not the engineer officer attached to it', and when Elliott

persisted he was told angrily to go away. The unnamed major was present but said nothing at the time. Later he hinted to Elliott that it was a matter of the honour of the Corps and advised him to say nothing more, advice which he followed as long as he remained a Royal Engineer. The whole affair, though not important, was decidedly curious.

Wellington wasted no time, and by 20 January working parties had started levelling the approaches, although the work was somewhat impeded by snow. Work began on buiding up the breaches, and a new advanced work was started on the Great Teson, some 500yds north of the old one so as to be able to look down into the valley where the siege park had been located. Although Wellington's next objective was likely to be Badajos, the siege guns and remaining ammunition were sent back to Lamego, to be embarked on their storeships at Oporto, on the grounds that they were too heavy to be moved overland. The only guns to be sent by road were the six 5½in iron howitzers which were sent off southwards as soon as bullocks became available.

General Craufurd, who died from his wounds four days after the assault, was buried at the foot of the lesser breach with all ceremony, while at the other end of the scale a number of British deserters who had been taken in Ciudad Rodrigo were tried and sentenced to death. Those who could get a testimonial as to previous good character were reprieved but a number were shot, six of them being from the Light Division. Another, whose trial was delayed for some reason, was court-martialled and shot seven weeks later; Capt Kincaid noted with a certain respect that the soldier protested strongly about the sentence being carried out until he had received the arrears of pay due to him up to the date of his desertion.

Before the end of the month, Spanish masons were hard at work laying foundations for the new revetments for the breaches. By then the snow had turned to heavy rain which greatly hampered them and it was then realised how fortunate the besiegers had been to have frost and snow, for any attempt at digging found water rising immediately.

On 19 February three thousand Spanish troops marched in as the new garrison and on 5 March Wellington formally handed over the place to its new Governor, General Vivas, and his Chief Engineer General Calvet. Part of the proceedings included the provision of 12000 dollars in cash to pay for the repairs. The British troops had marched south in the meanwhile, the last to go being the 5th Division who left their cantonments on 26 February.

The taking of Ciudad Rodrigo, the first successful operation of its type conducted by the British Army in the Peninsular War, was a notable achievement for which Wellington very properly received an earldom. It went very much according to plan, and although the decision to assault from the second parallel instead of carrying the works forward to the counterscarp probably increased the casualties, it undoubtedly saved time, which was its main object. A good many lessons had clearly been learnt from Badajos, in particular perhaps the need for the best siege artillery available, although as we shall see later it was not always remembered. The French were undoubtedly taken by surprise; Marmont did not even hear of it until 15 January and although he ordered an immediate concentration it was of course far too late, for the place was in British hands after a siege of twelve days, without him having been able to take a single step to hinder it.

# CHAPTER FIVE

## The Third Siege of Badajos— The Approaches

Wellington had selected a good time to attack Badajos, for his enemies were in some disarray. In Andalusia, Soult, tied down by the hopeless siege of Cadiz and the activities of Spanish troops and guerrillas, had practically no troops to spare; nor was the army of Portugal in much better state. It was easy for Napoleon, furious at the loss of Ciudad Rodrigo, to fulminate orders at Marmont to fortify Salamanca, concentrate his army, and assemble a siege train, with a view to drawing Wellington back north, but as the unfortunate marshal had no money, no supplies, no transport, and had also lost his siege train in Rodrigo, he could not in practice comply with any of them. Nor were things improved by the fact that the French Emperor was steadily withdrawing troops from Spain for his Russian expedition. Wellington thus felt justified in leaving Ciudad Rodrigo and Almeida to fend for themselves, with only a skeleton force of British troops to observe Marmont and delay him if he should make a move.

By 11 March Headquarters had been established at Elvas, the bulk of the army being in cantonments in the neighbourhood. Gen Hill was at Merida, covering the northern and eastern approaches while Graham was at Llerena to watch the southern side. As Badajos has already been described in chapter 2 it is proposed here only to consider some of the changes made in the place by the garrison as a result of their experience in the siege of the previous year. San Cristoval had been repaired and considerably strengthened, and a redoubt had been built on the site of the breaching battery established by the British. The castle had also been strengthened with internal retrenchments, and more guns had been

*The city of Badajos as painted by Harry Smith. To the left is the castle dominating the town with, in the foreground, the bridge-head fort covering the crossing of the Guadiana.*

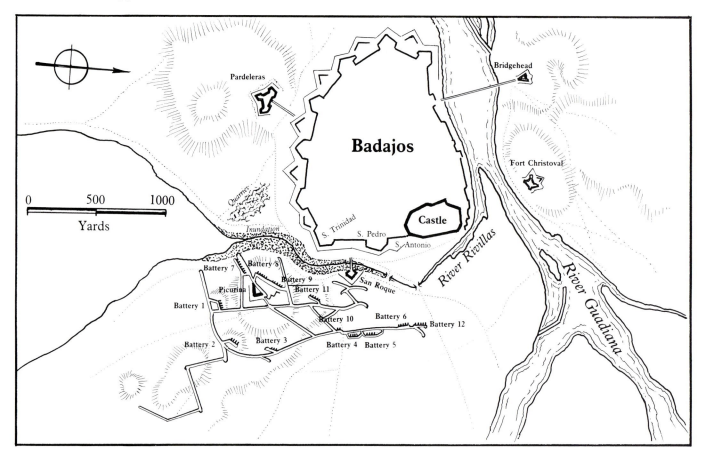

mounted on it to make it less susceptible to attack from Cristoval. A good deal of work had been done on the south face of the main *enceinte*, and much of the south and south-west had been protected by extensive counter-mines, although very fortunately a French sergeant-major of Sappers had deserted to the British as a result of some affront offered to him by an officer, taking with him all his maps of these. A *cunette* or supplementary ditch, deep enough to drown a man, had been dug in the bottom of the main ditch, and the Rivillas stream had been dammed at the San Roque redoubt, causing an inundation stretching about 1000yds upstream. There had been a considerable shortage of money, workmen and material of all kinds, so that other projected improvements had not been started, amongst these being a proper bomb-proof shelter for San Cristoval. The fortification mounted one hundred and forty guns but was rather short of ammunition, since the earlier activities of Gen Hill had foiled various attempts to get convoys through from Seville. Food was adequate for six or seven weeks, and as many of the Spanish inhabitants, reluctant to undergo yet another siege, had deserted. The garrison, which numbered about 5000, was able to supplement its rations by cultivating the various gardens and small farms in the

*The siege works during the third Siege of Badajos were extensive, being directed first against Picurina and, following its capture, against the city itself.*

vicinity. The morale of the garrison was high, and it was fortunate in being commanded by Gen Phillipon, an excellent officer.

On 14 March the Guadiana was bridged, the crossing being further secured by a flying bridge drawn by artillery horses, and two days later the place was invested on the south side by Marshal Beresford, having under him the 3rd Division (Picton), the 4th Division (Colville) and the Light Division (Barnard, still officiating since Ciudad Rodrigo). A vedette post was established on the height on San Miguel, about 1400yds east from which point the Chief Engineer was able to make a detailed reconnaissance of the works on that side.

The final plan differed very considerably from the one tried unsuccessfully in the sieges of the previous year. It was decided to leave San Cristoval and the castle severely alone, and to concentrate instead on the south-eastern face of the works, where an unfinished counter-guard made it possible to see from the high ground of Fort Picurina the base of the wall of part of the Trinidad bastion. In order to achieve this it was proposed to establish the first parallel as close to Picurina as possible, extending it well to the right so as to allow the construction of batteries to keep the main defences under fire. Picurina would then be stormed and used as a base for breaching batteries; two breaches were to be made initially, with a third, last-minute one between them, so as to turn any retrenchments, the same technique in fact that had been used at Ciudad Rodrigo with such success.

The question of the artillery was, as before, a difficult one, although for a different reason. Brief reference has been made in the previous chapter to the problems of moving the guns used at Ciudad Rodrigo by road, and because of this other arrangements had to be made. A further sixteen good iron 24 pounders had recently arrived from England and were available in the Tagus, but although these would form a good basis for a train, experience had shown that more guns would be needed against a strong place such as Badajos. The obvious person to turn to was Admiral Berkeley, commanding the Royal Navy in the Tagus, since naval maindeck guns were virtually identical to siege guns, except that they were often shorter. The admiral replied that he had no ship on station carrying such heavy metal as 24 pounders, but would be happy to let Wellington have twenty 18 pounders, complete with ammunition and stores, and after some consultation with his artillery and engineer advisers it was decided that, given a nucleus of 24 pounders, 18 pounders would be acceptable, although as has already been discussed in the section on siege artillery the difference in battering power was very considerable, due to the more rapid loss of velocity of the lighter projectiles.

Almost inevitably the task of assembling and moving this new train fell to Major Dickson, who at the end of January moved off to Setubal, a small port at the mouth of the river Sardao, some twenty miles southeast of Lisbon; from there it was proposed to move everything by boat to Alcacer do Sol, and thence by road to Elvas. The Commissary-General was ordered to send an intelligent commissary to the area to make the necessary arrangements for boats for the first stage, and bullocks and carts for the second. In the meanwhile the iron howitzers and various stores were sent off by road, followed a day or two later by twenty spare carriages for 24 pounders and five for 18 pounders. Each howitzer was drawn by eight bullocks, but as the animals which normally draw the bridge equipment were sent off at the same time it was possible to provide replacements and reliefs. All these had arrived safely at Elvas by 3 March.

When Dickson arrived at Setubal he found that the 18 pounder guns supplied by the Navy were Russian pieces which had been found in store in Lisbon. On examination they were found to be in poor condition with their bores very rough and their shot rusty. Even worse was the fact that owing to differences in calibration the windage was almost half-an-inch, which was certain to have a seriously adverse effect on both velocity and accuracy. Dickson protested as vigorously as he dared to Hardy, Berkeley's Fleet Captain, but got no satisfaction and so accepted the guns. He wrote to Wellington on the subject on 18 March, and received the following reply:

> Freneda
> 23 Feb 1812
>
> 'My dear Sir,
> I received only this evening your letter of 18th. I do not know what answer you were to expect from me upon the subject of Russian 18 pounders. I wrote to the Admiral to express my disappointment; but there was no use in discussing with you by letter the resources which occurred to my mind to extricate us from the scrape into which we had got, notwithstanding all the pains I had taken to avoid it, *in consequence of the busy meddling folly of those whom I had been inclined to trust on this occasion.*
>
> I do not know whether the Admiral will send you English guns or not. If he should not we must separate carefully, and mark, the English, Russian and Portuguese shot; and we must use those of each nation in different batteries. The artillery officers must then calculate upon the windage of the different descriptions of shot in their charges, and the direction and elevation of their guns; and as the shot in each battery will always be the same there will not be so much difficulty in managing these pieces as we experienced in the last siege under similar circumstances.
>
> I hope however that if the Admiral has them, he will send English 18 pounders,
>
> Believe me etc,
> Wellington'

This letter seemed to be worth reproducing in full because it is perhaps characteristic of the writer, including as it does a certain philosophical acceptance of what could not be cured, a flash of sarcastic anger (this is the sentence in italics, which it should be noted was tactfully omitted in the published despatches), the absolution of the obviously worried Dickson from any

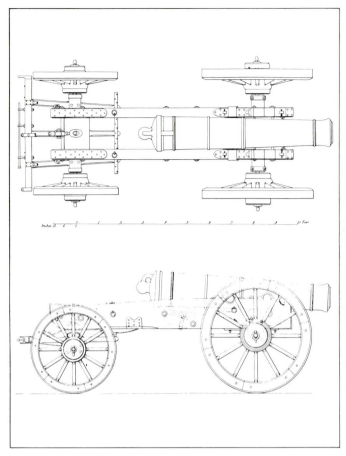

*British 18pdr siege guns, here in travelling order complete with limber, ten of which were eventually sent by the Royal Navy to Badajos.*

serious disadvantage in single ship encounters with American frigates when the United States declared war on Great Britain in 1812. Even more notable is the fact that the series of American successes was only broken by one of the Royal Navy's real advocates of accurate and scientific gunnery; this was Capt Philip Broke of the frigate *Shannon*, who in 1813 battered the United States frigate *Chesapeake* into a bloody wreck within a few minutes.

It is possible that some inkling of Wellington's displeasure may have filtered back to his naval opposite number, for some time later the latter sent to Alcacer do Sol ten English 18 pounders. Dickson was reluctant to accept them because they added yet another problem of calibre, but finally did so and transported them to Elvas, although there appears to be no indication that they were actually used against Badajos.

Inevitably there were the normal troubles over finding bullocks and carts in south Portugal, but Dickson and

blame, and the production of a neat solution to the problem. Here perhaps it may be desirable to explain certain differences between naval and military gunnery of the period. The Royal Navy was not, generally speaking, very worried about long-range accuracy, but relied on seamanship to place their ships so close to those of the enemy that rapid mechanical gunnery was bound to hit them, a concept resembling in some ways the employment of infantry volleys in land warfare. Siege artillery, on the other hand, had to be able to place shot after shot in the same place at ranges of five hundred yards or more, which needed a different type of gunnery and the very best guns available. It is of interest to note that the gunnery tactics of the Navy were to prove a

*Siege work called for accurate, long-range artillery whereas normal Royal Navy tactics employed massed, close-quarter broadsides. One notable exception was the frigate action between the **Chesapeake** and **Shannon**, the latter commanded by Capt Broke, an advocate of accurate and scientific naval gunnery.*

his staff overcame them all, so that by 8 March, the very day stated by Wellington in his original memorandum, the new train, consisting of sixteen iron 24 pounders, twenty Russian iron 18 pounders, and the sixteen 5½in howitzers, were all drawn up on the glacis at Elvas, together with their stores. Two days later the assembly of the engineer stores and tools was also complete, and the pontoons and Spanish boats for the construction of the bridge were ready.

The engineer resources for the siege were a good deal better than they had been in the previous year. Lt-Col Fletcher was again in charge, with two majors and twenty-one other officers and one hundred and fifteen Royal Military Artificers. The hundred and twenty surviving volunteer sappers of the 3rd Division had also been re-employed, together with a further eighty carpenters from the line. The next few days were employed in setting up an engineer park about one mile south-east of the stronghold on the Talavera road, the

site being well screened by the heights of San Miguel. This work was completed by 17 March and on that night the first parallel was opened by 1800 workmen, with a covering party of 2000. The parallel had been marked out at dusk by the chief engineer while the troops were assembling. This in itself did not take long, but the ground across which the approaches to it lay was very rough and irregular, and this, combined with heavy rain and strong winds, impeded things so much that it was three hours before work actually began. One thousand men were first set to work on the communication trench which was about 4000ft long (it had of course to be built in zig-zags so that the garrison could not fire straight down it at daybreak) while the remainder began to open the parallel. So many of the workmen had made their way to the rear to seek cover from the storm that only six hundred were available, so that no more than 600yds of the southern end could be opened that night.

The parallel was so close to Picurina, 160yds according to Jones (but 300m according to Belmas) that the covering party had to be stationed in various hollows behind it, which made it nerve-racking for the workmen. One fortunate result of the bad weather was that it effectively prevented the garrison from discovering that the work was in progress until daylight on 18 March, by which time the trenches afforded reasonable cover. The garrison of Picurina was soon re-inforced from the main works via the communication trench with San Roque, and a considerable fire of muskets was kept up from the covered way. Several field pieces and one light howitzer also opened fire from the outwork, and a few shots were fired from the main ramparts. None of this fire was very effective and some work continued on the parallel during the hours of daylight.

The weather had improved somewhat by the night of 18 March and the work went well with a working party of 1800 and a covering force of 1500. Batteries No1 and No2 were traced out and work began on them by four hundred men, the remainder working on the parallel which was extended to the right about 450yds, and to the left about 200yds.

At daybreak on 19 March it was found that the garrison of Picurina had erected sandbag head cover for their sharpshooters along the parapet of the covered way, and to counter this fire as many men of the covering party who could be accommodated in the parallel without hampering the workmen were given the task of returning the fire. There was a good deal more fire from the town but it was mostly roundshot, probably due, as Belmas noted later, to the shortage

of shells. The effect of roundshot, both morally and materially, was much less than that of the huge shells which had so plagued the besiegers at Ciudad Rodrigo, and the workmen were able to continue without much disruption.

Just after midday the garrison, who had noticed that the new right hand extension to the parallel was largely unsupported, launched a sortie. Fifteen hundred infantry filed out of the town unobserved under cover of a thin fog and formed in the Picurina-San Roque communication, whence they charged the parallel. They were followed by forty cavalry who galloped off towards the engineer park.

Lt Grattan, by his own account, was supervising work on one of the batteries further to the left, when he noticed the bustle and activity in the communication, and at once got his workmen equipped and their muskets loaded, so that he was able to hold on; but further right, where the main blow fell, the guards and workmen were completely surprised, and driven out of the parallel in considerable confusion. They soon rallied however, and counter-attacking briskly, drove the French back in their turn, although they lost about one

*On 19 March, fifteen hundred French troops from Badajos launched an attack from the Picurina-San Roque communication trench against the 2nd parallel.*

hundred and fifty killed and wounded in the affair. Included in this number was Lt-Col Fletcher, the Chief Engineer, who was struck in the groin by a musket ball. Fortunately for him the bullet struck a silver dollar in his pocket, and so saved his life, although the coin was driven an inch which caused a painful wound. He continued to direct the attack from his bed, Wellington conferring with him in his tent each morning at 8am to plan the day's work. Picton, who was Duty General in the trenches on that day, was quickly on the scene. He was followed by Capt Cuthbert of the 7th Fusiliers, one of his aides-de-camp, who somewhat rashly rode forward to the parallel, where he was struck by a roundshot and killed while supervising a counter-attack by elements of the 3rd Division.

Very little damage was done, but the French, who had been promised a dollar for every tool they took back, succeeded in carrying off five hundred and forty-five. The cavalry raid on the park did little material

**Distribution of pieces against Badajos 24 March 1812**

| Battery | Pieces | Target |
|---|---|---|
| No1 | 3 × 18 pounders | To enfilade the east face of Picurina and its communications |
| | 3 × 5.5in howitzers | To concentrate on the interior of Picurina and the rear palisades |
| No2 | 4 × 24 pounders | Direct fire on Picurina |
| No3 | 4 × 18 pounders | Direct fire on the south face of San Roque |
| No4 | 6 × 24 pounders | To enfilade the south face of the Trinidad bastion |
| | 1 × 5.5in howitzers | To enfilade the south face of the Trinidad bastion |
| No5 | 4 × 18 pounders | To enfilade the south face of the St Pedro bastion |
| No6 | 3 × 5.5in howitzers | Direct fire on the north face of San Roque |

damage either, although it caused consternation amongst the troops there, many of whom were unarmed. After this, one squadron of cavalry and a troop of artillery was kept constantly mounted in the vicinity of the park, an observation post being set up on the Sierra de Viento, a piece of high ground to the south of the town whence a good view of the eastern side of the fortress could be obtained. The episode provided a salutory lesson for the British, although at rather heavy cost.

The night of 19 March was very wet and the trenches mostly flooded, but work continued next day to extend the parallel even further to the right. When it reached the Talavera road the surface was so hard that the tools would make no impression on it, so the gap of 20yds had to be screened with sandbags. Although the batteries had not yet opened, the French were obviously apprehensive regarding the communication between Picurina and San Roque, because they erected a screen on poles to mask it, a fairly common device when there was no time to construct proper works.

On the night of 20th work began on three more batteries, Nos4, 5 and 6, at the north end of the parallel. These had to be dug slightly in the rear because of the swampy state of the ground. The parallel had by then stretched so far north that there was a risk of it's being enfiladed from the north bank of the river, which was not invested, and sure enough on the morning of 21 March the French had two field pieces in position which did some damage, even though the range was over 1000yds, until they were driven off by riflemen firing from the south bank.

At this stage of the siege the French, presumably misled by the new batteries, had come to the conclusion that the breach was likely to be made in the curtain wall north of No8 bastion (San Pedro) and began to strengthen the internal defences of that sector. The weather continued very wet, and on 21 March most of the trenches were knee-deep in water. The French sited

more guns across the river, so Gen Leith was ordered to invest the place on that side, which disposed of the nuisance once and for all. Some work continued on the new batteries, but by evening the soil was of the consistency of soup, the works began to crumble, and it was quite impossible even to consider moving guns. Fortunately things improved on 24 March, and the batteries were finally finished. The fire from the town was greatly increased, but as it was almost all from guns it did relatively little damage. The 5th Division was ordered up to invest San Cristoval.

On the night of 24 March the batteries were all completed and armed with very little interference from the garrison. Adequate ammunition was placed in the magazines in readiness to open fire next morning, Dickson's gunners having spent long and tedious hours in gauging the 18 pounder shot and painting it in three different colours according to its calibre. All preparations had been made to replenish as required from Elvas, by any means available. Even men were pressed into service, for Kincaid wrote:

> 'Our batteries were supplied with ammunition, by the Portuguese militia, from Elvas, a string of whom used to arrive every day, reaching nearly from one place to the other, (twlelve miles) each man carrying a twenty-four pound shot and cursing all the way and back again.'

On the morning of 25 March all the batteries opened fire, and the two outposts of Picurina and San Roque were very soon silenced by the weight of fire directed against them. The works appeared to have suffered very little material damage, but in spite of this Wellington decided to take Picurina by assault the same night. Unfortunately the notice was so short that it was not possible to launch the attack before 10pm, which at that time of the year gave the garrison several hours of dusk and darkness in which to work, a benefit of which they took full advantage. The ramparts were repaired with woolpacks, which as the British had found in the earlier sieges, made excellent hasty defences, and fascines, and as an attack was anticipated bombs, shells and powder bags were placed in readiness, together with two hundred extra muskets so that the first, vital fire should be heavy.

Picurina was in effect a detached bastion, the two front faces being covered by ditches. Only the bottom 9ft of the rampart were revetted, the upper part being of earth and therefore standing at an angle up which men could scramble, although it was protected by a row of *fraises*, sharpened stakes set horizontally into it. The most vulnerable part was its gorge, or rear. This was closed with a treble row of palisades, so that should it be taken the guns of the main fortress could with luck make it untenable for the besiegers. The castle was commanded by Col Gaspard-Thierry, and had a garrison of some three hundred men with seven light guns.

The actual assault was planned by Maj-Gen Kempt, commanding a brigade of 3rd Division, and was essentially simple, as any plan for a night attack must be. Basically a party of two hundred men, guided by an engineer officer and accompanied by a party of miners, sappers and carpenters carrying tools and ladders, was to pass round the southern face of the outwork and break in at the rear. A second party of similar size was to pass round the north face and leave half its number to cut off communications with the town, while the remainder assisted the southern detachment. A further reserve of one hundred men was left in No2 battery to make a frontal attack if it became necessary to reduce the pressure on the flanks.

The southern attack reached the gorge undetected, but on attempting to break in through the palisades came under such heavy fire of musketry at point blank range that they could make no progress. The northern attack, only a hundred strong by the time it reached the actual work, was similarly repulsed. They then raised the ladders against the north flank, where there

was no ditch, and attempted an escalade, but they too were beaten back. Seeing that things were held up, Gen Kempt then launched his reserve in a frontal attack. This too was initially held, but by then the application of pressure all round had taken effect and the garrison suddenly broke and ran for the main fortress. Three officers (including the Commandant) and eighty men got back, but the remainder were killed or captured, many being drowned in the inundation caused by the dammed Rivillas, into which they plunged in their desperate attempts to get away. In a sense it may perhaps be said that the attackers were rather fortunate to succeed, which they did at a cost of over 60 per cent of their numbers killed or wounded. Gen Phillipon had no hesitation in censuring the garrison for what he considered to have been a very feeble defence. Most of the damage to the attackers was done by musket and bayonet, and virtually none of the shells and other combustibles, which had proved so useful in earlier sieges, were used.

As soon as the attack was known to have been successful, three battalions were brought up from the trenches and posted close to the defences in case the garrison should counter-attack. In the event no such attempt was made, but the alarm was sounded in the town where the defenders opened a heavy but random fire of both guns and muskets. The besiegers replied equally at random, and as is always the case when wild fire is opened at night time, it took some time to stop. By midnight however, all was quiet and at once a party of workmen under engineer supervision began a lodgement on the *terreplein*. A ramp was made up the exterior of the front face to give access to this lodgement and the place connected to the first parallel by a *boyau*, or communication trench. Thus by the morning of 26 March Wellington could be well satisfied with the results of the previous night's work, which had advanced the progress of the siege very considerably.

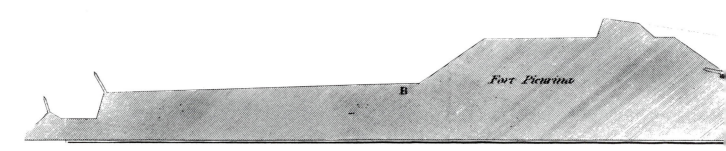

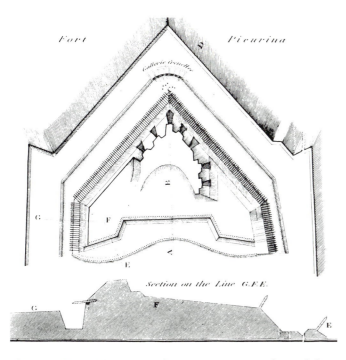

*Above: Fort Picurina, whose capture was planned by Maj-Gen Kempt. Essentially a detached bastion, the place was defended to the front by a ditch and partly revetted rampart protected by **fraises**. Following two unsuccessful attacks on the rear palisade, a frontal assault by the British reserves caused the defenders to flee, many drowning in the inundation between the fort and the city.*

*Below: This cross-section of Picurina shows the front of the fort to the right and rear to the left. When occupied by the French, the rear palisade had succeeded in keeping out the attacking infantry. However once the British had secured the position, the palisade was destroyed by heavy fire from Badajos itself, opening up the **terreplein** to direct gunfire.*

The 26th was a day of considerable artillery activity. Nobody but the sentries were allowed into Picurina, which was just as well, for the guns in the town deluged it with heavy fire which soon wrecked the lodgement made with such trouble the previous night. In the course of the day the sappers completed a second lodgement, but this time under the exterior walls of the work which provided some protection. The British batteries were also extremely active, and began to use ricochet fire in which roundshot with reduced charges were lobbed in enfilade just over the parapets, after which they skipped along like stones skimmed across a pond. When the direction and elevation were exactly right a 24 pound shot moving in this way down a line of guns could do great damage. The Portuguese gunners disliked this kind of fire because they could not see any result.

By that evening the second parallel was sufficiently far advanced to afford cover along its full length, although work continued to improve it. No1 and No2 batteries, having completed their tasks, were dismantled, and three new ones were started. No7, to take twelve 24 pounders, was sited just to the west of Picurina, its task being to breach the southern face of the Trinidad bastion; No9, to take eight 18 pounders, was to breach the eastern flank of Santa Maria, and No10, for three howitzers, was to enfilade the ditch in front of the main breaches so as to prevent the garrison from working there. These last two batteries were being built in the gorge of Picurina. Once the latter had fallen, it became clear to the French that they had been in error regarding the site for the breach, and had wasted much time and effort. Once they had finally identified the real site they quickly started work to improve the defences, mainly by raising the unfinished raveline and making sure that the covered way was in good order. This latter was then lined with infantry, who kept up a steady fire of musketry on the workmen in the new batteries. The range was about 400yds, and thus well outside the effective range of individual muskets, so presumably they used volleys, although the fact is nowhere stated.

Artillery fire on both sides also continued briskly; the batteries had been covered in front by a screen of filled gabions, but the guns from the place soon knocked these over, thus exposing the workmen to the musketry, which in spite of the range, caused so many casualties that those outside were withdrawn.

It was then decided to extend the second parallel to the right and sap forward from it with a view to taking San Roque and destroying the dam, thus doing away with the inundation and allowing free approach to the breaches. There was again some difficulty in crossing the Talavera road, due to the hardness of the metal, and as there was a bright moon on the night of the 27 March a number of casualties were suffered. The light artillery in San Roque had been withdrawn, but the concentrated musketry fire from the place was still very effective.

Artillery fire continued on 28th; No6 battery came under such effective plunging fire from the castle that it had to be dismantled, and other guns were also damaged, so that the night was mainly spent in repairing damage both to guns and walls. The Talavera road was finally crossed and work was also begun on an east-west trench just north of Picurina, this being intended to be used by riflemen to keep down the effective French musketry. It was of this time that Kincaid of 95th Regt later wrote:

> 'One day's trench work is as like another as the days themselves; and like nothing better than serving an apprenticeship to the double calling of grave-digger and game-keeper, for we found ample employment for both the spade and the rifle.'

George Simmons, of the same battalion, was sent out with ten men to conceal themselves opposite a particularly effective gun in the garrison, and after they had put a few shots through the embrasure it was blocked with sandbags. Simmons, watching like a hawk, soon spotted the head of a French officer, presumably a marksman, who was firing back with muskets passed up to him, and being anxious to dispose of this danger he lent his shoulder to one of his riflemen as a steady rest and had the satisfaction of seeing the Frenchman tumble over. Unfortunately the lock of the rifle was very close to Simmons's ear which got badly scorched by the flash of the priming, an event which his unfeeling brother officers thought extremely funny.

On the night of 28th the engineers continued to sap forward towards San Roque. The line of the sap had been traced out with tapes and according to Belmas this had been spotted from the fortress. At dusk therefore a gallant French sapper, Cpl Stoll, crept out and altered

*Above: A British officer, accompanied by one of his engineers who is carrying tapes and pickets used for marking-out the intended lines of trenches and saps. At Badajos, an enterprising French sapper moved the tapes to bring the approach trenches into line with the enfilading-fire from the defenders. Fortunately the tampering with the markers was detected before any work began.*

*Below: Cross-section through the Santa Maria bastion showing the breach in its left flank, and the retrenchment which linked this bastion with La Trinidad.*

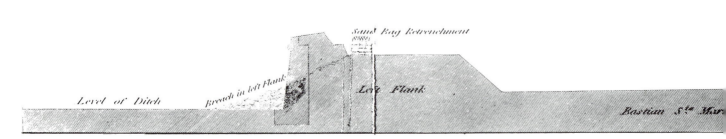

*General Sir Thomas Picton, whose division comprised two British and one Portuguese brigade for the attack on Badajos. His troops were to escalade the castle.*

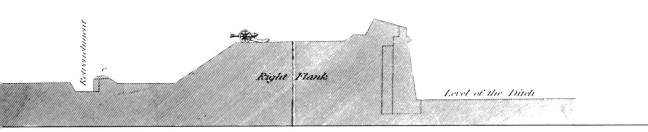

the tape so as to bring it into line with the guns of the castle. Very fortunately Capt Ellicombe of the Royal Engineers, who was on duty in the trenches next evening, went out at dusk to check the traces and detected the change in direction, which he was able to rectify before work started on it. At that time nobody had any idea of how the supposed error had occurred, and it was generally assumed that the marking line had been deflected by catching on a bush or rock. It was not until after the citadel had fallen that captured documents revealed exactly what had happened. On 29 March a new battery, No11, was started against San Roque and the new No9 and No10 batteries were also completed and armed. Next morning steady fire continued from 3, 4 and 5, and No9 began to breach Santa Maria. The shooting was good but the masonry was very tough and progress was slow. Soon after fire was opened from No9 battery, a shell from the town struck its magazine and almost a ton of powder exploded, killing and wounding a number of gunners. New cartridges were at once brought in from neighbouring batteries so that there was hardly any interruption in the fire. The gunners of this battery also suffered some casualties from musketry until a detachment of riflemen opened fire and soon subdued it.

On this day there were reports that Soult was approaching, and the 5th Division was withdrawn from the north bank in consequence and marched south, some squadrons of Portuguese cavalry being sent to watch that side in its place.

By 31 March affairs were beginning to reach a climax, batteries Nos1-10, containing between them fifteen 24 pounders, seventeen 18 pounders, and six howitzers, all being in more or less continuous action. Although some work had been done on No11, which was intended to be armed with six Portuguese iron naval guns, it was never in fact used, and the guns remained at Elvas. In spite of the excellence of the artillery fire the state of the breaches remained disappointing, partly because of the long range and partly because some of the guns were 18 pounders. The French worked each night to clear the outside debris so as to make the slope as difficult as possible, and otherwise to improve the defence in every way they could. Certain of the besiegers' batteries were nominated to maintain a fire of roundshot, grape, and shell onto the defences by night so as to prevent, or at least greatly hamper, this kind of activity, but on the morning of 1 April it was clear from the improvements visible that the batteries concerned had been neglecting their duty. The General Officer in the trenches that day was Picton, a somewhat irascible

officer with the reputation of having the finest flow of invective in the Peninsula; his Reserve Order of that day simply threatened to report to Wellington every officer who neglected his duty, but from the known character of the man it is probable that he visited the batteries personally and addressed the delinquents in his usual forcible way. Certainly it was noticeable on the next night that the guns fired almost continuously with a mixture of case, grape and shrapnel.

Breaching continued slowly, and although the masonry came down in great quantities the clay behind it remained obstinately vertical, being held in place between the counterforts, the internal buttresses supporting the wall. In spite of the almost continuous nightly shower of missiles, the French continued to work devotedly at clearing the debris from the breaches and building up their ruined parapets with woolpacks and sandbags. Their own counter-battery fire had by then begun to be hampered by the shortage of shells, and their casualties were heavy.

At this stage it was clear that in spite of their great courage and devotion to duty, the partly-trained sappers drawn from the 3rd Division could not sap up to San Roque in time for it to be useful, so on the night of

2 April an attempt was made to reduce the inundation by making a direct attack on the dam. Lt Stanway of the Royal Engineers went out with another officer and twenty sappers with nearly a quarter of a ton of powder with which to blow it up. Unfortunately there was so much water pouring over the dam that the powder had to be placed some distance away. The first slow match failed to function and Stanway gallantly went back and re-lit it, but the explosion did not have the hoped-for effect and he had to withdraw under heavy fire from the, by then, thoroughly aroused garrison.

The time for an assault was fast approaching, but by 4 April there were reports that Soult was at Llerena and Wellington had to prepare a provisional plan to leave a blockading face in the works and move out with the rest of his army, although in the event this did not become necessary. The works were by then so far advanced that an assault appeared practicable. According to Belmas, French non-commissioned

**Right:** *The standard of the Hesse-Darmstadt Regiment, captured by the British at Badajos.*
**Below:** *A sketch from the gorge of La Picurina during the third Siege of Badajos.*

officers had checked the breaches at dusk in full kit and found them easily accessible, and as carts full of ladders had also been seen coming into the British camp, it was clear to the besieged that an attack was imminent. Wellington had in fact decided to assault the place on the night of 5 April, but as his engineers reported the breaches heavily retrenched and capable of a long and possible successful defence he decided, on their recommendation, to open a third breach and then take the place before the garrison had a chance to retrench it. On the morning of 6 April therefore eight 24 pounders and six 18 pounders were turned on the east end of the curtain wall between Santa Maria and Trinidad, and a third breach knocked in it very quickly. Jones says it was practicable by 4pm but Belmas says it only took three hours to make. As it had to be defended, Gen Phillipon had to draw some of the Hessians from the garrison of the castle, leaving only a bare 250 in the place. As will be seen later this was to have an effect out of all proportion to the number of soldiers concerned.

# CHAPTER SIX

## The Third Siege of Badajos— The Assault

Wellington's arrangements for the assault on Badajos were originally made on 5 April, but had to be amended slightly for the actual attack on 6 April.

A battery for fourteen howitzers had been hastily constructed at the north end of the 1st parallel. This was to be unmasked as late as possible, and its fire directed against a battery which the French had sited just south of the castle so as to cover the breaches. This fire was to be controlled by signals previously concerted between the battery commander and GOC 3rd Division. All these operations were to start at 10pm. The 4th and Light divisions were to move side by side in column from the south, passing between the quarries on the left and the inundation on the right. Each was to drop off a reserve in the quarries; each was to be preceded by an advance of five hundred men with twelve ladders and haybags for the ditch; and each was to detail a party to line the top of the glacis and attempt to keep down the fire of the garrison. The main bodies were to keep back under cover as far as possible until they saw their stormers ascending the breaches, when they were to advance at the double. Once up the breaches they were to turn outwards, the 4th to its right, the Light to its left, each taking care to leave an adequate reserve at the breaches themselves.

The French, on their side, can have been in no doubt that the assault would come that evening, and had made extensive preparations to receive it. Retrenchments, solid breastworks of wool packs and sandbags, had been built behind the breaches so as to bring heavy fire on the attackers as they reached the top, and the breaches themselves had been closed by *chevaux-de-frise*, solid

*Hell before La Trinidad bastion, during the third Siege of Badajos, at the moment the French fired their mines. Clearly visible are the barricaded breaches.*

## Deployment of troops for the assault on Badajos 6 April 1812

| Unit | Objective |
| --- | --- |
| 4th DIVISION | To attack the breach in Trinidad and the new one just to the west of it |
| LIGHT DIVISION | To attack the breach in Santa Maria |
| 3rd DIVISION | To escalade the castle |
| 5th DIVISION | (a) One British brigade to escalade the bastion of San Vincente |
| | (b) One Portuguese brigade to escalade the outworks of Pardeleras |
| | (c) One British brigade held in reserve |
| TRENCH GUARD | To escalade San Roque |
| (Found that night by 4th Division) | |
| POWER'S PORTUGUESE BRIGADE | To make a false attack on the bridgehead on the north bank of the Guadiana |

baulks of timber a foot square, bristling with sword blades and firmly anchored into position, while the actual slopes were covered with nail-studded planks. The ramparts on either side of the breaches were piled with shells, powder bags, rocks, baulks of timber and other missiles, while narrow trenches had been dug to the forward edges of the ramparts for individual sharpshooters, with slots through which they could fire down into the ditch itself, and each defender had three or four loaded muskets ready to hand so that the first fire would be rapid and deadly. They had even launched a fortified raft on the inundation to bring small arms fire on to any attack. Worst of all, perhaps, were the numerous mines and shells which had been buried in the ditch at the foot of the breaches, with covered quick matches leading back onto the ramparts. The British guns had stopped firing at 7.30pm so that the defenders had ample time to connect up their fuzes without any risk of their being cut again by artillery fire.

The night was dark and a good deal of mist was rising from the Rivillas inundation. Most battalions were in their assembly areas by 8pm, and having piled their arms were fallen out to wait impatiently in small groups for the affair to begin. Many officers reported an air of savage determination in their men, very different from their usual good-humoured demeanour. They had worked hard under appalling conditions for weeks and had watched their comrades killed around them, and now they apparently felt that the moment for revenge had come. Most were clearly looking beyond the assault to the time when the successful survivors could break loose from all the bonds of discipline and restraint and have a night, and perhaps more, of loot, drunkenness, and rape as a reward for all their sufferings. Some of them had even concocted business-like plans to make the most of their opportunity. One of these was Lawrence of the 40th Regt, who had discussed the matter in some detail with two friends, for he later wrote:

> 'Through being quartered at Badajos after the battle of Talavera, all three of us knew the town perfectly well and so understood the position of most of the valuable shops; and hearing a report likewise that if we succeeded in taking the place there was to be three hours' plunder, we had planned to meet at a silversmith's shop that we knew about, poor Pig even providing himself with a piece of wax candle to light us if needed.'

It was of course unfortunate that the Spanish inhabitants of the town were allies, but not many people seem to have taken that into account. The few who did consoled themselves with the quite erroneous idea that most of the loyal inhabitants had already fled, and that those who remained were French sympathizers who deserved all they got.

By 9.30pm all was ready and the men fell into their places in the ranks and unpiled arms. The Peninsular army was not famed for its sartorial standards and it is probable that most of them looked more like bandits than soldiers. Months of living in the open air in bad weather did nothing to improve the appearance of shoddy, badly-dyed coatees, most of which had bleached and faded to a colour more akin to khaki than red; their trousers were torn and patched, and their felt shakos

had long since lost their shape. Nor was their appearance much improved by heavy whiskers and presumably in many cases full beards, for there is no real indication that men shaved regularly on campaign. Each company apparently had a barber, for when one of them belonging to the 88th Regt was killed in the siege, lots were at once drawn for his razor and soap which were found in his pocket. It is difficult to know how often the razor was used—or for that matter, what it must have felt like when it was.

The first troops in action were the trench guards of 4th Division, who at about 9.45pm, opened heavy musketry on the front faces of San Roque, under cover of which an escalading party got in at the rear and mastered the place in a few minutes. The sudden rattle of fire alerted the defenders of the castle who threw down fireballs, by the light of which the 3rd Division was seen advancing from the first parallel. Heavy fire was at once opened from the fortress, and as there was no point in remaining as stationary targets the division was ordered forward a few minutes prematurely. The order was given by Maj-Gen Kempt, Picton not having reached the division. There we must leave them for the moment, and return to the main breaches.

The 4th and Light Divisions advanced in good order in parallel colums, the Light apparently a little ahead of the 4th. The heads then began to converge, so that there was a momentary alarm in the Light Division that they were about to be attacked on their right flank, but this was soon resolved and the leading elements reached the edge of the glacis without incident. Many of the palisades in front of the covered way had been smashed by the heavy artillery fire so that they were able to get into the covered way without difficulty. The four companies of the 95th Regt under Col Cameron detailed to give supporting fire on the front of the Light Division's attack apparently led the way, because Kincaid, who was acting adjutant of the detachment, later wrote that they succeeded in bringing them to the very spot agreed on. He went on:

'(they) then formed line to the left without a word being spoken, each man lying down as he got into line, with the muzzle of his rifle over the edge of the ditch between the palisades all ready to open. It was tolerably clear above, and we distinctly saw their heads lining the ramparts; but there was a sort of haze on the ground, which with the colour of our dress, prevented them from seeing us, although only a few yards asunder. One of their sentries challenged us twice, '*qui vive!*', and receiving no reply he fired off his musket which was followed by their drums beating to arms; but we still remained perfectly quiet and all was silence again for the space of five or ten minutes, when the head of the forlorn hope at length came up and we took advantage of the first fire while the enemy's heads were yet visible.'

The stormers of both divisions (which in spite of Kincaid's assertion seemed to have veered inwards), then lowered their ladders and, flinging in their haybags, began the descent into the ditch under a heavy fire of musketry. On the right, in front of the 4th Division, a deep *cunette* had been dug in the bottom of the original ditch and flooded from the inundation, and many of the leading troops, thinking it to be no more than a string of puddles, leapt into it and were drowned.

When the advanced columns of the two divisions, some thousand men in all, were fairly down in the ditches and attempting to form for a concerted rush at the breaches, the French fired all their mines with terrible effect. Only two officers of the Light Division remained unscathed and almost all the Engineer officers, the only ones with any detailed knowledge of the breaches, were killed or wounded in the first blast, as were hundreds of others, many of whom were dreadfully burnt. Much of the floor of the ditch has been covered with obstructions in the form of old carts, hand barrows (presumably those used earlier by the garrison for clearing rubble) broken gabions, and even one or two old boats, and these being almost all of timber, blazed up immediately and gave ample light by which to shoot.

Harry Smith of the 95th Regt, then a brigade major in the Light Division, was well to the forefront of the attack, and saw a rifleman actually standing amongst the sword blades on top of one of the *chevaux-de-frise;* he wrote:

'We made a glorious rush to follow, but alas! in vain. He was knocked over. My old Captain, O'Hare, who commanded the storming party, was

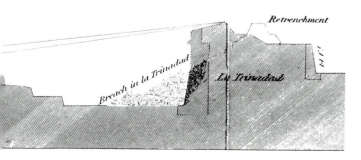

*Cross-section through the Santa Maria bastion showing the breach in its left flank and the retrenchment.*

*Two of the three points of attack on Badajos are shown in this illustration with, in the centre, the chaos at the breaches and, right, the castle assault.*

killed. All were awfully wounded except, I do believe myself and little Freer of the 43rd. I had been some seconds at the breach and my red-coat pockets were literally filled with chips of stones splintered by musket balls. Those not knocked down were driven back by this hail of mortality to the ladders. At the foot of them I saw poor Col Macleod with his hands on his breast—the man who lent me his horse when I was wounded at the bridge on the Coa. He said "Oh Smith, I am mortally wounded. Help me up the ladder". I said "Oh no, dear fellow!". "I am" he said "be quick". I did so and came back again. Little Freer and I said "Let us throw down the ladders; the fellows shan't go out". Some soldiers behind said "Damn your eyes, if you do we will bayonet you!" and we were literally forced up by the crowd. So soon as we got on the glacis, up came a fresh brigade of the Portuguese of the 4th Division. I never saw any soldiers behave with more pluck. Down into the ditch we went again, but the more we tried to get up, the more we were destroyed.'

By this time the main bodies of the two divisions were pouring into the ditch, and as those of the 4th naturally veered to their left to avoid the *cunette* they were soon inextricably mixed. Many of the men mistook the

unfinished ravelin, which had been badly battered by artillery fire, for the breach and rearing their ladders against it scrambled up, only to find themselves marooned on a great mound of torn earth with the main ditch still in front of them. Some opened fire, but others slid down again and made for the breaches. By then all semblance of order had been lost and the assault had degenerated into a series of gallant but hopeless attempts made by individual officers with such men as they could gather behind them. One example was Lt Shaw of the 43rd Regt, who seeing Capt Nicholas of the Engineers, (probably the only uninjured officer of his Corps in the ditch at that time) well up the breach, collected a handful of men and attempted to support him. Nicholas however was at that moment desperately wounded by a charge of grape or cannister and the attempt failed, as indeed it was bound to do. Nevertheless men were still scrambling into the inferno in the ditch until even the reserves from the quarries had been absorbed. Perhaps unfortunately, very few made for the new central breach, which was by far the easiest to ascend, because the approach to it was blocked by the *cunette*.

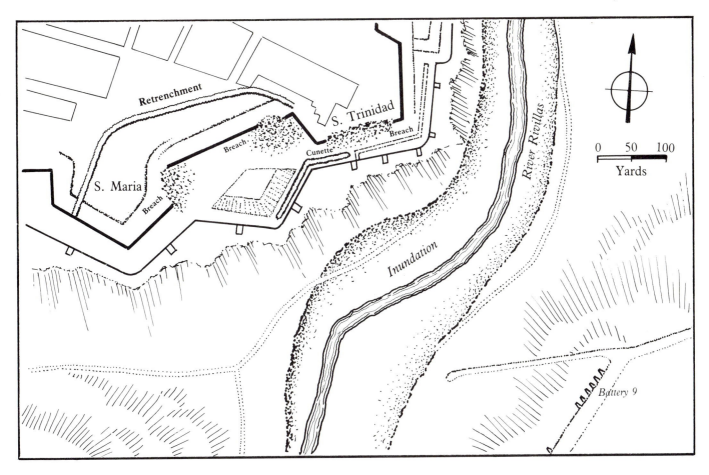

*The 4th and Light Divisions were to attack the breaches in the S Maria and S Trinidad bastions, but the recently improvised and flooded* cunette *in the ditch was to prove disastrous to their assault.*

Pte Lawrence of the 40th Regt, badly wounded in the leg, managed to get back by dragging himself up a ladder with dead men hanging from every rung, and crawled away. On his painful way to the rear he passed Wellington who asked him about his wounds and enquired if anyone had got into the town, to which Lawrence replied 'No'. One of the staff officers present then bound up his leg with a silk handkerchief and directed him to an aid post behind a hill where he actually encountered the doctor of his own regiment. Lawrence was clearly by no means the only man who replied 'No', and finally, after two hours Wellington bowed to the inevitable; the recall was sounded and the survivors of the two divisions, exhausted, blood-stained, and filthy, withdrew suddenly. Wellington, refusing to admit defeat, ordered them to re-organise and renew their attacks next morning, a prospect which filled even the dashing Harry Smith with horror. In the meanwhile a succession of urgent messages were sent to Picton to

take the castle, whatever the cost. Once the tumult at the breaches had died down, some distant firing could also be heard far off to the north west, but its portent was not then known and it seemed as if everything depended on exertions of the 3rd Division.

Gen Picton caught up with the head of his division as they were crossing the Rivillas on the wall of a mill-dam, over which water was flowing in some depth and which was so narrow that it had to be crossed in single file, a slow and tedious process for several thousand men, especially since it was under fire. The advance troops of three companies of the 60th Rifles appear to have got across with few casualties, as did the leading brigade of 1st/45th, 74th and 1st/88th Regts, although their Brigadier, Maj-Gen Kempt, was wounded there. A palisade on the far side was pushed aside and the troops scrambled across as fast as they could, and it was there that Picton himself was hit in the groin. Fortunately for him he had a wad of papers in his breeches pocket which deadened the impact and prevented the projectile, presumably a partly-spent musket ball, from penetrating, but which nevertheless shocked him considerably and put him temporarily hors-de-combat.

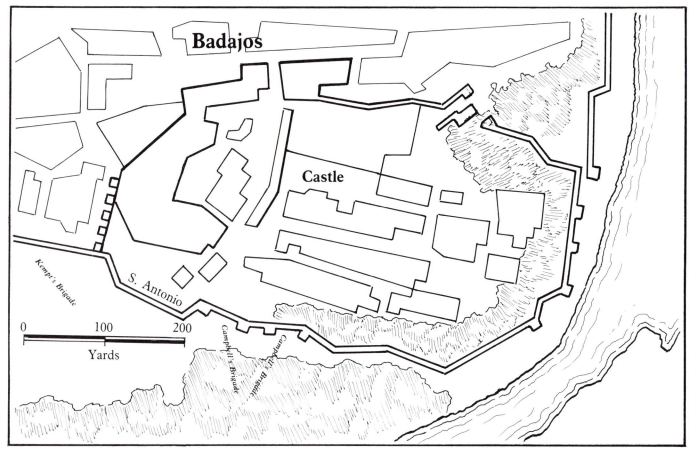

The Portuguese followed and then Campbell's brigade of 2nd/5th, 77th, 2nd/83rd and 94th Regts and it seems likely that by then the fire on the crossing place had intensified. George Hennell was serving with the 94th as a volunteer, that is, he was a young man of officer type who hoped to get a commission by service in the ranks. This was his first time in action—he had to borrow a red coat, a musket and a pouch of ammunition a little earlier, and his impressions were very much those of a novice. He later wrote to a friend that:

> 'Just as I passed the palisade ditch there came a shot from a 24 pounder directly above this flat place and twelve men sank together with a groan that could have shook the soul, the nerves of the oldest soldier that ever carried a musket. I believe ten of them never rose again, the nearest was within a foot of me, the farthest not four yards off. It swept like a besom all within its range. The next four steps I took were over this heap. You read of the horrors of war, you little know what it means.'

Kempt's brigade, temporarily leaderless, reared its ladders not against the castle, but against the curtain wall a little further south and thus in a crossfire from the castle and a neighbouring bastion, and the troops

mounted them, but every effort failed. A man scrambling up a ladder is an easy target for an enemy on top armed with a pike and three or four muskets, so that the few who got to the summit unscathed were there killed. Of the five or six ladders reared, several were pushed down and according to Major Burgoyne, the conducting engineer with the division, at least one was actually drawn up by the garrison. The ladders were 24ft long and of the solid type commonly used by builders. As they normally constituted a heavy and awkward load for four men their weight was

*Left: Kempt's Brigade attacked too far to the left, against the town walls, but Picton directed Campbell's Brigade to assault the Castle proper.*
*Bottom left: A private of the 5th Regiment, part of Campbell's Brigade, mounting a ladder during the escalade of the Castle.*
*Below: Mounting pressure is brought to bear against the Castle.*

considerable and it must have taken a good deal of strength to haul it up over the parapet.

The Portuguese then tried, but they too failed, and the two leading brigades withdrew baffled, having suffered considerable casualties, and it was at this stage apparently that Picton hobbled back on the scene. He was a very tough general indeed, sparing neither himself or his men, and he was determined to get into the castle if it took his whole division. The furious uproar still coming from the breaches made it obvious that the main attack had been held up, and it seemed clear to him, as indeed it did to Wellington, that the success or failure of the whole business depended on him. He saw at once that the place selected was too far south, and directed his third brigade to put their ladders against the castle wall and try there, and this they duly did. They had some difficulty in finding suitable places on which to rest their ladders on the steep slope, for if the ends were too close to the wall they became very easy to push away from the top. Several ladders were eventually got into

position and the third brigade began to scramble up.

The division was by then somewhat mixed up and according to Lt M'Carthy of the 50th Regt, one of the volunteer assistant engineers, the first man into the castle was a soldier of the 45th who died as he scrambled over the parapet. Col Ridge of the 5th had better luck for he got two ladders reared and he and Lt Canch, the officer commanding his grenadier company, mounted them swiftly, followed by a yelling, cursing crowd of soldiers. Both officers reached the top safely at a point where the defenders were few, and with the help of a dozen soldiers held the entry point (which was at an empty embrasure), until fifteen or twenty more had entered, when they at once charged the thin line of defenders and drove them off. By this time the division were streaming up the ladders, one of the first up being Mackie of the 88th who had led the forlorn hope at Ciudad Rodrigo a few weeks earlier. Volunteer Hennell, noticing as he said that men were tending to stand round calling out for their regiments, went up a ladder shouting 'Here is the 94th' and was glad to see that the

*A tribute to Lt-Col Ridge of the 5th Regiment, one of the first men into the Castle at Badajos. He was subsequently killed when the French launched a counter-attack which was repulsed.*

troops began to follow him. The best way for a volunteer to gain the commission he wanted was to distinguish himself in action, and it is clear Hennell's conduct had been noted, for within a few weeks he had been gazetted as ensign in the 43rd, one of the regiments of the Light Division.

The castle was vital to Gen Phillipon, for in it was stored his food and ammunition, and as soon as its fall was reported to him he ordered a battalion of his reserve, the French 88th, to counter-attack. Most of the gates had been blocked up, so this could only be done on a narrow front, and one charge by the 5th Regt stopped it very quickly, though at great cost, for in the course of it the gallant Col Ridge was killed. It was of him that Napier later wrote 'no man died that night with more glory—yet many died and there was much glory'—as noble an epitaph as any soldier could expect.

There was thereafter a good deal of apparent inaction. Capt Tyler, one of Picton's ADCS, at once galloped off to Wellington with the good news and was greeted with relief by him and actual cheers from his worried staff. According to Col Jones, a message was sent back to Picton to blow down the gates but otherwise remain quiet until morning and then sally out with 2000 men, which may of course account for it, but no other authority mentions such an order. It is by no means clear where Picton was at this time, but having regard to the obvious difficulties in hoisting a heavy, elderly man up a slippery, bloodstained ladder in the dark while suffering from the effects of a violent blow in the groin,

*General Picton exhorting his division to take the Castle. He had been wounded in the groin early in the battle and is therefore unlikely to have scaled the walls himself.*

*The 88th Regiment pouring into the Castle, whose fall preceded the final collapse of French resistance. For the 88th, as for other Peninsular veterans, 'the capture of Badajos had long been their idol'.*

it seems reasonable to suppose that he stayed at the foot of the wall, at least until daylight, leaving Campbell, the commander of his third brigade, in actual command in the castle itself. It is also very probable that Picton, having had first hand experience of events in Ciudad Rodrigo immediately after its fall, was reluctant to let his troops into the town in the dark. Wellington's despatch is not clear on this point.

Things started badly for the 5th Division, since the officer sent to draw the scaling ladders from the engineer park got lost, and did not rejoin the division until 11pm; during the interval General Leith had ordered one of his Portuguese battalions to make a false attack on Pardeleras which they did with great energy, and as soon as the ladders arrived the two British brigades moved off towards the bastion of San Vincente, which was at the northwest angle of the Badajos, whence the curtain wall ran eastwards along the river. The defences, although only lightly manned, were formidable in themselves, with a ditch and a thirty foot high rampart,

but the leading brigade under Maj-Gen Walker, was not deterred. They climbed down the ladders into the ditch, which was there twelve feet deep, with a *cunette* in its centre, crossed that, and reared their ladders against the ramparts, all under heavy fire. The ladders were only 24ft long, but fortunately the rampart was only vertical for the first twenty feet, the remainder being an earth bank, steep but able to be climbed, and the brigade was soon on the summit, from which they drove the French defenders in confusion.

General Walker, re-forming quickly, then led off southwards, along the ramparts, having detached half the 4th Regt to clear some houses on his flank. He cleared bastions No2 and No3, not without hard fighting, but fell desperately wounded at No4. A

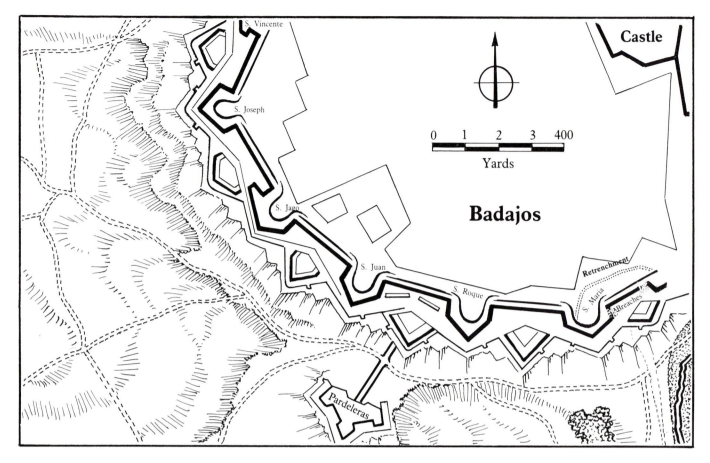

smouldering port-fire, presumably dropped by a French artilleryman, then caused the cry of 'mine' to be raised, and the brigade, seized with a sudden irrational panic, fled back the way it had come, and actually reached San Vincente, with the French in hot pursuit. Here however General Leith had the 38th Regt drawn up ready, and as soon as the fugitives had passed through them they fired one terrible volley which brought the French to a halt with fearful casualties. Walker's brigade then quickly recovered itself and General Leith, having got the rest of his second brigade up the ladders and called in the detachment of the 4th Regt (which had suffered some loss in the meanwhile), formed into two columns and marched off southward, with his buglers all sounding the advance to the limit of their lung-power. This was decisive, and the gallant French defenders of

*Above: The other defences of Badajos away from the two breaches and castle. The 5th Division, following a feint against Pardeleras, finally escaladed the bastion of San Vincente to gain entry into the town. From here the Regiments were to fight their way along the walls and so come upon the defenders of the breaches from the rear.*

*Below: A section through the defences of Badajos at the San Vincente bastion. The British siege ladders could reach to the top of the lower, vertical face of the bastion itself and the attackers were able to scramble up the steep bank to the summit.*

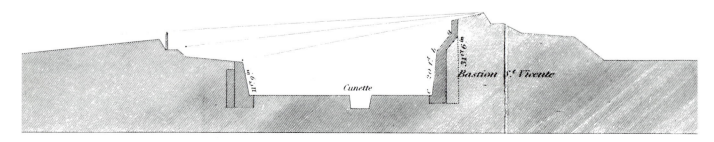

the main breaches, realising that the British were in the town behind them, finally broke and ran, most of them making for the bridge. Major Gomm, on the staff of the 5th Division, wrote to his brother Henry:

> 'It was some time before we could establish our footing on the rampart, but through General Walker's exertions it was at length effected and we had thrown, or rather lifted, four regiments into the town by midnight. Imagine what an effect our buglers, sounding in this part of the town immediately behind the breaches, must have had upon those defending them.'

Wellington, having certain news that Leith was in the town and the breaches deserted, at once ordered the 4th and Light Divisions forward again. They were at first certain that they were marching to their deaths, but the breaches were silent and they scrambled up them marvelling at their change in fortune in an hour or so. Even without defenders, the breaches were by no means easy of access, particularly since they were heaped with dead and wounded, but they eventually

*General Sir James Leith who commanded the 5th Division. Both he and Picton had claimed the glory for the victory at Bussaco. At the third Siege of Badajos each was assigned objectives on opposite sides of the town.*

*With British troops in both the town and castle, the defenders of the two breaches withdrew and the remnants of the 4th and Light Divisions were at last able to move up out of the ditches. The looting and plundering of the town then started.*

got in and by first light were formed up on the ramparts, with *picquets* in front of them. At this stage of the proceedings, and with recent memories of Ciudad Rodrigo in mind, considerable efforts were made, particularly by the Light Division, to keep the soldiers out of the town.

Phillipon, seeing that the situation was hopeless, collected what few officers and men he could find and crossed the Guadiana to the bridgehead, which in spite of the orders to Power's Portuguese was still in French hands. He made his way thence to San Cristoval, which was of course intact and fully garrisoned, and was there summoned to surrender by Lord Fitzroy Somerset of Wellington's staff some six hours later. He made a bold attempt to discuss terms, but was given ten minutes

*Governor Phillipon addresses his troops in Badajos before crossing the river to Fort Cristoval where he finally surrendered to Lord Fitzroy Somerset. He was evacuated under British guard.*

to surrender unconditionally which he duly did. By this time most of the prisoners had been collected and according to Kincaid were on their way to Elvas by 10am the same morning.

The horrors of the sack of Badajos by the British Army in April 1812 are a matter of history, rivalling as they do some of the worst atrocities of the Thirty Years War, but from their very nature it is difficult to give any coherent account of them.

At Ciudad Rodrigo virtually all the troops concerned had swarmed up the breaches together, so that the rioting and looting which followed broke out almost spontaneously, but at Badajos things turned out somewhat differently due to different circumstances. There can be little doubt that the great bulk of the assaulting troops were grimly determined to have their reward for their labours by sacking the town thoroughly, and as systematically as their drunken state would allow, and all were eager to begin. The general impression is that it started with the 5th Division, simply because

they were first into the town, and spread rapidly as more and more troops gained access. It was probably not far short of daylight before the 4th and Light Divisions had managed to penetrate the breaches, and then there was clearly a general rush to join in; Cooper of the 7th Regt states very definitely that:

> 'As soon as the French had left the breach the beam was removed and our maddened fellows rushed into the town by thousands. Wine shops were broken open and horrible scenes commenced. All order ceased. Plunder was the order of the night.'

So it is clear that the 4th Division, to which his unit belonged, wasted no time.

The Light Division, or at least some of it, was kept in restraint for some time, for its commander Barnard, (who in spite of his gallant exertions in the ditch earlier had escaped injury), was steadfastly against looting of all kinds. Kincaid, speaking of his own battalion, says that it sent *picquets* into the town but was otherwise kept in hand until day should throw some light on the situation. He himself commanded one of the *picquets*, whose prime function seems to have been rounding up prisoners, and soon collected a good many, one of whom, an officer, presented him with a handsome black mare which was the only legitimate plunder an officer could legally accept. As he made his way back to the battalion many more Frenchmen joined him, all presumably eager to get out of the town before the British got in, and they talked so loudly that they were near to being fired on by a Light Division *picquet* which was obviously well in hand. Kincaid goes on to say that the whole of the garrison had been marched off to Elvas by 10am after which 'our men were then permitted to fall out, to enjoy themselves for the remainder of the day as a reward for having kept together as long as they were wanted', but although he may have believed this, it was by no means official, for Colonel Barnard and many of his officers did all they could to stop the looting, Barnard it is said being at one time in very great personal danger.

The 3rd Division, being cooped up in the castle which had only one easily guarded exit into the town, had no choice but to stay where they were. Pte Donaldson of the 94th tells us that:

> 'When the town surrendered, and the prisoners were secured, the gate leading into the town from the castle was opened and we were allowed to enter the town for the purpose of plundering it ...'

After first drinking inordinate quantities of spirits (according to him some men fell into the casks and drowned) the real atrocities started, but he goes on to say:

> 'They were not general, and in most cases were perpetrated by cold-blooded villains who were backward enough in the attack. Many risked their lives in defending helpless females and although it was rather a dangerous place for an officer to appear I saw many of them running as much risk to prevent inhumanity, as they did the preceding night in storming the town.'

Lawrence of the 40th, whom we left crawling back to a doctor, felt better by next morning and decided to hobble into town with the aid of a sergeant's half-pike, which he used as a crutch, presumably to see what he could find. His earlier designs on a silversmiths had come to nothing because of course he had been wounded; even so he was more fortunate than his two confederates who were both lying in the ditch in front of the breaches. It was also very noticeable that as soon as it was possible to enter the town hundreds of the soldiers' wives also swarmed in, although on the whole they were more interested in plunder than drink.

One of the many officers who strove hard to prevent the worst horrors was Capt Robert Blakeney of the 28th. He had in fact been promoted to a company in another regiment, but happened to be passing close to Badajos just as the siege was beginning and attached himself unofficially to the 4th Division as a sort of extra ADC to General Bowes, whom he later managed to get out of the ditch when he had been wounded. He really summed up the general situation by noting that:

> 'The infuriated soldiery resembled rather a pack of hell hounds vomited up from the infernal regions for the extirpation of mankind than what they were but twelve short hours previously—a well-organised, brave, disciplined and obedient British Army, and burning only with impatience for what is called glory.'

He had several narrow escapes; on one occasion a sergeant actually struck him with his pike upon which Blakeney, not in the least the man to tolerate that sort of treatment, drew a pistol and snapped it full in the man's face. Fortunately for the sergeant it mis-fired but he was so shocked at his narrow escape that he made an awkward apology and disappeared.

It is perhaps understandable that soldiers who survived such hardship and danger should have got briefly out of hand, but unlike Ciudad Rodrigo, where order was restored next morning, it was not until 9 April that firm action was taken. *Picquets* sent in earlier had been drawn into looting, but on that day a brigade was

marched in and a gallows erected. Kincaid says that the sight of a few suspended red coats did the trick, but Blakeney disagreed. His view was that:

> 'A general order was proclaimed that the first man detected in plundering should be executed; but no execution took place. The soldiers well knew how far they might proceed and no farther did they go. The butcheries and the horrible scenes of plunder and debauchery ceased in Badajos; and it became an orderly British garrison.'

One can only wonder at the sheer stamina of the participants, unless indeed they slept at the scene of their debauchery and returned to it refreshed in due course. The real problem however is to explain the long delay in stopping the affair, for although Wellington was furious he seems also to have been powerless, a very strange condition indeed for him. It is impossible to believe that he condoned the sack, although being a realist he may have regarded it as inevitable. He once

*Wellington stands in the S. Trinidad breach, cheered by his victorious troops. Casualty figures of over 3500 killed or wounded contributed, in part, to excesses during the plundering of the town.*

described his army as being the scum of the earth, enlisted for drink, and although this was probably an exaggeration one has but to consider the aftermath of Badajos to see that there was a considerable element of truth in it. Most commanding officers would have readily agreed that their battalions contained up to two hundred incorrigibles, who in the last resort could only be kept under control by the fear of death or the lash, and there must have been many more who, although not in the same class, were easily led astray by a bad example. The line between discipline and anarchy was, and in many ways still is, a very narrow one, and once it has been crossed chaos can soon result. Fresh troops might have been put in to clear the place but this could have made things worse, either because they might have joined the rioters, or because if they had attempted to use force, they might have been resisted. The troops in the town were all armed, and drunk as they were they might well have caused a bloodbath.

Presumably one can return to the laws of war which, imprecise though they were, did at least suggest propriety of a surrender when a practicable breach had been made, to which Phillipon might very justifiably have retorted that 'practicable' was not a recognisable description of breaches which two of the best divisions in the British Army had failed to make any impressions, even though the extent of their effort can be measured by their losses. These were very large indeed. The total losses in the siege were 72 officers 963 men killed, 306 officers and 3483 men wounded, and about 100 missing, of whom 59 officers, 744 men were killed in the course of the actual assault and 258 officers and 2600 men wounded, the great bulk of these being at the breaches. Several regiments lost almost half their effectives, including four battalion commanders killed, and six generals wounded. These figures are perhaps the more terrible when we consider that the losses of the garrison in the actual assault could be counted in less than three figures.

The evacuation of casualties from the breaches was slow, for reasons which have already been made clear. William Surtees of the 95th, being a quartermaster, was not actively engaged in the actual siege, but he and his Commanding Officer, Capt Perceval, were at the breaches soon after first light and worked unceasingly to get the wounded away. Perceval rounded up drunks for the purpose, using his stick freely, but they were not much use as Surtees reported:

'... many who from the nature of their wounds, required great care and attention in carrying, the half-drunken brutes whom we were forced to employ exceedingly tortured and injured; nay, in carrying one man out of the ditch they very frequently kicked or trod upon several others whom to touch was like death to them, and which produced the most agonising cries imaginable.'

The same writer, a most serious upright, character, goes on to tell us with ill-concealed distaste, that while they were busy at this work of mercy:

'an officer with yellow facings came out of the town with a frail fair one leaning on his arm, and carrying in her other hand a cage with a bird in it; and she tripped over the dead and dying with all the ease and indifference of a person moving in a ball-room, —no more concern being evinced

by either of them than if nothing extraordinary had occurred. It really was lamentable to see such an utter absence of all right feeling.'

Even amongst these scenes of horror there was a place for romance. During the sack two Spanish ladies fled the town and sought refuge in the camp of the 95th. One of them, no more than fourteen years of age, was very beautiful and captured the heart of every young officer in the battalion. The lucky man was Henry Smith who married her on the spot and she soon became a most popular member of the Light Division. She accompanied Smith on almost all his travels and campaigns and died in 1872. In view of her long military connections it was perhaps appropriate that a town in South Africa to which she had given her name, Ladysmith, was to become famous militarily nearly thirty years after her death.

Once the looting had been stopped and the troops got back to their camps, they were given a day to recover

*Juana Maria de los Dolores de Leon, who with her sister, fled from the sack of Badajos, their ears bleeding from where the earrings had been ripped off. She sought sanctuary in the British camp and there married Harry Smith of the 95th Regt. Years later, Ladysmith in South Africa was named in her honour.*

(which most of them presumably badly needed) and then, sobriety and discipline restored, they were put to work. Due to the efforts of a number of devoted officers of the type of Perceval and Surtees, many of the wounded had been dealt with, and now it was possible to identify and bury the dead. The trenches were also filled in and the siege guns sent off to Elvas, all being complete by 13 April when the Army marched off elsewhere.

Marmont, too weak to interfere at Badajos, and lacking the siege train with which to menace Ciudad Rodrigo, had led a raid into Portugal which got as far as Castello Branco but did little harm, except to alarm the small covering force left in the area by Wellington. As was usual with any French army, lack of supplies soon compelled him to withdraw, so that the British were not involved with him. General Hill was left to guard Badajos with his corps while the place was restored by Spanish masons and other workmen under the supervision of Colonel Sir Richard Fletcher the Chief Engineer, (by then well on the way to recovery from the wound received during the siege) and at a cost of 65000 dollars.

On 10 April Wellington had performed a kindness to Capt Nicholas of the Royal Enginners, who it will be remembered had been desperately wounded in the breach, when he wrote the following letter to Colonel Torrens, Military Secretary at the Horse Guards:

'In my last letters I omitted to recommend to His Royal Highness's favour Capt Nicholas of the Engineers, because he is so desperately wounded that I thought it impossible he could live, but I understand that he is likely to do well; and it is but justice to him to make known his merits to his Royal Highness...'

It was a kind and generous thought on the part of Wellington but in the event did not achieve anything, for the very favourable medical reports on Nicholas were over-optimistic, and he died soon afterwards.

In spite of the shadow cast over it by its sacking, the capture of Badajos was a remarkable feat of arms of which the British Army could be proud. Wellington, deeply conscious of its cost, later wrote to Maj-Gen G. Murray, who had been his Quarter-Master General:

'The assault was a terrible business, of which I foresaw the loss when I was ordering it. But we had brought matters to that state that we could do no more, and it was necessary to storm or raise the siege. I trust however, that future armies will be equipped for sieges with the people necessary to carry them on as they ought to be; and that our engineers will learn how to put their batteries on the crest of the glacis, and to blow in the counterscarp, instead of placing them wherever the wall can be seen, leaving it to the poor officers and troops to get into and across the ditch as best they can.'

These strictures on the capacity of his engineers seem to be somewhat unkind. The officers concerned, although inevitably lacking extensive practical experience, knew well enough what to do, but lacked the means to do it. The volunteer sappers from the Line were brave and willing, but did not have the skill and training of properly trained workmen, so that they tended to be slow. It was also the case (then as now) that soldiers work better under officers of their own corps, so that although it was perfectly acceptable, to use working parties in the early stages, they lacked the knowledge of, and faith in, their officers which was essential when it came, for example, to sapping forward

*Capt William Nicholas RE who, though terribly wounded in the assault on the breaches, survived the siege. Wellington's kindness in recommending him to London was regrettably wasted, as he died soon after.*

*Officers and men of the Corps of Sappers and Miners in 1812. Following Wellington's request, the corps was raised to provide troops trained in siege warfare.*

to the counterscarp. Wellington himself was well aware of this, and soon after Ciudad Rodrigo he had written to the Prime Minister to urge the immediate formation of a Corps of Sappers and Miners; this proposal had been accepted and arrangements were at once made to comply with his wishes by converting the old Corps of Military Artificers. The new Royal Corps of Sappers and Miners came into official existence in August 1812, although the British Army in Spain did not see any of its members until almost a year later.

It is interesting to speculate how Wellington would have liked to see the business conducted if full facilities had been available. If he had decided to make his breaches in the same places, the approach via Picurina would have been impossible without a preliminary operation to take San Roque and destroy the dam so as to do away with the inundation. He might have decided to tackle the south face although the comprehensive system of mines which covered it would have caused problems. Both Phillipon and his chief engineer considered the front to the south of the castle to be the most vulnerable, but this was not necessarily obvious at the time, while many of the French

considered that a large-scale series of escalades on the first night would have been just as effective, and less costly, than the method adopted, but this again was to be wise after the event.

When we consider that in 1811 the French, fully equipped for siege operations, took forty-one days of open trenches to take Badajo's (which finally surrendered in suspicious circumstances before any assault was actually made), it will be realised that the twenty-one days taken by the British was not excessive. As we have seen in the earlier sieges, Wellington was always to some degree vulnerable to outside interference, so that time was the important factor, and one is driven to wonder whether Wellington could ever have contemplated spending six weeks to reduce a fortress. Had he but had ample mortars and howitzers to prevent repairs to the breaches, and in particular to destroy the trains of powder to the mines, Badajos might well have been taken through the breaches on 6 April without excessive casualties.

Nor in a discussion of this kind, must we forget the skill and ingenuity of General Phillipon and his engineers, and the devoted backing they received from their garrison. There is little doubt that at the time the assault was launched, the breaches constituted the strongest part of the perimeter and they were gallantly defended.

# CHAPTER SEVEN

## Three Minor Sieges—
## The Bridge of Almaraz
## The Forts at Salamanca
## The Retiro at Madrid

### The Bridge of Almaraz

Although the British were not to be involved in another fullscale siege for some months, it is necessary to deal with the intervening period in some detail, partly because of its intrinsic importance but largely because the operations, although mainly mobile in character, nevertheless involved the reduction of three small fortified places. As soon as Ciudad Rodrigo and Badajos were safely in allied hands—repaired, revictualled, and properly garrisoned—Wellington found himself in possession of a secure base from which he could conduct offensive operations into Spain. He was still heavily outnumbered by the French, although their superiority was not as great in practice as it appeared on paper. The British, operating in a friendly country and possessed of an efficient supply system, were able to conduct mobile operations for long periods whereas the French, an army of occupation living off the country, found it difficult to concentrate. Even when they managed to do so, lack of transport made it exceptionally difficult to carry food and ammunition except for relatively short periods.

As Wellington's army was usually stronger than any of the various armies on their own, some degree of co-operation on the part of the latter was essential. This needed good communications, in a country where roads were few and in poor condition and haunted by guerrillas, and the French made much use of fortified posts for this purpose. One of the most important of these was the group of works covering their boat bridge at Almaraz on the Tagus which was on the direct route between Soult and Marmont and which had been

*The taking of the bridge at Almaraz, consistently drawn by contemporary illustrators as a rigid structure, when it was, in fact, a bridge of boats.*

**Forces deployed for the attack on the bridge at Almarez 1812**

| Command | Units |
| --- | --- |
| MAJOR-GENERAL HOWARD'S BRIGADE | 50th, 71st, 92nd, Coy 60th Rifles |
| COLONEL WILSON'S BRIGADE | |
| (incomplete) | 28th, 34th, Coy 60th Rifles |
| PORTUGUESE BRIGADE | 6th Line, 18th Line, 6th *Cacadores* |
| MAJOR-GENERAL LONG | 13th Light Dragoons |
| ARTILLERY | 6 × 24 pounder howitzers |
| | 3 × 9 pounder guns |
| ENGINEERS | With tools and twelve 32ft scaling ladders, together with six pontoons to make flying bridges |

established by the latter in the previous year. It was used extensively by everything from small escorts to whole armies, and Wellington knew that if it could be destroyed it would compel the French to communicate by the bridge at Toledo, which meant that for practical purposes they had to travel via Madrid, a distance of some four hundred miles. The French could not establish another one because Soult's own boat bridge had been taken in Badajos. Wellington therefore decided to eliminate it, while at the same time re-establishing the old Roman bridge of Alcantara, which would reduce his own line from Ciudad Rodrigo to Badajos to little more than a hundred and fifty miles.

The task of dealing with Almaraz was given to Lt-Gen Hill, one of Wellington's most trusted subordinates, who quickly assembled a suitable force at Merida. It is perhaps indicative of the importance Wellington attached to the operation that he wrote to Hill on 24 April, 'See Dickson in regard to this equipment and settle the whole with him. You had better take him on the expedition with you'.

The expedition was soon formed at Merida, and as soon as the bridge there had been repaired the whole crossed over and set out for Almaraz via Truxillo and Jaracejo. The bridge was strongly defended by a group of works which the French regarded as being capable of resisting attack by artillery for eight days, which would have allowed ample time for a relief expedition to be launched by the nearest French troops which were only two marches away.

The main work was Fort Napoleon, which mounted nine guns. It was situated at the north end of a ridge of high ground and overlooked the river. It had a proper ditch and a central loopholed keep, and was garrisoned by about 450 men. Then there was the actual bridge-head itself, which mounted three guns, while on the north bank of the river was Fort Ragusa, a solidly built pentagonal work, also with a central tower. It was

on high ground some distance from the northern end of the bridge, the local defence of which was provided by a *flèche*, *i.e.* a simple earthwork shaped like a broad arrow head. The barracks, stores, and extensive and well-equipped workshops were in the Spanish hamlet of Lugar Nuevo, on the south side of the river and about half a mile east of Fort Napoleon; its original inhabitants had of course been ejected when the defences were first built. The whole complex lay with a horseshoe-shaped ridge of steep hills, the only access to it for wheeled vehicles being by the Truxillo road. This, at the point where it crossed the high ground, was defended by the ancient Moorish tower of Miravete, which the French had strengthened by surrounding it with a lower wall and rampart twelve feet high, and mounting nine cannon in it. It was flanked by a fortified house actually on the roadside, with two small earthworks between,

*A trooper of the 13th Light Dragoons, who under Maj-Gen Long, were tasked with providing the cavalry screen for the attack on the Pass of Miravete.*

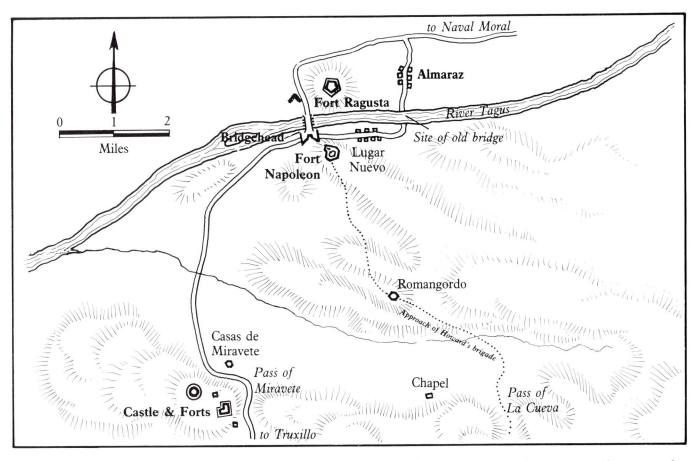

*The plan of attack against the new, temporary bridge at Almaraz. Unforeseen difficulties delayed both lines of advance before the bridge was finally taken.*

the whole constituting a formidable defensive line across the pass. There was a second pass, that of La Cueva, about three miles further east, but the path over it was little more than a goat track, quite impassable for wheeled vehicles.

The original plan had been for the centre column, which was under the command of Maj-Gen Long and consisted of the cavalry, artillery, and the two Portuguese line battalions, to advance towards the pass of Miravete and demonstrate against the secondary defences, while the left or western column under Lt-Gen Chowne (in temporary command of 2nd Division) and consisting of Wilson's brigade and Portuguese *Cacadores*, should escalade the castle from the other side. The right, or eastern column, which was led by Hill in person and consisted of Howard's brigade, was to cross the ridge at the pass of La Cueva and deal with the bridge defences, the whole being roughly co-ordinated to take place at first light on 17 May.

In the event, the programme went very wrong in practice, due mainly to the difficulties experienced by

Howard's brigade in moving over rough country by night on a goat track. This brigade was therefore halted out of sight of the French while the others continued their advance. Chowne however, having reconnoitred Miravete, came to the sensible conclusion that it would be quite impossible to take it by a surprise escalade and thus abandoned the operation, apparently to the no small relief of his troops. Young George Bell of the 34th, then a new-comer to the Peninsula, had been given the duty of supervising the placing of the ladders against the ramparts and later said that it was 'a position I considered at the time equal to a wooden leg', and it is certain that his feelings were shared with others. The abandonment of this project naturally stopped the centre column, so for the moment the whole force was held up. The remainder of the 17 and 18 May was largely occupied with an extensive search by staff officers for some other point where the guns could be got over the ridge and down into the valley, but in the event their search was fruitless, so Hill came to the bold conclusion that he would attempt a surprise escalade on the works covering the bridge with his infantry only, and trust to them to overcome the disadvantages occasioned by lack of artillery support. He therefore reinforced Howard's brigade with 6th *Ccacadores*, a company of the 60th Rifles, and a detachment of artillerymen, and at 9pm on 18 May they set off across country.

As a result of previous experience the long and clumsy ladders were cut in half so as to make them more portable, but even so they proved to be a fearful burden in the dark and across exceptionally rough and difficult country. Sergeant Robertson of the 92nd, who was in charge of one ladder party, had sixteen men in two shifts of eight. He noted that the road was the roughest he had ever travelled, and that when any of the ladder men lost their footing away went the whole party down a steep hill along the side of which the path lay. Nevertheless, soon after dawn, the 50th Regt and a wing of the 71st were under cover in a thicket no more than a couple of hundred yards from Fort Napoleon, and although many of the troops were still scattered across the hillsides to the rear like sheep, Hill decided to attack as quickly as possible. He had previously arranged for Chowne to create a diversion by making a false attack on the works at Miravete as soon as the light was good enough; this he duly did, and very soon the French garrisons round the bridge were all lining the south parapets, listening to the roar of the artillery and watching shells bursting on the high ground.

Although accounts vary as to the exact time, it was probably almost 7am when the attack was launched. The 50th and a wing of the 71st crossed the open space with a rush, their ladder parties panting along with them, and scrambled into the ditch leaving the open space behind them scattered with fallen red-coats. They then raised their ladders under showers of missiles—rocks, stones, roundshot, and even bottles—which caused a good many casualties; a soldier of the 71st later

*Fort Napoleon at the southern end of the bridge across the Tagus. During the difficult approach march, the scaling ladders had been sawn in half but fortunately, by using the ledge in the fort's rampart, the ladders could be hauled up to reach the parapet.*

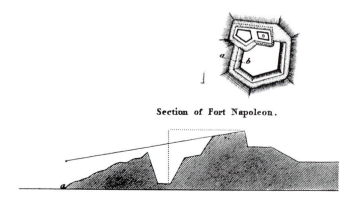

Section of Fort Napoleon.

stated that the French dared not actually raise their heads over the parapets at this stage because of the musketry of the besiegers, although Capt Patterson of the 50th speaks feelingly of the 'Fench grenadiers whose great bearskin caps and whiskered faces ornamented the breastwork overhead'. The half ladders were too short to reach the top of the parapet but fortunately the rampart had been built in two steps with a wide berm, or ledge, half way up. The attackers therefore scrambled on to this first and hauling the ladders up behind them, planted them on the berm and mounted them again. The first man over was Capt Robert Chandler, commanding No4 company of the 50th, who was at once killed, but on the other side of the fort, where the rampart was somewhat lower, the grenadiers soon made a lodgement, as did the 71st, upon which the garrison was seized with panic and made a wild dash at the sally port leading out of the work in the direction of the bridge. The Governor who was in Fort Napoleon, was however made of sterner stuff, for as Patterson tells he:

> 'refused to surrender to our men, and being resolved to sell his life as dearly as he could, he placed his back against the round tower in the centre of the work where with his sabre he chopped away right and left, cutting down any rash

desperado who ventured to approach his weapon. At length Sergeant Checker, of 50th Light Company, a fine soldier, exasperated by the stubborn obstinacy of the Frenchman, put an end to his existence with his halberd, giving to the valiant governor the fate which, in his despair, he so resolutely courted.'

He was in fact only mortally wounded at that stage, but died at Merida where he was buried with full military honours. It is said that Checker, who later became Sergeant-Major, always regretted the necessity for having to dispose of so gallant an enemy.

The garrison then raced for the shelter of the *tête-du-pont*, with a few of the 50th and 71st amongst them, but they had little chance to make a second stand there for the 92nd, who were by that time up and formed, at once charged and swept them across the bridge which then broke in the centre. The reason for this is not wholly clear. Some accounts say that the leading fugitives cut the ropes behind them, although the French General Foy later stated that the bridge was linked in the centre by a light country boat which could be pulled out easily, and that it had collapsed under the weight of the fugitives, which seems a reasonable explanation. A good many of the French were drowned

and the remainder had no choice but to surrender. This would normally have been the end of the affair, since the bridge could hardly have been repaired under the steady close-range fire from Fort Ragusa. The British gunner detachment however then turned the guns of Fort Napoleon onto Fort Ragusa, and to the great surprise of all concerned the garrison streamed out, making for Naval Moral as fast as they could go. Some grenadiers of the 92nd at once stripped and swam the river to retrieve some boats on the other side, by means of which the bridge was quickly restored.

The whole complex was then destroyed. The guns were thrown into the river and the towers and magazines blown up, in the course of which activity Lt Thiel of the Artillery was killed. He had gone back to inspect a fuze which was believed to have gone out, and was standing near the charge when it went off somewhat belatedly. The well-equipped workshops and stores full of rope, tools, timber, and other materials were all burnt, and once the destruction on the north bank was complete the troops recrossed the river and burnt the bridge behind them. The only items spared were the food and drink, which everyone present agreed to have been in considerable quantity and of excellent quality. The bonus was made even greater by the fact that the force had been without bread or biscuit for several days. It is true that a double ration of meat had been issued in lieu, but an unrelieved diet of ration beef cannot have been particularly palatable, especially since the beasts from which it came had marched for hundreds of miles behind the army and had been slaughtered, butchered, cooked and consumed within the space of an hour or so. Sergeant Robertson mentions bread, pork, and brandy, while Capt Patterson fairly rhapsodised over 'provisions to gratify the palate of the most fastidious gourmand'. He goes on to describe the scene where:

> 'Collected together in knots and parties, with the greensward for our tablecloth, forgetful of the past, and careless about the future, we feasted most sumptuously, drinking to our foes in their own generous wine, and wishing that, in future campaigns, our adventures might be terminated in an equally agreeable and fortunate manner.'

Although it is clear that a somewhat desperate venture had ended in a picnic atmosphere, the bill was by no means light, for thirty-three officers and men had been

*The attack on Fort Napoleon and the bridge (again a solid structure) at Almaraz by the 50th, 71st and 92nd Regiments. To the left can be seen Fort Ragusta, which was abandoned by the French without a fight.*

*General Rowland Hill. The Almaraz bridge taken, his forces burnt it and blew-up the supporting forts.*

killed and one hundred and forty-four wounded, most of them from the 50th. The French losses were also high, since Hill reported two hundred and seventy-nine prisoners, which together with those killed in action or drowned in the Tagus must have pushed the French losses up to some four hundred. Fort Ragusa and the *tête-du-pont* were held by a Prussian regiment in the French service, and there was probably by that period a certain amount of disillusionment amongst its members, since many of those who escaped never rejoined their colours and must be presumed to have deserted, unless they were destroyed by the guerrillas. The Commandant of Fort Ragusa was later condemned to death by the French which in all the circumstances seemed proper.

The only unsatisfactory part of the business was Hill's failure to take Miravete, although it was in no way his fault. Once the bridge defences were in his hands he could probably have taken it without difficulty, but he had received apparently authentic information from a responsible officer that Soult was close at hand with his army and therefore withdrew. In fact it made no difference; the bridge was never re-established and the events of the next few months so changed the situation in the Peninsula that it lost all importance.

## The Forts at Salamanca

Wellington now had the chance of tackling Soult or Marmont, and after some consideration settled on the latter. Soult was heavily committed in Andalusia with the siege of Cadiz and various operations against the Spaniards and would be reluctant to move north, so that he might be disregarded for the moment, especially since a successful Allied blow against Marmont would leave him hopelessly isolated. The British Army therefore moved north, and after re-victualling Ciudad Rodrigo (which the Spaniards had neglected to do) made for Salamanca, from which Marmont withdrew on its approach. After the fall of Ciudad Rodrigo, Napoleon had ordered Salamanca to be strongly fortified as an alternative French base, and although both money and material had been in short supply a good deal had been done to implement the Emperor's instructions in the time available.

The principal position consisted of a triangular group of three forts, standing on high ground in the south-west angle of the city. They had been made by the ingenious conversion of three very strongly built stone convents and almost all the other buildings in the vicinity had been demolished so as to afford them a clear field of fire. The largest, that of San Vincente, stood in the extreme south-west corner of the old wall and was well protected on the south side by a cliff above the river Tormes, and on the east by a deep ravine. About 600yds to the south-east of it, on the other side of the ravine, was La Merced, similarly protected on its south and west sides by the river and the ravine, the third fort, San Cayetano, being about 250yds north of it. The destruction of virtually all the surrounding buildings had resulted in vast quantities of cut stone and good timber being available, and much use of this material had been made to strengthen the three original structures. The walls had been thickened and windows blocked, and a great deal of internal re-inforcement had been carried out. On the more vulnerable sides the forts had been surrounded by dry stone walls, complete with bastions and covered ways, and hundreds of tons of stone rubble had then been piled on the outside to form a regular glacis, the space between comprising a ditch with its bottom at ground level. The roofs of the two smaller places had been removed and replaced by strong oak beams with six feet of earth on top, the resulting bomb proof surface being sufficiently strong to support light guns in sandbagged embrasures. The vast quantities of timber available had also made it possible to put in extensive palisades, so that all in all the strongholds were well defended, having a garrison of

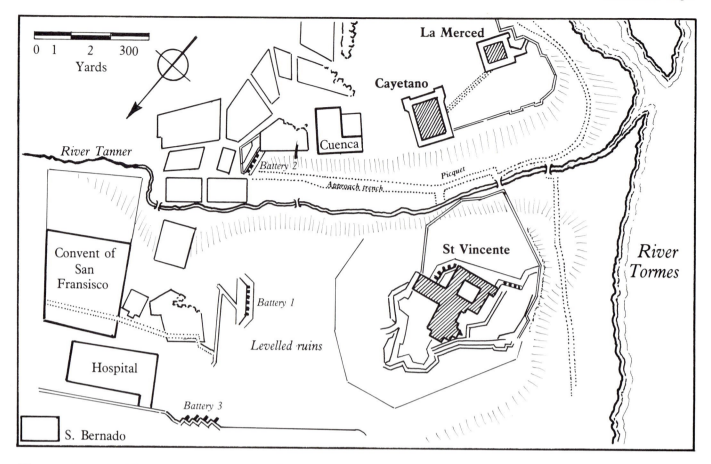

*The attack on the Forts at Salamanca. The French had raised the surrounding buildings and levelled the ruins to provide uninterrupted fields of fire.*

some 800 men, thirty guns, and ample supplies.

According to Belmas the work had been done in fewer than three months by a colonel and lieutenant of engineers, with six companies of sappers and about six hundred infantry, and although one must regret the virtual destruction of much of the university quarter of the city, it is nevertheless impossible not to admire the remarkable combination of ingenuity and hard work which had been devoted to the work. The original idea had been to surround the whole complex with a proper, bastioned rampart, which would have made it stronger still, but even so it was a formidable proposition. Wellington, whose only previous information had been a rough sketch made by a Spanish agent with no military knowledge, was disagreeably surprised, and it is clear that his artillery and engineer arrangements were somewhat inadequate for the task facing him.

His artillery personnel were adequate, but his actual battering guns consisted of four 18 pounders only, with a hundred rounds per gun. Six heavy, iron howitzers were on the march to join him but had not arrived, but

similar weapons could be borrowed as a temporary measure from the field artillery, as could field guns. The overall number of pieces is surprisingly difficult to ascertain accurately, because field guns and howitzers were borrowed and re-borrowed in a confusing way, and no two contemporary writers agree on the final total, which does not however appear to have exceeded twelve at any one time, four 18 pounders, two 6 pounders, and six howitzers, although not necessarily the same ones. Engineer support consisted of Lt-Col Burgoyne and two junior officers, together with nine rank and file and a limited supply of tools. The task of conducting the siege was given to the 6th Division, and as Marmont was still in the vicinity with his army, the remainder of the British Army took up a covering position on the heights of San Cristoval, three or four miles north of the town. In view of the unexpected strength of the defences and the limited resources available, the plan necessarily had to be a simple one and it was decided to attempt to breach St Vincente from a battery to be constructed about 250yds north-east of the place. There were still a number of partially demolished buildings at this distance from the work, which afforded a good covered approach to the besiegers.

Work started after dark on 17 June, but progress was

slow. The 6th Division had had no previous experience of siege work, and things were made worse by the fact that the ground was almost entirely covered with old foundations which made the digging difficult, and meant that soil had to be carried forward in baskets. As it was a clear night with a good moon, all this activity was visible to the defenders who were able to shoot with some effect, which further discouraged the working parties. Lt-Col Burgoyne noted with some scorn that the Portuguese amongst them actually crawled along, dragging their baskets behind them, although as his diary indicates a chronic dislike of people of their race, this need not be taken too seriously. During the night an engineer officer went forward with twenty men to investigate the possibility of blowing in the counterscarp opposite the point selected for breaching. There were enough ruins on the ground to provide cover for a small party and they got to the ramparts undetected, but a dog, possibly trained, then began barking incessantly. This brought a French patrol to the scene and the party had to retire, having sustained several casualties. All in all it had been a disappointing night and by daylight so little had been achieved that the whole party had to be withdrawn.

Next morning Burgoyne asked for riflemen to keep down the fire from St Vincente, and very soon three hundred men of a rifle battalion of the King's German Legion were ensconced amongst the ruins. They went some way towards silencing the French artillery, but could not subdue the musketry, since the French *tirailleurs* were firing through loopholes which presented a very small target indeed. Two 6 pounders from a field battery were also hoisted onto the first floor of the convent of San Bernardo, about 500yds north, and opened fire, as one of the participants noted 'out of the drawing room window'. The exchange went on for some hours during the course of which an officer was killed and a gunner wounded. In spite of these counter-measures, work by the besiegers had to be confined to the communications during the hours of daylight. As soon as it became dark however work was re-started and battery No1 was completed and armed with the four 18 pounders and three 24 pounder howitzers borrowed from a field brigade. A second battery was also completed about 250yds south-east of No1, and on the other side of the ravine, this being intended as an alternative position from which fire could be brought to bear on San Vincente. Fire was opened from No1 battery against the north-eastern face of San Vincente at 6am on 19 June, and soon brought down part of the wall, although the existence of the stone counterscarp

*A sharpshooter from the Light Battalion of the King's German Legion loads his Baker rifle at Salamanca.*

meant that the damage was rather high. Two more borrowed howitzers which had been installed in No2 battery then also opened fire, but as No1 ceased fire to save ammunition soon afterwards, all the French guns then concentrated their fire on them and casualties were high. As the effect of the fire was negligible it was then stopped, particularly since ammunition for the howitzers was getting low.

That night two 18 pounders were shifted to No2 battery and next morning the howitzers arrived from Elvas. Two of these were placed in No2, the remainder having been given to the field brigade to replace the ones borrowed from them, and at midday 20 June fire was re-opened on St Vincente. After a few shots some vital load-bearing wall must have been shattered, for a great part of the side of the convent, together with much of the roof, suddenly came down with a fearful crash, burying in the ruins many of the garrison who were firing at the battery through loopholes. Carcasses, that is, shells filled with combustible material were then fired into the interior in the hopes of setting it on fire,

but any that started were extinguished by the garrison who appear to have recovered from their disaster very quickly. An outside battery, built in a south-east facing re-entrant angle of the building, was indeed quickly abandoned, but fire from the shell of the convent continued briskly and effectively.

This day's firing practically exhausted the remaining supplies of ammunition, and as by that date Marmont was apparently threatening to attack the British position on San Cristoval the siege was suspended, and the heavy howitzers used in the siege were moved up to cover the British right flank. In the event Marmont declined battle (and very sensibly, for he was numerically inferior to his opponent who was well posted in a strong, defensive position) and the siege was then resumed, although so little ammunition remained that not much could be done. In view of this reduced capacity for breaching it was decided to batter down the north-western rear wall of San Gayetano, which was less substantial than the main fort with the few rounds which remained, in the hopes that the place could then be stormed out of hand and used as a base from which to mine under San Vincente. A new battery No3 was therefore constructed during the night and at about 11am on 23 June fire was opened from it with the 18 pounder and three of the howitzers which Wellington had sent back to the siege.

This fire was largely ineffective, for the battery was at an oblique angle to its target, and the remaining ammunition had all gone in a few hours. Many of the palisades had been broken off however, and the parapet badly damaged, so that Wellington decided to escalade both Gayetano and La Merced that evening, trusting, as he had often done before, that the gallantry of his troops would compensate for all other deficiencies. The duty fell on the light companies of the brigades of Hulse and Bowes of the 6th Division, which consisted of between three and four hundred men of the 2nd, 1st/11th, 1st/32nd, 1st/36th, 2nd/53rd, and 1st/61st Regts, and it is regrettably, if understandably, clear that there was no great enthusiasm for what all considered a hopeless venture. There was apparently no forlorn hope; the whole force charged together, preceded by twelve ladders, and at once came under heavy fire from Gayetano in their front and an even heavier fire from San Vincente in their rear. Many ladders, hastily knocked together from green wood, fell to pieces before the objective was reached and of the remainder only two were actually placed. No one apparently attempted to mount them and the attack collapsed with a loss of over 120 killed and wounded amongst them being Maj-Gen Bowes; he had been slightly wounded in the early

*Major Ross-Lewin of the 32nd Regt was one of the many officers present who considered the hasty attacks against La Merced and Gayetano a pointless waste.*

stages, but had his wound bound and went on, apparently hoping that his example might achieve the impossible. Major Ross-Lewin, then a subaltern in the light company of 1st/32nd later summed it up, 'the result was precisely such as most officers anticipated—a failure attended with severe loss of life'.

General Jones says that 'by a truce in the evening the killed and wounded were removed'. By this he presumably meant removed into the fort, because Ross-Lewin states very definitely that the flag of truce was not received, the wounded having been taken into the place, and supports this claim by giving details later of an officer of the 2nd Regt who was recovered from the place after it finally fell. He suffered the amputation of a leg and had been treated with great care in a well-run hospital. It is possible that there was a later unofficial truce, not unusual in such circumstances, to allow the removal of the dead, and it is to something of this sort that Jones may perhaps be referring.

In order to keep some sort of siege activity in progress during the period required to bring forward fresh

supplies of ammunition, work was begun on an approach running south-west from No3 battery which could be used by riflemen to bring fire onto some of the guns in San Vincente which could be seen from that side. A further trench was begun along the ravine from a point just below No2 battery towards Gayetano, and a *picquet* was posted just below the rear face of the place so as to cut off its communication with San Vincente. The garrison, appreciating its object, brought a good deal of fire to bear on it and inflicted many casualties. Nevertheless the work was pressed forward and by the late evening of 26 June it had reached the old town wall. This enabled *picquets* to be posted in various ruined buildings, thus achieving its object of isolating the minor works from the major one.

On the morning of 26 June the fresh ammunition finally arrived and the guns, which had been withdrawn for safety reasons, were at once replaced, the 18 pounders (one of which had been badly damaged) going into No3 battery, and four howitzers into No2. The guns were to continue battering Gayetano, the howitzers to fire hot shot into the roof of San Vincente. Fire was opened at midday, and before sunset San Vincente was burning in several places, although by great exertions the garrison succeeded in extinguishing all of them. Two 6 pounders and a brass howitzer from field battery were also replaced in San Bernado, to keep the French artillery in check.

That evening an alternative approach was begun from Cuenca towards Gayetano with a view to mining the place should the guns not breach it. Work was also begun on a mineshaft under La Merced from the south; there was a natural hollow in the cliff which gave some initial cover to the work, and as the cliff was of soft and easily worked sandstone, progress was good. The approaches to the mine were covered by *picquets* lodged in the various ruins in the vicinity. At daybreak on 27 June the batteries resumed their fire with great effect; the breach in Gayetano soon becoming practicable under the battering of the 18 pounders and San Vincento was soon enveloped in flames.

No time was wasted. Troops were soon in position in the ravine below Gayetano and the assault was about to be launched when a white flag went up in the building. The Commander then proposed to surrender both Gayetano and La Merced, but felt it his duty to consult his Commandant in Vincente, for which he requested a two-hour truce. Wellington however would have none of it, and gave him five minutes to surrender, after which he might march out with his baggage. The French officer, perhaps fearing the vengeance of

Napoleon against any officer who surrendered a fort before assault, refused, upon which he was told to haul down his white flag as an assault was imminent. The Commandant of San Vincente then also offered to surrender in three hours, but Wellington, suspecting this to be no more than a ruse to allow the French to extinguish their fires unmolested, gave him five minutes also, and as soon as that time had elapsed fire was re-opened briefly. Gayetano was then carried through the breach, only a few shots being fired at the stormers, while La Merced was successfully escaladed at the same time. A battalion of *Cacadores* of the 6th Division, concealed in the ravine and surrounding buildings, then rushed San Vincente but the garrison offered no opposition and the siege was finally over.

The siege, although eventually successful, was not a particularly satisfactory operation, due mainly to the fact that the capacity of the forts to resist had been seriously under-estimated. This was hardly Wellington's fault, since his sole piece of information on them had been sketchy, and he naturally did not want to be encumbered by more siege guns than were necessary, on what was to be primarily a mobile operation against Marmont's field army. As a matter of fact the 18 pounders would have been adequate for the task had they but had sufficient ammunition to keep up the sort of relentless fire needed. The hot shot from the

*Within weeks of the fall of the garrison, Wellington gained a decisive victory over Marmont just south of Salamanca, precipitating a French retreat to Burgos.*

that he could beat the British soundly, and be back in Salamanca while the forts were still holding out, if indeed they had been attacked and not simply blockaded. If he really did believe this to be a reasonable possibility it was of course sensible to leave the garrison, if only to keep out the Spanish civil population who would otherwise have been in instantly. In the event no reinforcements materialized and Marmont then realised that he had abandoned 800 men for no good reason. This according to General Foy, (not perhaps one of his greatest admirers), was why he kept manoeuvring in the vicinity, anxious to save them, but not quite daring to risk a battle with the troops he had in hand. There may be some truth in this, for it is certain that once the forts fell he moved off northwards and left Salamanca alone, at least for the moment.

## The Retiro at Madrid

The first three weeks of July 1812 were largely taken up by extensive manoeuvring between the two armies, until 22 July when Marmont, having made a serious tactical error, was decisively beaten by Wellington at a great battle just south of Salamanca. The French Marshal was badly wounded there and his army was brought out of action by Clausel in such a state of disarray that the General hastily retreated with it past Burgos. King Joseph, who heard of the defeat of Marmont while on his way to join him, at once returned to Madrid where he arrived on 5 August. Having thrown a garrison in the principal strong place there, the Retiro, he then evacuated the capital and retreated to Valencia on the Mediterranean coast, followed by a vast and unhappy swarm of francophile Spaniards who knew only too well the kind of fate they were likely to receive from their countrymen if they remained there without French protection.

The Retiro was in many ways typical of the sort of strongpoint constructed by the French in the Peninsula, although being in the capital itself it was somewhat larger and more elaborate than most. It had been designed so that a comparatively small force might defend it against guerrilla attacks in the absence of the main garrison, or similarly use it to over-awe a hostile population, and it had been made sufficiently large to offer some protection to the many francophile Spaniards living in the capital. The palace and museum, both barricaded and capable of defence, stood in park-like grounds surrounded by a normal estate wall, which with the addition of a few *flèches*, constituted the outer line of defence. Inside this was an extensive bastioned

howitzers had eventually proved particularly effective, due mainly to the vast amounts of timber used to re-inforce the convents, and the two types of weapon in conjunction might well have settled the business in a couple of days. Here again however we must consider that an extra initial supply of ammunition of, let us say a thousand rounds for the 18 pounders and five hundred for the howitzers, would have amounted to a weight of some 25 tons, which on a bullock cart basis would have required a great deal of transport.

The lack of experience of the 6 th Division may also have slowed things down. They did not show much enthusiasm after their attack on the night of 23 June, although in the circumstances this was understandable. The same troops fought with great distinction and very heavy casualties a month later, from which it is clear that there was nothing wrong with their morale.

It is not wholly clear why Marmont decided to leave a garrison in Salamanca at all. When he marched out he had considerable hopes of receiving sufficient reinforcements from the Army of the North to allow him to meet Wellington's troops on equal terms, and being by nature a confident officer he may have thought

*Wellington's triumphal entry into Madrid on 12 August 1812, despite the Retiro's still being in enemy hands.*

earthwork, roughly oval in shape, which constituted the second line, and within this again was the old china factory, which had been surrounded by a quite elaborate octagonal star fort with a good ditch and well palisaded. The garrison consisted of 78 officers and 1982 men, a heterogeneous collection consisting almost entirely of drafts awaiting onward transmission to Andalusia. The place was packed with stores and munitions of all kinds, many of which had been dumped there in the final few days before Joseph retreated south. Wellington entered Madrid with his Army on 12 August amongst scenes of wild rejoicing, and a bold sortie by the garrison that night might have caused a good deal of consternation. The Governor however remained quiet, and on 13 August arrangements were made to capture the place.

That evening elements of a brigade of 7th Division, consisting of 51st, 68th, and the *Chasseurs Britanniques* entered the botanical gardens, (which were adjacent to the place on the south-west side), under a smart fire of musketry, but got up the park wall without casualties. The garrison was too small to hold the outer line, and the orders had been given to the Commandant to withdraw to his second line when attacked. A copy of these orders had been found and given to Wellington,

so that little opposition had in fact been anticipated. Once established in the gardens the *Chasseurs* set to work on the wall and by daylight, according to Pte Wheeler, they had demolished about forty feet of it. The noise drew a good deal of fire from the second line and a soldier of 51st was wounded, but otherwise most of the troops seem to have got some sleep. Next morning detachments of the 3rd Division attacked from the north, and those of the 7th Division from the gardens, upon which the defenders withdrew promptly to their second line, having inflicted a dozen or so casualties. Preparations were then made to bring up guns, upon which the Governor sent out a flag of truce, noting these preparations and stating that if batteries were erected the garrison would fire into the town.

According to Burgoyne, Wellington replied that there were no batteries, but that he was not surprised at their intention, adding ominously that 'the time will come, and that not before long, when all these accounts may be settled'. This clearly sounded ominous to the French emissary, who therefore changed his tune and soon agreed to march out with the honours of war. In this he was wise for the French were in a hopeless position; they had only one small well, the aquaduct which originally supplied the china factory having been cut, and the whole area was littered with combustible stores of all kinds so that a few shells would have quickly blown everything up with disastrous results to the garrison. As soon as they had time to assemble their baggage they marched out, most of the soldiers being too drunk to do more than stagger along cursing. Included in the surrender were over four hundred sick; they had been in a hospital outside the defences, and had perhaps been lucky to escape the attentions of the angry inhabitants.

The place was found to be full of stores of every kind. There were nearly two hundred guns, twenty thousand muskets, nine hundred barrels of powder, and several million musket cartridges. There were also vast supplies of more immediately useful universal items, such as boots, shirts, socks and trousers, and even some of the blue coats of the French were handed over to the Royal Artillery for conversion to their pattern. There was also much food and a good deal of drink, although there was so much of the latter commodity available free in the town that for once even the British Army had as much as it could possibly manage.

Although all was for the moment well, it was unlikely that such a happy state of affairs would continue. The

*The Retiro, with a garrison of over two thousand and unlimited supplies, fell within twenty-four hours.*

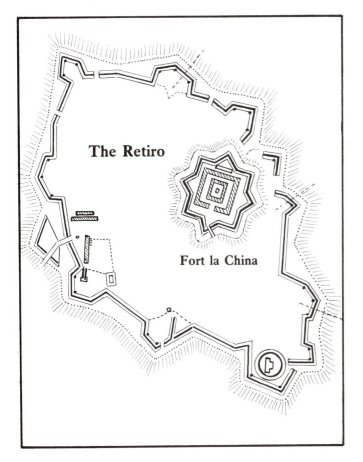

**The Retiro**

Fort la China

very magnitude of the success of Salamanca had disrupted French arrangements all over Spain and they were being forced by circumstances beyond their control to do what they ought to have done earlier, that is, to abandon to a great extent their role as an army of occupation and assemble as strong a field force as possible with a view to driving the British out of the country once and for all. Only by doing so could they hope to keep possession of Spain in the long term.

Whole armies were on the move. By the end of August even Soult had been compelled to abandon Andalusia and was withdrawing eastwards to join King Joseph, while in the north Clausel was busy rebuilding his shattered army. This he had achieved with so much success that early in September Wellington had considered it desirable to move against him with part of his army. He had at once withdrawn to Burgos, where he joined forces with General Cafarelli, who left a garrison in that place as he passed it, a decision which was to have a greater effect on the campaign than anyone could have foreseen. The Army of the North was also preparing to send troops south, so that of the whole French establishment in Spain almost the only one not on the move was Suchet, for the good reason that a British expedition from Sicily, planned earlier by Wellington, was hovering off the Mediterranean coast. It was therefore only a matter of time before Wellington might find himself attacked by something approaching double his own numbers, he himself being in a very advanced position with a long and vulnerable supply line stretching back to Portugal.

The situation was not, however, wholly black. The French supply system, based entirely on requisition and never at best very reliable, had been hopelessly disrupted, and although their armies were not yet starving, their supply problems were difficult and would get appreciably worse with the onset of winter. In these circumstances it was just possible that the British might maintain themselves in New Castile, provided that they could take and hold Burgos as a barrier against Clausel, and also providing that the autumn rains would be sufficiently heavy, and early, to fill the Tagus and so make it impossible for the French to construct and maintain bridges over it. The latter was of course dependent on circumstances quite outside Wellington's control, but the first appeared to be well within his capacity. It would take Soult and Joseph several weeks to get within striking distance of Madrid, which gave him ample time to take Burgos, and on 19 September he invested the place as a first step to establishing himself in his newly conquered territory.

# CHAPTER EIGHT

## The Siege of Burgos

The town of Burgos lay on the main highway from France to Valladolid, at a point where the road to Madrid forked off it to run southward to the capital, and was therefore an important place on the French lines of communication, particularly since its ancient castle commanded the bridges over the river Arlazon. In the early days of the war Napoleon, then commanding in Spain in person, had made it a main depot and had ordered it to be fortified, but over the years the war had rolled on to the south and west, so that by no means all the improvements originally envisaged had been completed. The works were based on the old keep, which stood on a steep, conical hill to the north of the town. It had been burnt out some seventy-five years previously, but the shell remained sound and had been strengthened by the French engineers to the extent that it had been possible to mount a battery (named after Napoleon) on top of it. Some 40yds to the north-west, and linked to the keep by a covered communication, was the church of La Blanca, which was poorly built and suitable only as a store, the whole being surrounded by a powerful earthwork having a ditch 30ft wide, and usually referred to in contemporary accounts as the third, or upper, line.

The next complete perimeter defence was based on the medieval wall of the castle, which had been strengthened with an earthern rampart with additional tambours, ie small external works like miniature bastions and designed for the same purpose, that is, to bring flanking fire onto the curtain wall. This line also had a good ditch. On the eastern and northern sides of the hill the slope was so steep that the two lines were

*The British repulsed at Burgos. With some notable exceptions the infantry were generally reluctant to assault, and the place could not be carried.*

so close together that a third was neither necessary nor possible, but on the western side, where the slope was more gradual there was an intermediate line, constructed as a powerful field-work and covering about one third of the perimeter. Somewhat confusingly this, where it existed, was known as the second line, the part of the medieval wall outside it being there referred to as the third line. Reference to the map should make this clear.

Immediately to the north-east was a second hill of almost equal height to the main feature, its summit being little more than 250yds from the castle, and the intervening valley very deep. This feature was defended by a hornwork, a roughly rectangular earthwork with a demi-bastion at each of its forward angles. Although incomplete, it had a steep scarp some 25ft high, and a ditch with a 10ft counterscarp, the difference in height being due to the steep slope on which it was built. The rear of the hornwork was closed by a stout palisade, and both its interior and its flanks were well covered by the battery on the keep. Three small, external earthworks had also been constructed on the forward slopes of the hill so that *picquets* from the garrison could look down into the deep valley below it. The whole place was adequately provisioned, although water was in short supply and had to be rationed as soon as the place had been invested. The live bullocks, on which the garrison depended for meat, all had to be slaughtered and salted down for the same reason.

Apart from nine heavy guns, eleven field guns, and half-a-dozen howitzers the hornwork also had a great deal of reserve artillery and ammunition, so the Governor could afford to be lavish with his defensive fire. There was practically no shelter for the garrison of some 2000 men, who thus had to bivouac wherever they could find room, often just behind the ramparts which it was their duty to defend. All in all then, Burgos could be classed as perfectly proof against guerrillas or even Spanish regular troops unprovided with siege guns, but should have been vulnerable to an army with a siege train and a proper engineer establishment. These however were the very assets which Wellington did not have, for his only battering guns consisted of the survivors of the siege of the Salamanca forts, three 18 pounder guns and five of the inadequate 24 pounder howitzers, the deficiencies of this train being made worse by the fact that the supplies of ammunition easily available were limited. His engineer sources were correspondingly small, consisting as they did of Lt-Col Burgoyne and four other officers, eight Royal Military Artificers, ten assistant engineers and eighty-one

assorted tradesmen, the members of these last two categories being volunteers from the line. Even the supply of tools was inadequate, although by sheer good fortune a store of French ones was found in the town, which went some way to making up the deficiency.

On 19 September Burgos was invested by the 1st and 6th Divisions and two brigades of Portuguese, while the 5th and 7th Divisions were pushed out to the north-east as a covering force. The first across the river were the 1st Division, and a Portuguese brigade, which closed in on all sides, the light companies driving in the small posts in the *flèches* outside the hornwork. The whole place was reconnoitred immediately, and like the Salamanca forts its strength seems to have come as something of a surprise. Lt-Col Robe commanding the Royal Artillery, wrote to Dickson (by then also a lieutenant-colonel) on 18 September, noting that, 'we have had a view of the castle which appears a more tough job than we might have supposed', and it is clear that his views were widely shared.

In view of the shortage of guns, Wellington's plan was based on a concept of digging and mining, using his guns chiefly to support attacks or keep breaches clear. His first requirement was to capture the hornwork, from which an excellent view of much of the northern face of the main work could be had. The steepness of the hill on which the castle stood meant that all the successive ramparts could be seen one above the other, so that if necessary guns could be brought to bear immediately on the inner line. The hornwork having been taken, a battery would be constructed just to the west of it, at a point where a slight rise in the ground protected it from the main French battery, but enabled it to fire on the defences at the western end of the church of La Blanca. This was the general area selected for the final attack, partly because it was screened from the main battery by the church, and partly because the ground fell so steeply below it that not even light guns could be depressed enough to bear on it. Sapping would start simultaneously from this battery, and from the suburb of San Pedro, so as to give a continuous communication between the two points. This would provide a convenient base for the miners to drive their shafts under the place so as to form breaches in the successive lines of defence.

Arrangements were at once made to seize the hornwork by a surprise escalade that same evening at

*The fortifications of Burgos in 1812, comprised three major lines of defence. The high ground to the north-east was commanded by the hornwork of St Michael.*

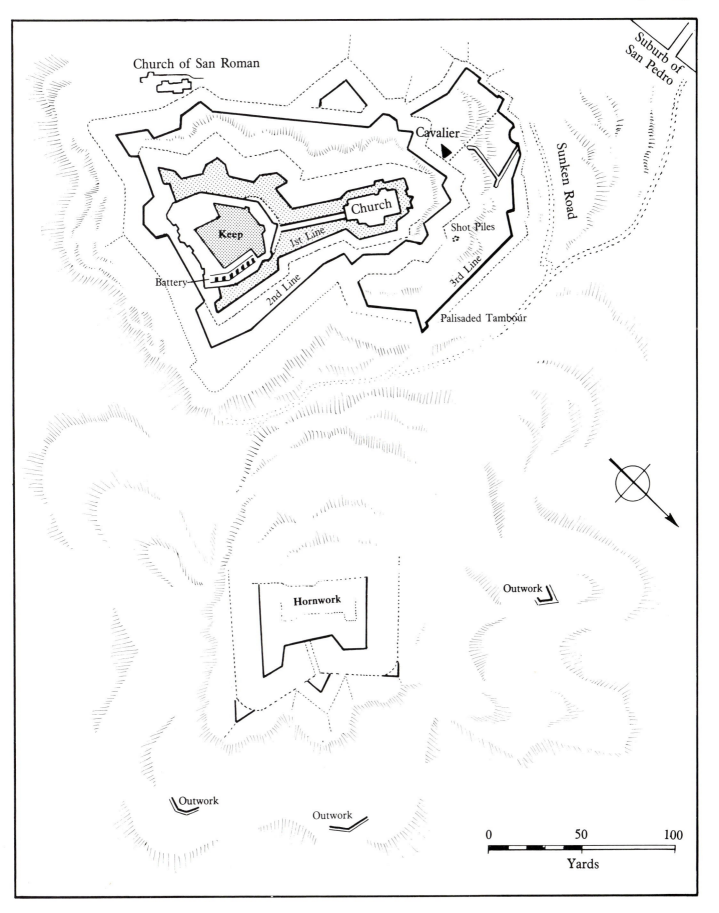

Church of San Roman

Cavalier

Church

Keep

1st Line

Battery

2nd Line

3rd Line

Shot Piles

Palisaded Tambour

Sunken Road

Suburb of San Pedro

Hornwork

Outwork

Outwork

Outwork

0          50          100

Yards

*Above: Major Somers-Cocks (here in the uniform of his former regiment, the 16th Light Dragoons) rallied the flagging attack on the hornwork of San Michael and led the light companies in driving the French from this position. He was later killed at the siege.*

*Below: A cross-section of the ground between the hornwork and the tiered defences of Burgos. With the hornwork in British hands, two batteries were started there, one of which was to remain concealed until needed.*

8pm, in very much the same way as Colborne had captured the Redoubt Renaud at Ciudad Rodrigo. The plan was that three hundred men of the 1st/42nd Regt should line the counterscarp on the northern face and keep down the heads of the defenders on the ramparts by musketry, under cover of which two columns of Pack's Portuguese, each two hundred strong, were to escalade the outer faces of the two demi-bastions. These were to be preceded by ladder parties and forlorn hopes from the 1st/42nd. Lastly the light companies of the brigade concerned (1st/42nd, 1st/24th, and 1st/79th regts) would attempt to force their way in from the rear.

Things went badly from the start. The covering party was detected early on, but continued to advance steadily under heavy and accurate fire. The stormers ran out and raised their ladders, and the British forlorn hope mounted them gallantly, but the Portuguese hung back and no progress was made. Fortunately the situation was saved by the light companies under Major Somers-Cocks of the 79th. He was an active and intelligent officer, who as a captain in the 16th Light Dragoons had been one of Wellington's most trusted reconnoitring officers, and now he led the light companies, a total of fewer than 150 men, forward with great dash. Fire was opened on them from the main works behind them as they charged up the steep slope, but they broke in through the palisades upon which Somers-Cocks, having left a small party by the postern gate, at once attacked the garrison from behind. The French, surprised and dismayed, broke at once and dashed out through the postern gate towards the main fortress in such numbers that the small guard there was fairly tumbled over in the rush.

The Allied losses were very heavy, six officers and sixty-five men killed, and fifteen officers and three hundred and thirty-four wounded, the great bulk of them being British. The French losses did not reach

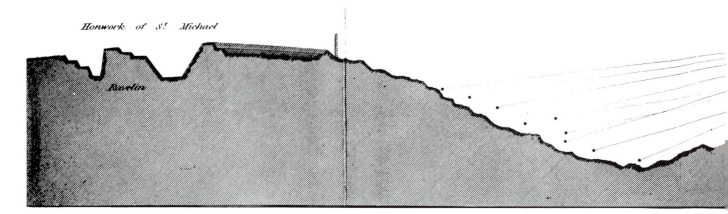

Honwork of St. Michael

Ravelin

two hundred, which included sixty prisoners, and seven field guns fell into British hands. Wellington ascribed the British losses to the inexperience of the 1st/42nd, who, new to Spain, made no attempts to seek cover, but it is clear that if the Portuguese had done their duty the French would have been otherwise engaged.

Once the hornwork had fallen a lodgement was immediately made in it, and the workmen, knowing what daylight would bring, got themselves under cover with such commendable speed that work was able to continue after dawn. This work included the construction of a covered approach from the north side of the hill, this being completed next night; and work continued on 21 September, during which the besieged kept up a heavy but not very effective fire. That night a trench was dug to the south east of the battery, and next morning a part of the trench guard was installed in it. In spite of heavy fire from the main garrison they kept up a heavy and effective fire of musketry at a range of about 200yds.

On the night of 22 September Battery No1 was completed and armed with two 18 pounders and three howitzers, its intended role being to support an assault, while a second, No2, was started in the gorge of the hornwork, whence an uninterrupted view of the keep could be obtained. This battery was to be held in reserve until the time came to breach the keep.

In view of the shortage of artillery, and also in order to save valuable time, Wellington then decided to escalade the outer wall the same night, and establish a lodgement on its summit, a decision perhaps influenced by the success of the similar, earlier operation on the hornwork. The place chosen was on the north face of the outer wall at a point where the scarp was about 24ft high, but where the ditch was shallow and without a revetted counterscarp. Its chief advantage was that a sunken road, completely covered from the fire of any French gun, led to within sixty yards of it from the suburb of San Pedro, and thus offered an excellent avenue of approach. The storming party was to consist of two hundred volunteers from the 1st Division, with a similar number to bring musketry to bear on the defenders lining the parapet. Once the lodgement had been made, this second party was to become a workforce and start breaking down the masonry scarp with a view to making a practicable ramp up the work. A further party of workmen under engineer control was also to be brought forward at the proper time to help with this task. A detachment of *Cacadores* from the 6th Division were to make a diversionary attack on the south side of the perimeter at the same time. The orders were peculiar in that the stormers were to be in sections of twenty men with an officer, and once the ladders had been reared these were to run out and mount them in succession, no section leaving cover until the preceding one had gained the summit.

The attack, which was launched at midnight, was a disaster. The Portuguese diversion achieved nothing, since the few men who ventured out from the shelter of the ruined houses near the ramparts were driven back with no difficulty by a small French guard. In the main body the ladder party got four (or possibly five) ladders reared, but the troops following were in columns of four and had straggled badly. Attempts were made to form them in the open space between the sunken road and the wall under a heavy and accurate fire from the defenders. The covering party never got into position, but simply crowded forward with the stormers; the few men who managed to get to the top of the ladders were promptly bayoneted, while the rest were showered with shells and other missiles, including apparently some type of incendiary, which caused many of their cartridge pouches to explode. The officer commanding the attack, Major Laurie of the 79th, was killed early on, and as

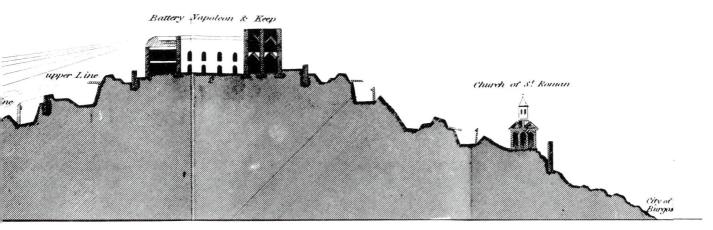

no one knew who was the next senior the slaughter continued for a quarter of an hour until someone finally gave the command to retire, by which time it is probable that most of the party had already anticipated it and sought cover. The attack cost the attackers a hundred and fifty-eight casualties in all, and the Governor of the castle later reported forty dead in the ditch alone. The French lost twenty-two, of whom nine were killed.

Most contemporary writers have their own theory for the cause of the shambles, but there is a certain thread of unanimity amongst them. Burgoyne, the Commanding Engineer, who had already received a severe contusion from a spent ball but who remained at duty, blamed the Portuguese, which in view of his expressed dislike of the soldiers of that race, is not altogether surprising. Nevertheless he was by no means alone in his views, and it seems to be an undeniable fact that they were going through a bad phase at that time. At one stage of the siege Burgoyne suggested to the Adjutant-General that there should always be a high proportion of British troops with the Portuguese; this suggestion being forwarded as an official complaint, which brought down the wrath of the British commanders of the Portuguese on the head of the engineer. He was however completely unrepentant and

appears to have been supported by Wellington himself.

The most general view seems to be that the use of detachments was a mistake, whole units being greatly preferred, while the use of twenty-man sections for the actual assault was generally condemned. Wellington's idea was that it limited casualties, but it must be clear to any soldier of experience that a party of that size would have felt hideously naked and alone when attacking a rampart defended by hundreds of very determined Frenchmen.

Wellington seems to have been disposed to blame the officer commanding the assault for rushing on like a common soldier, and although it may be unfair to blame an officer who died bravely there may be a good deal in what he said. Even allowing for the problems of handling strange detachments in the dark, one is driven to the conclusion that there was a great lack of organisation. The sunken road gave an ideal place in which to form up, and if the two hundred men of the covering party had been put into position on the bank behind it, and the sections for the assault properly formed up, the result might have been different. All reports make reference to the defenders standing on the parapet, which could hardly have been possible if it had been swept by effective musketry at the time that the sections ran forward to the ladders.

Next morning, 23 September, the garrison began a heavy fire on the communication trench through the rear of the hornwork and did much damage to the parapet, but at midday a two-hour truce was agreed to allow the besiegers to remove their dead and wounded. In other circumstances the latter would have been regarded as prisoners of war, but the Governor, Brig-Gen Dubreton, allowed them to be taken back to their own lines. In view of the shortage of water and the lack of covered accommodation in the castle this was both sensible and more humane.

The escalade having failed, it was decided to resort to mining, and with this end in view the stretch of hollow road which had been used as a covered approach for the stormers was converted into a parallel, an approach from San Pedro being marked out at the same time. By next morning, in spite of heavy rain, the workmen in the new parallel were well under cover and work was able to continue in daylight. Although no

*Left: A Royal Engineer officer at the siege of 1812. Regrettably their work could not bring down Burgos.*

*Right: The batteries, trenches and saps directed against the western defences of Burgos.*

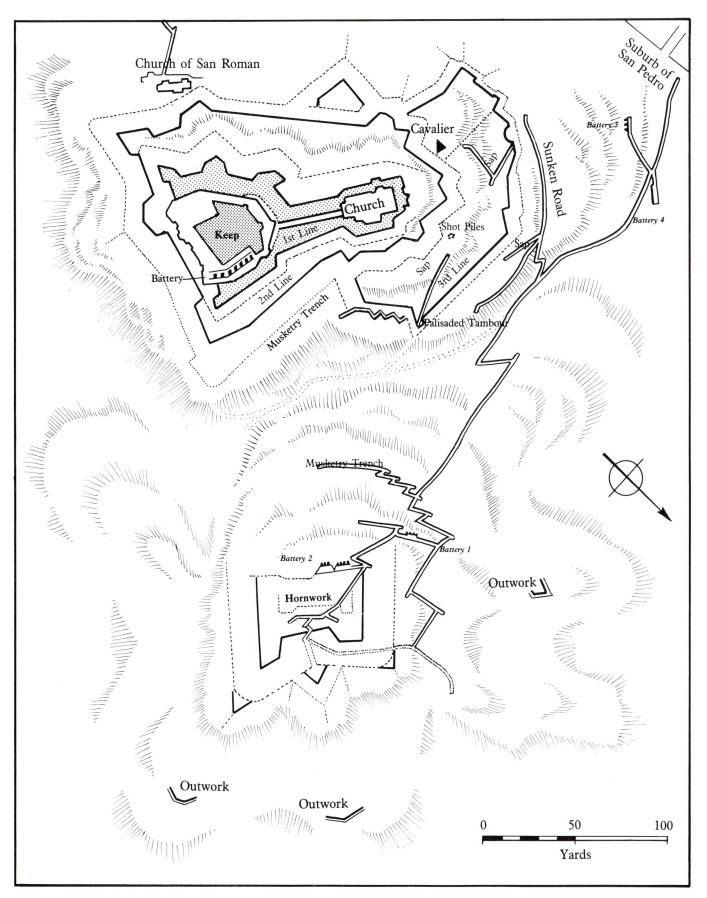

Church of San Roman

Suburb of San Pedro

Cavalier

Battery 3

Sap

Sunken Road

Church

Battery 4

1st Line

Keep

Shot Piles

Battery

2nd Line

Sap

3rd Line

Musketry Trench

Sap

Palisaded Tambour

Musketry Trench

Battery 2

Battery 1

Outwork

Hornwork

Outwork

Outwork

0       50       100

Yards

French guns could be brought to bear, considerable small arms fire was used by the defenders, and in view of their commanding position the parallel had to be both deep and narrow to afford any real protection. Some relief was also gained by interspersing the workmen with musketeers who did much to discourage the defenders. Only from one point, where a palisaded *tambour* allowed enfilade fire down the trench from behind good cover at a range of about forty yards, did fire continue, chiefly, it was believed, by only one man. The common musket, particularly when loaded rapidly, was not a very accurate weapon, but a well-made one in the hands of an expert would shoot well enough to eighty or ninety yards, particularly with a carefully measured charge and a well cast ball, possibly wrapped in a fragment of linen to make it a tight fit in the bore.

On the night of the 24th a sap was begun diagonally from the new parallel towards the wall, with a view to reaching a point where mining could be started. This work was desperately dangerous, since even a narrow trench six feet deep with a row of gabions above it hardly afforded shelter from musket fire from the wall. The besieged, knowing full well what was intended, also rolled down lighted shells which caused so many casualties that on the morning of the 25 September the mine was started. At the same time the howitzers in No1 battery opened fire at the palisade which had sheltered the marksman, but these pieces were not effective with roundshot and after a good many rounds had been fired without any apparent effect it was decided that the whole thing was a waste of valuable ammunition, and the practice was stopped.

No2 battery in the gorge of the hornwork was completed that day, but the embrasures were left filled with earth so that it could not be recognised as such from the castle, until it was actually required.

That night a series of zig-zag trenches was started down the hill from the vicinity of No1 battery, with a view to opening a second trench for musketry at about a hundred yards from the outer wall. As the work was on a forward slope less than two hundred yards from the castle the workmen were terribly exposed and subjected to showers of grape which caused very heavy casualties amongst them, although work continued almost uninterrupted.

*One of the few remaining 10in howitzers of the type used by the British at the Siege of Burgos.*

By the end of 26 September the mine had advanced eighteen feet; it was four feet high and three wide and the soil was a type of clay which required no revetment. As soon as it was dark the original parallel was extended southward to within twenty-three yards of the wall, with a view to starting a second mine. The zig-zags from No1 battery were also carried further down the hill and the musketry trench was opened. The enemy, who had been anticipating this, opened heavy fire and caused some casualties and it was therefore decided to carry forward the gabions separately, two men being employed. These retired once the thing was in position and another pair then ran forward. This method, although slow, greatly reduced casualties, but once the gabions were all in position the workmen were able to carry on behind reasonable cover and things went well. When work stopped at daylight there was enough cover for a few men who were left behind with orders to concentrate their fire on the palisade which had previously caused so much annoyance to the workmen in the parallel by the first mine.

By 27 September it was clear that the garrison had anticipated the probable loss of their outer line and were seen to have strengthened their second line quite considerably. They had cut a covered way along the top of the counterscarp and had also planted a new stockade in front of the gate so as to give themselves safe access to and from the counterscarp. That morning the besiegers started the gallery of their second mine, and also improved the trench to the extent that a firing party could be posted in it. Work also continued on the first mine but by evening only twenty-eight feet had been completed, due partly to the fact that the workmen were not used to military-type mining, but probably largely due to the size and weight of the picks and shovels which made them difficult to handle in a confined space. The garrison concentrated their efforts on the nearest part of the sap and hurled down stones and other missiles including hand grenades which Jones describes as having 'much the appearance in descending of cricket balls'. The new musketry trench, built on the slope below the hornwork also came in for a good deal of battering by the well-handled French artillery, and in the course of the day was rendered untenable.

On the night of 27 September work was started to connect the zig-zag trenches below the hornwork to the parallel which had been advanced eastwards from San Pedro. Five hundred men were ordered for the task although a hundred and fifty of these were absent when a count was taken. The remainder worked well but the communication lay for the most part along a steep,

forward slope commanded by the castle guns at ranges nowhere exceeding two hundred yards. As soon as work started several light balls were thrown, followed by showers of grape, but the men worked hard and by daybreak were mostly under some sort of cover. The extreme angle of the slope, together with the degree of command by the castle guns, made it necessary to dig the trenches unusually deep. Once day had dawned on 28 September the garrison were able to fire with great accuracy at point blank range, and due to the slope many shells, which landed beyond the trench rolled back into it before exploding. During the night the musketry trench below the hornwork was also repaired so that the gunners in the castle could at least be kept under some sort of retaliatory fire. Work also continued on the mines, and by the evening the first was forty-two feet long and the second thirty-two.

On 29 September the garrison continued to fire heavily, mainly from small howitzers, while the besiegers replied with musketry. Work in the meanwhile continued on the mines, and by noon the miners in the

*A miner at work at Burgos during the siege. Three mines were blown but with only limited results.*

first one reported that they had come up against solid masonry which was taken to be the foundations of the scarp wall. A powder chamber was made underneath it and that night it was charged with just over a thousand pounds of powder, a *saucisson* or fuze being laid to it in an *auget* or wooden channel, and the whole tunnel then tamped solidly with bags of earth for fifteen feet so as to concentrate the force of the explosion in an upwards direction. Some attempt was also made that night to extend the musketry trench below the hornwork to its left, so as to bring increased fire onto the open ground between the second and outer walls, but so much French fire was concentrated on the work that heavy casualties soon compelled it to be abandoned.

As no time was to be wasted, it was decided to spring the first mine and assault the resulting breach the same night. A storming party of three hundred men, all detachments from the 6th Division, was thus assembled in the trenches, with a working party further to the rear, to be called forward when needed.

The mine was duly blown at midnight and brought down the scarp wall, although the earth rampart behind it remained very steep. Accurate reconnaissance was of course impossible in the dark but the assault was ordered and the troops advanced under a heavy supporting fire of musketry. The forlorn hope of an officer and twenty men was preceded by a sergeant and four men who quickly scrambled up the breach and found the summit deserted, the garrison having bolted at the shock of the explosion. So far then all was well, but things soon went wrong. The forlorn hope went too far to its right, and finding no breach promptly withdrew to the trenches and reported that the mine had produced no effect, upon which the whole party was ordered to retire. In the meanwhile the garrison had rallied and returned to the top of the breach where they soon drove down the sergeant and his gallant little party, whose bayonet wounds amply confirmed that the breach was practicable. Due to the serious shortage of engineer officers this was the first storming party not to have been accompanied by one of them, which is presumably how the error occurred. Daylight revealed that the breach was not in fact a very good one, and as the garrison had spent the remainder of the night in retrenching and obstructing it, there was no possibility of repeating the assault.

It was later decided that the foundations encountered by the miners had been ancient ones, some way in front of the scarp wall, which is why the results of the mine had been relatively ineffective, but whatever the cause the besiegers had begun to show distinct signs of discouragement. This was not wholly surprising since they had been working for twelve days in fearfully exposed conditions and under a heavy and effective fire of artillery which had been virtually unopposed by their own guns. The sap running up to the mine remained particularly vulnerable to accurate musketry from the stockaded *tambour* position, and so many men had been killed and wounded that it was finally decided that only artillery could deal with the problem. On the morning of 30 September a French 6 pounder gun, one of those taken in the hornwork, was run into No1 battery, together with a 24 pounder howitzer, and fire opened. The results were soon apparent, for although the garrison had done much to strengthen the position with sandbags and barrels filled with earth, forty rounds from the French gun and ninety-six from the howitzer totally demolished the *tambour*, and probably some of the concealed marksmen too. Although this solved one particular problem it did little to overcome the general discouragement which manifested itself in various ways, notably perhaps in the constant absence of men detailed for working parties (with the honourable exception of the Guards) and in a listless attitude on the part of those who did appear. Burgoyne wrote in his diary that:

> 'I had an opportunity of pointing out to Lord Wellington one day, a French and English working party, each excavating a trench; while the French shovels were going on as merrily as possible we saw in an equal space, at long intervals, a single English shovel-full make its appearance.'

This was probably true, but we must consider the different motivation of the two sides; the French, possibly facing years as prisoners of war, were only anxious to keep the British out as long as possible in the reasonable hope that relief would arrive. The British on the other hand, feeling (perhaps rightly) that they were attempting a hopeless task with quite inadequate support, were in no hurry to push their approaches forward to the point where they might face a further bloody repulse. Soon after the siege started a small reward had been offered for every roundshot brought in to the artillery park, and although this was largely in order to conserve existing stocks as far as possible, there was probably also the secondary motive of giving the soldiers something to interest them in their spare time, together with the chance to earn a few coppers, and so help, if only in a small way, to sustain their morale. In the first twelve days of the siege some fifteen hundred shot were brought in, so that the scheme was reasonably successful. Unfortunately there was no similar way of supplementing the dwindling store of

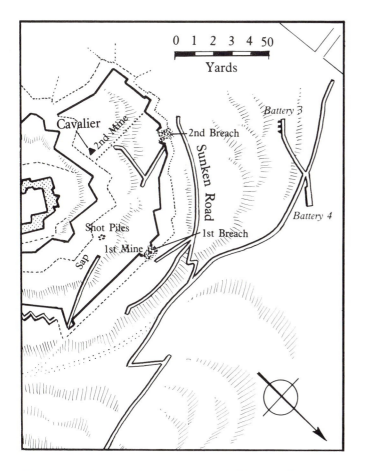

*The lines of approach to the west of Burgos. Two mine galleries were driven under the 3rd French defence line. No3 Battery was established to provide back-up if the mines failed. It soon became untenable, and No4 Battery was built to replace it.*

gunpowder, but on 24 September Wellington had written an urgent letter to Capt Sir Home Popham RN at Santander, asking if he had any to spare. That officer, who was commanding the British Naval vessels supporting the guerrillas in north Spain, responded so promptly and energetically that on 5 October forty ninety-pound barrels actually arrived at Burgos on the backs of mules.

In the meanwhile work continued on the gallery for the second mine, but in order not to have to depend on that means alone, Wellington ordered the construction of No3 battery, some sixty yards to the west of the outer wall, with a view to breaching it if necessary. The place was apparently well chosen since the church of La Blanca screened if from the main Napoleon battery and no other guns could be brought to bear on it. Work started on this new project at dusk and as it was not detected by the garrison the work went well. As none of the defenders' guns could bear on it,

the parapet was only made thick enough to be musket-proof which saved so much work that the place was virtually ready by first light on 1 October. The three 18 pounders had in the meanwhile been brought down by the Artillery from No2 battery and were ready to run into the new battery as soon as the carpenters should have laid the platforms. As soon as the garrison discovered the new work they opened a heavy fire of musketry but the workmen were behind reasonably good cover and had completed the work by 9am, when the guns were at once run in.

Unfortunately, and incredibly, no one on the besiegers' side seems to have considered the possibility of the French moving a piece, or pieces, to meet this new threat, but this is exactly what they did. Six-inch shells, lobbed from a howitzer firing at close range with very small charges, soon began falling into the new battery, doing terrible damage. To make matters worse the French also cut a temporary embrasure in the outer wall and opened fire with a 6 pounder field gun, which at a range of a bare hundred yards put shot after shot through the flimsy parapet. In a matter of minutes the battery was completely untenable and had to be evacuated, leaving the guns to their fate. The French then contrived to bring several other pieces to bear and hammered the abandoned pieces unmercifully, knocking a trunnion off one, smashing the muzzle of a second, and seriously damaging two carriages, without a shot having been fired from them in reply. Attempts were made to silence the French guns by musketry, but although very close, they were well elevated and the gunners difficult to see. General Jones comments later:

> 'Some officers, good shots who had frequently shown their skill in picking off individuals, attempted to play the same game on this occasion; but the French marksmen speedily drove them out of the field.—Lt N....., assistant engineer, lost part of an ear in this personal contention.'

It is by no means clear now why Lt N's ear should have merited particular mention in view of the daily carnage experienced at the siege; perhaps it was something of a Corps joke. Nor, tantalizingly, are we told whether or not the British were using rifles; there were brigade companies of the 60th Rifles present, so it is highly likely that they were, but the point is nowhere made clear. It is perhaps one of the sad things about this siege that with the exception of Ensign Aitchison of 3rd Guards, no one seems to have kept the sort of chatty, informative record so common, for example, in the Light Division.

That same evening, as soon as it was dark, a new

battery No4 was started, about 100yds north of the old one. A large quantity of woolpacks had been obtained from the town, for use as parapets, and the work was completed that night. At the same time the guns were withdrawn from No3 and moved into a piece of dead ground behind the new work, ready to run in at first light. The French however had other ideas, and as soon as there was enough daylight for them to locate the new battery they concentrated such a fire of heavy shells on it that it was destroyed in a very short period and no attempt was made to arm it, which in the circumstances was just as well, for daylight revealed the full extent of the damage to the guns; the whole attempt was therefore abandoned.

In the meanwhile the gallery for the second mine was going well and it was anticipated that it might be ready to fire on 3 October. Orders were therefore given to move the two surviving 18 pounders back to battery No1 on the night of 2 October with a view to supporting an assault on the 3rd; the damaged gun and carriages were to be moved to the artillery park at the same time. The weather was appallingly bad that night, and the bulk of the infantry working party detailed to assist the gunners simply did not appear, only the Guards reporting for duty. As a result the move could not be completed and the guns therefore had to be left concealed behind the hornwork when daylight made further activity impossible.

As it turned out, plans for an assault on 3 October were not practicable because the miners struck a huge rock and had to carry the mine over it, which naturally occasioned great delays. There was also considerable trouble with ventilation as the shaft got longer; the air got so bad that the candles by which the miners worked went out, and the mine had to be evacuated for increasingly long periods in order to allow the air to renew itself. It is perhaps surprising that no one ever apparently tried to improvise a simple airpump by which the difficulty could have been overcome.

This delay at least gave the artificers at the artillery park a chance to patch up the damaged guns. The piece with the missing trunnion was eventually mounted on a block carriage which had been converted with great ingenuity, and the only spare carriage was used to replace the damaged one, so that all three were again capable of being fired, although only one could be described as fully serviceable.

On the night of 3 October two officers measured the external length from the mine gallery entrance to the rampart and made it 73ft and 74ft. The internal measurement was by then 79ft, but another four feet were excavated to be on the safe side. Two guns were also finally installed in No1 battery, together with three howitzers, the object being to improve the partial breach made by the first mine so that both it and the new breach might be assaulted simultaneously when the time came. The French had apparently begun to suspect the existence of the second mine and had started a new retrenchment further back.

At about 9am on 4 October fire was opened by No1 battery. The gun with the split muzzle was at first loaded with a small charge only, but this was gradually increased to the full 6 pounds without any accident or apparent loss of accuracy or velocity. The other gun in the battery was the sole undamaged one, and between the two they had opened a 60ft breach by afternoon. The mine was also finished and charged with just over a thousand pounds of powder, and all being ready it was decided to launch the assault at 5pm; this would allow the important part to be carried out in daylight and still leave the night for consolidation. Possibly some of the adverse criticisms regarding assaults by detachments had come to the ears of Wellington, because on this occasion the duty was entrusted to a complete battalion, the 2nd/24th, under the temporary command of a Capt Hedderwick, although again the supports were composed of detachments.

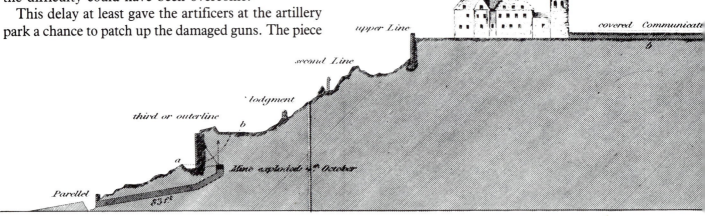

The troops were formed up in the hollow way, and although a bare fifty yards from the wall they seem to have been got into position without arousing any suspicion on the part of the defenders. Each breach was entrusted to a half battalion, each of which had its own forlorn hope under a subaltern, and everything went according to plan. The mine was duly fired, making a breach almost a hundred feet wide and killing many of the enemy, and before the smoke and dust had cleared the forlorn hopes were in the breaches with the supports close behind them. There was a short sharp fight and then the defenders broke and ran back to their rear entrenchments leaving the breaches firmly in British hands. This very successful assault, which cost the 2nd/24th no more than sixty-eight casualties had clearly been planned with care and intelligence and conducted with great dash, and did much to strengthen the views of those officers—and there were many—who deplored the use of detachments for serious services.

The reserve and a large working party with tools and defence stores then came up and work was started to make the breaches defensible under a heavy fire of guns and musketry, which greatly hampered the work and caused a further hundred and twenty-two casualties; amongst the latter was Lt-Col John Jones of the Royal Engineers, who subsequently wrote the standard English work on Peninsular sieges. At one stage there must have been the threat of a sortie, because the workmen were ordered to their arms, after which it was difficult to disentangle them from the guards, so that relatively little further work was done. Nevertheless by dawn the entrenchments at the breaches were complete and capable of a long defence. As by this time a final assault on the second line seemed at least a possibility, it was decided to make a new breach on the angle where

*A private of the 2nd Guards in greatcoat with oilskin foul-weather cover and a neck flap to his shako. Heavy rain caused particular problems during the siege.*

the first wall joined the second, the object of this being to be able to launch a flank attack on the defenders simultaneously with the main assault. On the night of 4 October therefore two 18 pounders and two howitzers were moved to battery No2 with a view to making the breach; four howitzers were also placed in battery No1 in the hopes that they could destroy the church of La Blanca with hot shot, a furnace for heating the shot being constructed close by.

*A cross-section from west to east under the defences of Burgos, showing the position of the 2nd Mine and, in anticipation of its explosion, the French retrenchment in front of their 2nd line.*

*Battery Napoleon & Keep*

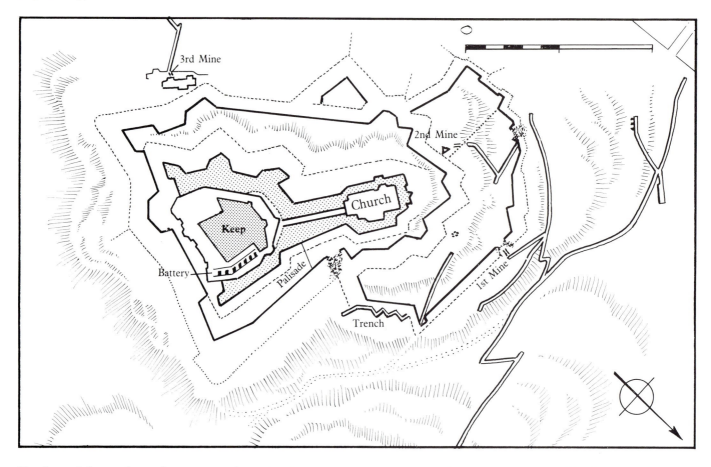

*Further mining and sapping attempted to gain the western defences while an assault, via the northern breach, failed to out-flank the 2nd defence line.*

The guns were ready on the morning of 5 October but fire was not opened immediately, although the howitzers in No2 tried a few rounds at the palisades in the ditch of the second line. Work also continued in the vicinity of the breaches, the parapet being turned into a parallel against the place. The French Governor however, always watchful, disliked the look of these preparations and at 5pm he launched a sudden sortie of three hundred men from the covered way of the second line. The positions were here only about thirty yards apart and the French, charging downhill with great determination, quickly drove off the besiegers with a hundred and fifty casualties, their own being small. They then began to level the works, destroy stores, and generally do what they could to delay the progress of the siege, until they were dislodged by a determined counter-attack. They then withdrew to their lines, carrying with them a considerable number of tools and presumably well satisfied with what they had achieved. The loss of the tools was in fact quite serious, but the damage was otherwise fairly superficial and had been restored by dawn on 6 October. During the night the besiegers also dug two saps outward from the lodgement on converging paths, the object being to join them on the glacis of the second line and so form a second parallel. The point selected for the junction was close to some conspicuous piles of roundshot on the glacis itself.

At 11am on 6 October the batteries opened fire, the guns in No2 against the new breach, and the howitzers against the same palisades that they had fired a few shots at the previous day. It was soon found that the embrasures in No2 were too high to allow the guns to be depressed sufficiently for their shot to strike the foot of the rampart, so firing had to be discontinued for the remainder of the day while the fault was remedied. Nor did the howitzers achieve very much against the palisades. At the same time the garrison kept up a brisk fire against the lodgement; they could not depress their artillery sufficiently for this purpose, but kept up a steady fire of musketry, and also from time to time rolled lighted shells down the steep slope of the glacis. These were sufficiently heavy, and the slope sufficiently steep, to knock over gabions and then roll on into the trench where they exploded, and work on the new saps came practically to a standstill as a result.

Some attempt was made by the howitzers in No1 battery to keep down the fire of the second line, but without much success. They were far too inaccurate to achieve anything with roundshot and the two sides were too close together to allow them to fire shells. On 7 October therefore two of them were withdrawn and replaced by two of the French guns taken in the hornwork, one an 8 pounder and the other a 4 pounder. There was ample shot available for these and they proved to be a very valuable addition to the besiegers' armament. Battery No2, having been modified, also re-opened fire at the same time, and by that evening a considerable impression had been made on the wall selected for breaching. The French maintained a heavy fire in reply and succeeded in knocking a trunnion off one of the guns, but by this time the artificers had perfected their method of mounting on block carriages so that the same night the gun damaged on the 1 October and the latest casualty were both back.

The weather then became so bad that virtually the whole effort of the working parties had to be directed to keeping the trenches drained. Early on the morning of 8 October the French took advantage of the storm to launch another sortie, which drove the besiegers out of their lodgements in a few minutes. They were quickly rallied by Major Somers-Cocks, who launched a successful counter-attack, he himself being shot dead as he led the charge. The situation was thus restored, although at considerable cost, for apart from some two hundred killed and wounded the French had had time to level some of the works and had again collected and carried off a considerable quantity of irreplaceable tools. The worst loss however was probably Somers-Cocks; he had already been recommended for promotion to lieutenant-colonel for his capture of the hornwork (some sources refer to him by that rank at the time of his death,

although he does not seem to have actually been gazetted) and it is clear that he was an officer of great promise. He had earlier done a great deal of reconnaissance and intelligence work for Wellington, who showed great distress at his funeral.

At daylight on 8 October the breaching battery re-opened fire at the new breach. Much difficulty was experienced in laying the two crippled guns on their improvised carriages, and it was soon found that they dismounted themselves when fired with a full charge of six pounds of powder. Some cautious experiment eventually revealed the maximum charge which could be employed with safety and fire continued, although the effect of the guns was naturally much reduced. Nevertheless by that evening the new breach appeared to be practicable on a front of at least twenty feet. That night a communication trench was begun towards the new breach. It started in the front line, near the point where the palisades at the salient angle had proved such excellent cover for the French sharpshooters, and thence progressed along the ditch in a series of zig-zags. When it had reached a point about thirty yards from the breach, a musketry trench was dug at right angles to it so that small arms fire could be brought to bear on the new breach at point-blank range; this to prevent its being scarped and obstructed by the French during the hours of darkness.

By 9 October the supply of small arms ammunition had got dangerously low, thousands upon thousands of rounds having been expended by the various trench guards as a substitute for artillery fire, and as it was of course essential to hold a sufficient reserve to fight a battle, even musket fire was stopped. In order however

*Low on ammunition the British guns tried to burn the church of La Blanca, to re-confirm their presence.*

to maintain a semblance of activity, orders were then given to try to burn the church of La Blanca with red-hot shot from both guns and howitzers. Temporary grates had already been built under cover near the batteries, and supplies of fuel dumped, and as it only required about forty minutes to raise an 18 pounder roundshot to red heat, fire was soon opened. The results however were disappointing, for although the roof of the church was seen to smoke a great deal the garrison was able to prevent any actual fire.

Attempts were then made to dig a mine under the church of San Roman. Although it was just outside the defences, the French maintained it as a store, and had themselves mined it for destruction if necessary; some ruined houses fifty yards from the place gave a secure starting point, and as the soil was easy good progress was made. That night the garrison attempted to work on the new breach, but the musketry trench dug by the besiegers proved its worth and they were repeatedly driven in by a party of 3rd Guards, the subaltern in command being killed. Belmas states that the breach had been scarped and rendered impossible except by escalade, but this is open to doubt. The fire of hot shot against the church continued on 10 and 11 October, but by then the remaining supplies of roundshot were so low that it was discontinued. According to Jones its lack of success was due to the difficulty of heating sufficient shot to keep up a vigorous discharge, but whether this was due to inadequate grates, insufficient fuel, or simply the teeming rain, is not stated. The situation regarding artillery ammunition was eased on 10 October by the arrival of the powder from Santander, and by the retrieval of a quantity of shot from the works. The bulk of these were French 16 pounders, which fitted the British 18 pounders reasonably well.

The weather continued bad, and much of the time of both sides was taken up with draining and repairing their works. The French, clearly anticipating another attack, had shells ranged ready along the parapet of the inner line, and had erected a row of palisades between their second and third lines just to east of the new breach. They also appeared to have mined the church, since two *augets*, the wooden troughs used to protect fuzes, were visible on the church wall, although they might have been no more than a bluff. In spite of the efforts of the trench guards they also succeeded in clearing much of the rubble from the front of the new breach, which they had also entrenched.

There was little artillery fire by either side during this period, but on the night of 14 October No2 battery was re-armed with the three 18 pounders, two of them

*British gunners of the period. Difficulties in siting suitable batteries, together with indifferent infantry support, led to the failures at Burgos.*

impaired and one howitzer, with a view to smashing the wall of the keep on which the Napoleon battery stood. Fire was duly opened on the morning of 15 October but the results were disastrous for the besiegers, for the French produced such a volume of artillery fire that the battery was completely silenced in less than an hour, although except for one broken wheel the guns escaped further damage.

As a result of this, Wellington ordered the angle of the embrasures to be changed so that the guns could be brought to bear on the new breach. A French 6in howitzer, originally taken in the hornwork, and two 24 pounder howitzers were also placed in No1 battery and succeeded in doing a good deal of damage to the second line. A supply of ammunition, both artillery and small arms, arrived at Burgos on 15th, but the heavy rain had so damaged the batteries that the whole of 16 October had to be devoted to their repair. On that day the French, with great energy began to construct a *cavalier*, a sort of small raised bastion, overlooking the sap from the second breach, from which they could see and fire into it. The mine towards the church of San Roman made good progress and was by then so near that the French could be heard talking there. In view of the risk of detection the tunnel was therefore only continued for a few more feet and then loaded with nine hundred pounds of powder.

On 17 October the besiegers' batteries re-opened fire, the guns on the new breach and the howitzers on the wall, and by mid-afternoon the breach was just practicable. Wellington however, after a reconnaissance, decided that a further day's fire was necessary to improve it and arrangements were made accordingly. The French completed their *cavalier* and killed nine men in the sap; the besiegers on their part ran a small mine from the sap to the *cavalier* and exploded it. It did little damage but caused the French to abandon the position hastily. Attempts were then made by the British to form a lodgement there, but a strong, French counter-attack soon drove them out.

Next day, 18 October, the artillery fire was resumed, and Wellington decided to attack the second line that afternoon. The signal for the assault was to be in the explosion of the mine under San Roman; the breach made by this was to be assaulted by Col Browne and a battalion of Portuguese with Spanish support, although as the effects of a mine could never be accurately predicted the actual form of the attack had to be left to the discretion of the commander on the spot.

The main attack was to be launched simultaneously, a signal being given by the waving of a colour from a prominent feature in case the mine explosion was not heard. On this signal three hundred men of the King's German Legion were to assault the new breach, while a similar sized party of the Guards came in through the original breach, both detachments then having been ordered to escalade the second line. The attack started well enough; the Germans entered the new breach without much difficulty and some of them reached the inner line, but they were met by greatly superior numbers in front and from the new palisades on their left and soon held up. The Guards' attack also went well initially and a good many of them got onto the second line in the vicinity of the shot piles, but they too were halted by superior numbers, after which a counter-attack drove them back. The losses of the two detachments were very similar, eighty-two for the Germans and eighty-five for the Guards. Both parties behaved remarkably well, but heavy musketry from the inner line, which was there only about ten yards from the second, proved too much for them.

The mine was not actually under the church and therefore did no damage to the building itself, although

*Hussar, infantry and light-infantry of the King's German Legion. The Legion's foot-soldiers were to be used in the last, abortive assault on Burgos.*

it wrecked the terrace in front of it. The French then withdrew and exploded their own mines and the Portuguese and Spaniards then occupied the rubble. The French claimed the destruction of several hundred of the attackers—Belmas calls them English, though there were none involved—but this appears to be a gross exaggeration. This final failure really marked the end of the siege, for although there was some renewed activity round the church of San Roman on the 19 October it was clear that there was by then no chance of taking Burgos. The French had allowed Wellington more time than he might have expected, but they were now on the move in such numbers that he had no option but to retreat. On 20th therefore the decision was finally taken and withdrawal began. General Pack was left before the place with a brigade of Portuguese and the guns were withdrawn, although a French howitzer and one French field gun were left in No1 battery with orders to fire intermittently so as to deceive the garrison as far as possible. All siege stores and other items which could not be moved were destroyed, the carriages of the captured French guns were burnt, and the guns themselves buried.

Withdrawal of the British 18 pounders, and howitzers, and remaining ammunition began at 11pm on 21 October. The guns had to cross the bridge within range of the fortress, but by muffling the wheels with straw the operation was carried out successfully. This phase of the retreat was however of short duration for it was soon found that the bullocks were too few and too weak to draw the guns. The carriages were therefore burnt, the remaining trunnions were knocked off the guns with sledge hammers, and the whole abandoned, although the howitzers and one captured French 4 pounder were able to continue so that something, if very little, was salvaged. Even the arrangements for the destruction of the hornwork went wrong, for although mines had been dug in readiness, the powder to arm them went astray, so introducing the final mishap into what had been a thoroughly unsatisfactory operation.

*British gunners move a heavy artillery piece. The lack of 24-pounder cannon contributed, in part, to the failure to take Burgos.*

It is clear that the failure to take Burgos came as an unpleasant surprise to an army which after a long series of unbroken successes was rapidly beginning to consider itself to be invincible. This naturally gave rise to a great deal of discussion regarding the reasons for the failure, and in general many of these seem to have been directed, if only obliquely, at Wellington himself, and perhaps with some reason. As with the Salamanca forts, it is clear that he had under-estimated the specialist resources needed to take Burgos; having never seen the place he may well have assumed that it was a guerrilla-proof strongpoint on the lines of the Retiro, which in a sense was true, although the commanding nature of the ground made it much more formidable. Even so, the resources which had been available, for example at Ciudad Rodrigo (which had a similar-sized garrison although under a far less enterprising governor), must have ensured the fall of the place in a matter of days.

In this context 'resources' must be taken to mean both guns and engineers, and it is of course difficult to separate the two because in any siege success depended on a scientific combination of guns and diligently plied shovels both supervised by experts. This was certainly the view of Col Jones, whose opinions must merit respect, and also to a lesser extent of Lt-Col Burgoyne who directed the engineers, although the latter considered that the lack of guns would not have constituted a bar had the troops concerned done their full duty. He noted a marked lack of confidence and much langour in the troops (always excepting the Guards) and there is clearly some truth in this. The surprisingly poor showing of the Portuguese was widely remarked on, and Burgoyne's views on the use of small detachments were generally agreed, but otherwise the troops seem to have behaved well enough, since the conduct of the 24th Regt, the Guards, and the German Legion was exemplary. It is true that they disliked siege work, no new thing, but this feeling must have been aggravated by the lack of supporting fire which made them feel that they were being sacrificed for an unobtainable object. Assuming this to be so, it is clear that the presence of, say, a dozen 24 pounders and a similar number of heavy howitzers, would have made an enormous difference to their morale. The consistent policy of using too small a number of troops was also a serious handicap, although perhaps understandable.

The British Army had already sustained heavy casualties that year, at Ciudad Rodrigo, Badajos, and Salamanca, and Wellington was right to be worried. Unlike the French army, which was kept up by conscription, the British relied on the voluntary system and at that late stage of the war it was becoming progressively more difficult to keep the ranks full. Nevertheless, when we consider that at no time were more than seven hundred men committed to the assault of a fortress held by at least three times that number of excellent soldiers, it is clear that the policy was a wrong one, which in the end cost him some 2000 casualties for no corresponding advantage. John Aitchison, then an ensign in the 3rd Guards, summed it up when he wrote of the assault on the second line:

'The whole of the men employed in the storm did not exceed 700. The breach was not above 10 feet wide and the garrison at least 2000 . . . in this case it will be answered perhaps that the numbers would not have been of use as from the smallness of the front attack no more could have been employed advantageously, but it must be recollected that they might have been in the trenches ready to support, and I am persuaded from what I have seen that a soldier knowing that whatever may happen his party is the stronger will go on to attack a large body with a confidence which will ensure success, whereas when his own party is inferior to that which opposes him both in numbers and situation, he is in a measure beaten before he begins . . .'

Subaltern officers tend naturally to be very severe critics of their superiors, but Aitchison was obviously an intelligent and thoughtful officer, and one speaking from first hand experience, and there is a ring of conviction in what he says.

Perhaps saddest of all was the fact that there were ample heavy guns available at no great distance. General Pakenham, Wellington's brother-in-law, offered to provide both guns and bullocks to draw them from Madrid but this offer was refused, and although some guns were finally borrowed from the Royal Navy at Santander they never actually arrived at Burgos. Even without adequate artillery, a body of well-trained sappers and miners might well have made it possible to take the place, but these were simply not available at the time, although as we shall see in the next chapter the deficiency had largely been remedied by 1813.

All in all therefore it is permissible to lay much of the blame on Wellington, although if we consider the enormous burden of responsibility he was bearing virtually single-handed at that period some degree of error must be regarded as inevitable. It is indeed a mark of his overall success that one single and comparatively minor failure should have been the cause of so much subsequent discussion.

# CHAPTER NINE

## The First Siege of San Sebastian

Wellington and Hill, heavily outnumbered, retreated on converging axes and met in the vicinity of Salamanca. Wellington offered battle on 15 November but Soult, in spite of his superior strength, declined, so the British were able to retreat to Portugal unmolested. There Wellington was able to rest and refit his army after a year of very arduous, and on the whole highly successful, campaigning and prepare it for a new thrust into Spain in 1813. By May of that year he was on the move again, moving north-eastwards on the line Salamanca, Valladolid, Burgos, but with a very strong left wing under Graham marching north of him across country which had always previously been considered impassable except to small bodies. The French, echeloned back along the same line, and in constant fear of being outflanked by Graham, withdrew steadily before him. They blew up Burgos as they passed through it, an event which gave the British great satisfaction, and by 19 June were concentrated at Vittoria where King Joseph offered battle. It was not an ideal place but the only alternative open to the French was to abandon their huge and unwieldy baggage trains which they were reluctant to do.

On 21 June Wellington defeated them decisively and they fled into France abandoning guns and baggage in their flight, a remarkable reversal of the situation of the previous autumn. The British commander halted his army along the frontier in order to consider his next move; he was reluctant to thrust into France until he knew what the general situation was in Europe, particularly since he had a strong French-held fortress at either end of his line, San Sebastian to the north and Pampeluna to the south, and soon decided that he must

*The Battle of Vittoria on 21 June 1813. Following this engagement the French retreated out of Spain.*

take at least one of them before going any further. His first reaction was to tackle Pampeluna, but it was so strong, and so well garrisoned, that his resources were not equal to it. As he knew that it was short of rations, he therefore decided to place it under blockade with a view to starving it out, and concentrate on San Sebastian instead.

The town of San Sebastian stands on a peninsula, shaped roughly like a comma and projecting northward into the bay of Biscay. The western face was protected by a simple curtain wall, which being on the edge of the sea was inaccessible except to a combined military/naval expedition. The south face, across the isthmus, was protected by a high curtain with a bastion at either end and a flat bastion and *cavalier* in the centre, the whole being covered by a hornwork, and by several hasty fieldworks further to the south. The eastern face, like the western, was defended by a simple curtain wall, but was much more accessible because it was covered on that side by the river Urumea, which was tidal. This meant that at high tide the wall was washed by four feet of water, but at low tide it was completely exposed, with a wide strand of rock and sand between it and the central river channel. On the other side of the river was an extensive range of sandhills which commanded the wall at ranges between five hundred and a thousand yards. The north end of the peninsula was steep and rocky with an ancient castle on its summit and three batteries on its eastern face.

The French, apparently secure in their occupation of Spain, had used the place as a depot but had never considered the need to defend it, except against possible minor guerrilla raids, until the whole situation was changed by the decisive British victory at Vittoria. General Rey arrived there on 22 June with some sappers and miners and a few other troops, mostly invalids, to find the place full of French and Spanish refugees, but once it was clear that the British were on their way these all fled. Foy handed over a couple of thousand men and Rey made hasty preparations for a siege. Although the population was said to be pro-French and ready to provide both workmen and food, he nevertheless gave the women and children forty-eight hours to get out so as to husband his limited resources, and a few days later found himself blockaded by Spanish irregulars;

*The defences of San Sebastian in 1813. The walled town straddled the isthmus of the peninsula, so protecting the Castle of La Mota. To the south was a major hornwork and the French had also fortified forward positions at the Convent of San Bartholomeo.*

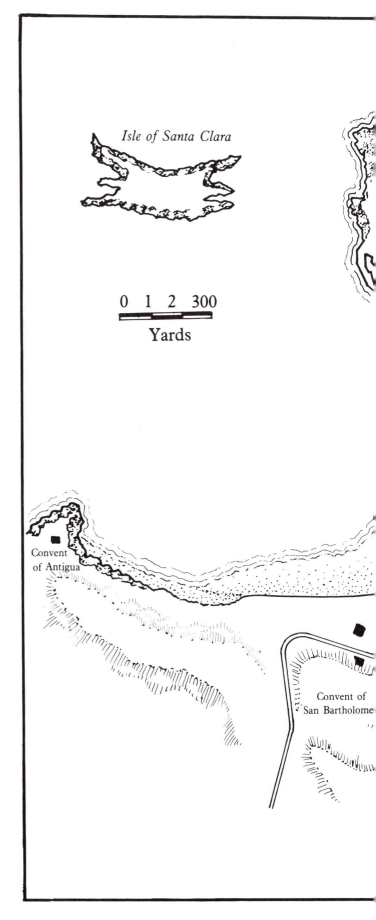

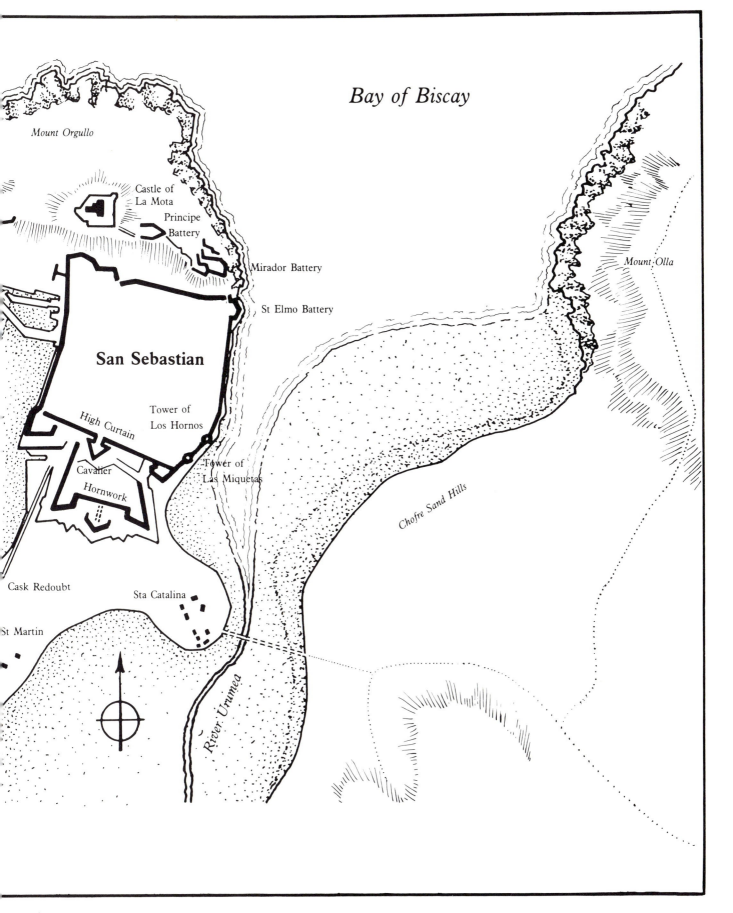

*Bay of Biscay*

*Mount Orgullo*

Castle of
La Mota

Principe
Battery

Mirador Battery

St Elmo Battery

**San Sebastian**

*Mount Olla*

Tower of
Los Hornos

High Curtain

*Chofre Sand Hills*

Cavalier

Hornwork

Tower of
Las Miquetas

Cask Redoubt

Sta Catalina

St Martin

*River Urumea*

these, though of poor quality, further increased his difficulties by cutting the main aquaduct through which came the town's water supply, leaving the place dependant on inadequate wells. By 12 July General Graham had assumed directions of the siege with the 5th Division and two Portuguese brigades, a slight naval blockade having also been established. Just before this occurred the small garrison of another French post had managed to get into the castle, raising the effective garrison to some three thousand men.

The resources available for the siege were indeed considerable. Wellington, having had experience of trying to move heavy guns by road, had handed the original train over to General Murray for the siege of Tarragona on the south coast and had arranged for a fresh one to be available for him on storeships at Corunna. This was then summoned eastwards, and after some uncertainty, due to the abandonment of the original plan to besiege Pampelun, was finally unloaded at the port of Passages, only a few miles away. The new train consisted of fourteen iron 24 pounders, four iron 10in mortars, six brass 8in howitzers and four 68 pounder carronades. To these were added six 18 pounders moving with the army, twenty-four French 12 pounder guns and ten 6in howitzers taken at Vittoria, and six short iron 24 pounders lent by Capt Sir George Collier, the naval commander on the north coast. There was also an ample initial scale of ammunition, although the precaution was taken of ordering further supplies from England. Everything was available for use at San Sebastian by 11 July with the exception of the mortars which were left for the moment at Santander because of the problems of transport. The artillery was commanded by Lt-Col Dickson, together with twenty-nine British or German officers, three hundred and sixty-nine other ranks of the Royal Artillery, eight officers and one hundred and seven men of the Portuguese artillery, and a Royal Naval detachment of five officers, two warrant officers, and fifty seamen.

The Engineer strength available consisted of Lt-Col Fletcher, (commanding), Lt-Col Burgoyne, and sixteen other officers, together with four sub-lieutenants and three hundred and five rank and file of the newly-formed Royal Sappers and Miners, (although these had unfortunately not arrived at the time the siege started). There were also ample supplies of tools and other specialised equipment.

The general plan for the siege was made as a result of a reconnaissance conducted on 12 July by Wellington, and Major Smith, at that time the senior engineer with the left wing of the army. The place had previously been

besieged and taken in 1719 by the Duke of Berwick, who had established his batteries on the Chofre sandhills and made a breach in the east wall, while at the same time establishing a lodgement and batteries on the isthmus in order to neutralise the fire from the southern defences of the place. It was decided to adopt a similar plan, although in view of the changed circumstances this did not turn out to be the best solution. In 1719 the Governor, in accordance with 18th century convention, had tamely surrendered the place once a practicable breach had been made, so that no experience had been gained of the difficulties of attacking along the comparatively narrow strip of dry land available below the east wall at low tide. It must have been clear that no French governor would give up the place without an actual and successful assault, but no one seems to have considered the implications of this at the time; even Fletcher and Dickson agreed, and on that basis the plan was accepted.

The first objective was the convent of St Bartholomeo which stood on a piece of high ground about 700yds southwest of the hornwork. The place had been considerably strengthened by the French, and was

*The unsuccessful Siege of Tarragona, invested by General Murray, who was provided with the original siege-train brought by Dickson to Ciudad Rodrigo.*

flanked by a redoubt which they had built in the churchyard between the main building and the river. Some preliminary attempt had been made to reduce it summarily on 7 July by the fire of a Portuguese field battery, but as this proved unsuccessful more orthodox methods had to be used and on the night of 11 July two batteries, No1 and No2, were started about two hundred and fifty yards west of the place. Two nights later work also started on batteries Nos 11-14 on the Chofre sandhills with a view to breaching the wall between the towers of Los Hornos and Las Miquetas, which were 110ft apart, the wall being 27ft high. As these batteries were on the other side of the river the risk of a sortie against them was considered to be slight and although they were linked by trenches no defensive parallel as such was constructed.

Early on the morning of 14 July Wellington set off southwards to the right flank of his line, leaving Graham to continue with the siege. The batteries against St

Bartholomeo had been completed and armed the previous night, No1 with four 18 pounders and No2 with two 8in howitzers, and on that morning fire was opened on the convent. Two of the guns were employed to fire hot shot while the howitzers concentrated mainly on keeping down the heavy fire of musketry from the place. A small field gun which attempted to return the fire from the belfry was soon silenced, while the fire from the main defences was ineffective.

Col Fletcher arrived next day from Pampeluna to assume command of the engineer effort and ordered fire to be continued. Much damage was done to the building and several small fires started, and by 2pm it seemed possible that the French were no longer present in force. A detachment of *Cacadores* was sent forward but met with heavy opposition and were compelled to retire. The artillery fire against the defenders was then augmented by five 9-pounder field guns and two 24 pounder howitzers which opened fire on the flanking redoubt from the east bank of the river. Fire was continued on 16th and 17th by which time the place was in such ruins that it was taken without difficulty by the 9th Regt, three companies of the 1st Regt and strong detachments of Portuguese, supported by two 6 pounder field pieces. The attackers then became over enthusiastic, and seeing a body of the garrison coming out of the town, at once charged towards them. This brought them under a heavy and accurate fire from the hornwork under cover of which the French reinforcements drove them back with a number of casualties. The convent however remained firmly in British hands, and work was at once started to strengthen its defences on the northern side. Two new batteries, No3 and No4 were also started on the ridge to the west of the convent, which was sufficiently high for them to enfilade the defenders on the eastern side of the town.

After the fall of the convent the French concentrated their efforts on improving the defences of the cask redoubt, so named because wine-casks filled with the local sandy soil had been used in its construction. This then became the next objective of the besiegers, who on the night of 19 July made a lodgement in the ruined suburb of St Martin, from where they proposed to dig approaches across the isthmus.

Work also continued on the batteries on the Chofre sandhills, and two new ones, No15 and No16, were started. By 19 July all were complete (with the exception of the two new ones), and armed, and at 8am on 20 July fire was opened against the stronghold. Some batteries were at rather long range, as a glance at the map will show; in particular, No11 on Mount Olla, was

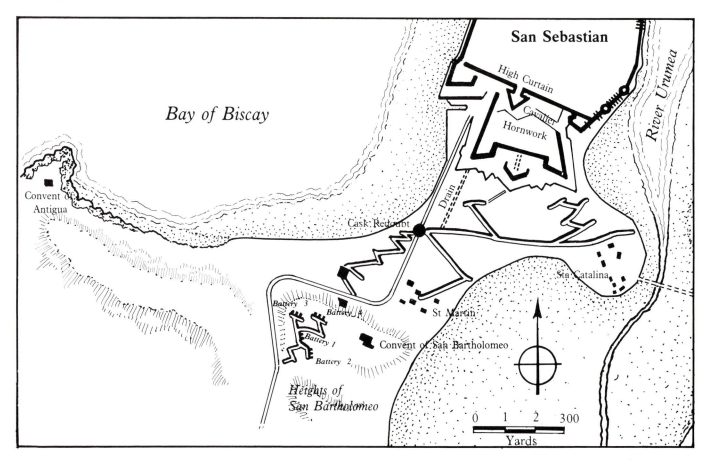

1500yds from the breach, but in spite of this its excellent observation over the whole place made its fire very effective indeed. In view of the difficulties of communication between the isthmus and the Chofre sandhills the two operations were to some degree independent and were known as the left and right attacks respectively. It was not long before the French had identified the point to be attacked and had begun extensive internal defences. At one stage, according to Belmas, the Governor considered a sortie across the river at low tide with a view to spiking the guns, but finally

*The British Left Attack during the first Siege of San Sebastian. By 17 July, the Convent of San Bartholomeo had fallen, and new batteries were started to bring fire upon the eastern portion of the curtain wall of the town. Engineers also started to dig trenches and approach saps across the isthmus. The chance discovery of a submerged drain running close to the western demi-bastion of the hornwork offered the opportunity of mining this place.*

**Distribution of pieces against San Sebastian 20th July 1813**

| Battery | Pieces | Target |
|---------|--------|--------|
| No3 | 6 × 18 pounders | To enfilade fire on eastern wall |
| No4 | 2 × 8in howitzers | To enfilade fire on eastern wall |
| No11 | 2 × short 24 pounders | The Castle, the Mirador battery and the land front generally |
|  | 4 × 8in howitzers | The Castle, the Mirador battery and the land front generally |
| No12 | 2 × 24 pounders | Defences generally |
| No13 | 4 × 24 pounders | Defences generally |
| No14 | 8 × 24 pounders | The Breaches |
|  | 3 × short 24 pounders | The Breaches |
| No15 | 4 × 68 pounder carronades* | The breach and land front generally |
|  | 4 × 10in mortars* | The breach and land front generally |

*not to be unmasked until required

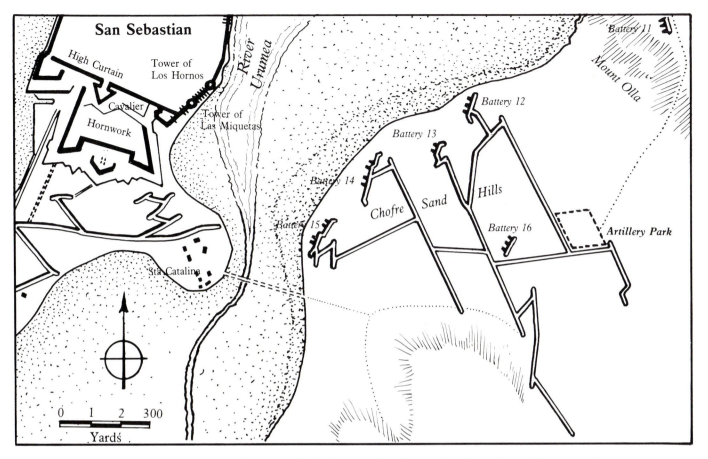

*The Right Attack at San Sebastian. Batteries were established amongst the Chofre Sand Hills, and on Mount Olla, to bombard the castle, town and French batteries, and to breach the eastern wall.*

rejected the idea as being too much of a risk, which in view of the number of men he would have needed to commit was probably a wise decision.

The artillery in the garrison replied briskly to this fire, concentrating their efforts to a considerable extent on No14 battery where they succeeded in knocking out one gun, while another was rendered temporarily useless by the breaking of a punch in the vent, although it is not clear how or why this happened. It is possible that General Jones may have used the wrong term and meant pricker, the thin metal rod pushed through the vent in order to pierce the serge of the cartridge and ensure that the flash from the priming reached the main charge. A careless ventsman might well have snapped-off one of these and caused the trouble. Several wheels were also damaged, although these were quickly and easily replaced. The three short guns in the same battery were mounted on ships' carriages; these were much lower than the standard travelling carriages, and the repeated vibration of their discharge quickly caused the embrasures to fill with sand, so that their fire also had to be stopped until that evening when three spare travelling carriages were brought up and the guns transferred to them.

The first day's firing produced a considerable

impression, and on the evening of the 20th the French, perhaps anticipating a sudden assault and wishing to concentrate on the vital points, evacuated the cask redoubt. Work had been scheduled to begin on a parallel from St Martin that night, but the weather was so bad that most of the Portuguese workmen absented themselves and progress was slow. Strangely enough Col Belmas, who usually follows Jones, his British counter-part, closely, states that the redoubt was taken by assault, but this must be an error on his part.

Heavy fire was resumed on 21 July until 10am when a summons to surrender was sent in under a flag of truce. This was done on the orders of Wellington who wrote on 20 July in a letter to Graham:

'I did not summons Badajos or Burgos, and the reason for not doing so has been confirmed in the King's (ie King Joseph's) papers, viz., that French officers are ordered not to surrender a place before it has been stormed. But as I hope the men will, on this occasion, employ themselves, when they get in, in destroying the enemy, rather than, as usual, in plunder, I think the place should be summoned. But as it is desirable that the summons should be given at a period when it will not convey notice to the enemy of our intentions, you had better send it in tomorrow.'

The meaning of this passage is obscure; with the experience of previous sieges before him it really was optimistic to have expected his troops to behave. He may have included in the letter to the Governor an appeal to conform to earlier custom so as to avoid unnecessary bloodshed, but if he did so it achieved nothing for General Rey returned the letter unopened, and fire was re-opened on the place not more than ten minutes after the emissary had returned to his lines.

The garrison continued to concentrate its fire on the breaching batteries and took little action against other attractive targets in the shape of working parties and the like. It was also noted that many of their shells, although fired with great accuracy, contained so little powder that they did not explode, all of which pointed to a shortage of artillery ammunition on the part of the besieged. The British fire continued to be rapid and effective, due both to good observation and to the fact that the arrangement of the batteries allowed every part of the defences to be taken either in reverse or enfilade. The garrison of the hornwork, which had no bomb-proof shelters, were particularly harassed by howitzer fire from No11, which although almost a mile away dropped shell after shell into it. These projectiles, which weighed 46 pounds, obliged the garrison to dig trenches for protection and communication within the work.

On the night of 21 July workmen digging the parallel across the isthmus discovered a drain, the top of which was just below ground level. It was four feet high and three feet wide and contained the pipe used to supply water to the town, although this had been cut off by the Spaniards of the original blockading force. Lt Reed of the Royal Engineers volunteered to explore this drain and on reaching the other end, 230yds away, found a door in the counterscarp opposite to the western demi-bastion of the hornwork. As it seemed likely that a good sized mine would damage the bastion sufficiently to offer a way into the work, thirty barrels of powder, each containing ninety pounds, were placed in position, with a fuze leading back to the southern end of the drain. All the batteries, with the exception of No12, continued to pound the town. The gun with the blocked vent in No14 had been cleared, so that ten guns were concentrated on the breach, firing with great accuracy at the unprecedented rate of 350 rounds each per day,

*King Joseph Bonaparte of Spain. Documents found in the King's papers instructed French commanders not to surrender their garrisons as least until after their defences had been stormed.*

which inevitably led to a good deal of enlargement of their vents. Lt-Col Frazer, commanding the artillery of the right attack, attributed this to the fact that the iron used was too soft, although he agreed that this greatly reduced the risk of guns bursting. The fire from the place was by then greatly reduced, but the few pieces still in action were also seen to be having vent trouble. Lt-Col Dickson commented that the flash and smoke from the breach end was so great as to give the impression of a double discharge.

The breach between the towers now appeared to be practicable which was not surprising for the wall, which was no more than eight feet thick, was being struck by some forty tons of roundshot in each fifteen hours of daylight. The French, clearly thinking an assault imminent, were seen to be very busy in preparing interior retrenchments, and in order to discourage them as much as possible four 68 pounder carronades were mounted in battery No15. The two 24 pounders from No12 were also moved to No14 to augment the breaching guns.

By mid-morning on 23 July the main breach appeared to be practicable, and a second breach was therefore begun a little further south between the tower of Las Miquetas and the eastern demi-bastion of the main curtain. General Graham had however received information from Spanish refugees that the wall further north was very thin, so fire was redirected to a point about 160yds north of the main breach. The information was clearly accurate, because by that evening a breach 30ft wide had been made. The remaining artillery fire was chiefly employed in making it as difficult as possible for the French to block or retrench the breaches, the bulk of it being from the four 10in mortars which had been brought forward and placed in No16 battery, from the howitzers on Mount Olla, and from the carronades. Almost inevitably the heavy shelling started a series of fires, and by mid-day many of the houses in the vicinity of the breaches were well ablaze. As it was intended to launch the assault at first light on 24th, a heavy fire of grape was kept up on the breaches during the night.

At dawn however, the fires still raging near the breaches seemed likely to be a barrier to the attackers and the assault was thus postponed and the troops, who were already in the trenches, were withdrawn. Steady fire was kept up against the new, northern-most breach, and some of the breaching guns also resumed their fire against the southern one which had been started but abandoned on 23 July. The officers of the Royal Artillery took advantage of the extra day to keep their telescopes trained on the place with a view to locating a variety of guns which had been moved into position to oppose any assault. They located two field guns on the *cavalier* bastion, two more in casemates on its flank, and another on the eastern branch of the hornwork. There were also two more pieces behind an entrenchment between the east end of the hornwork and the main curtain, two near the Mirador, and another behind the tower of Las Miquetas. These guns were concealed at the time but would have to be run out to fire, and when this happened the gunners were confident that with the weight of metal at their disposal they could neutralise them very quickly.

The troops carrying out the attack, who came from Maj-Gen Oswald's 5th Division, were all concealed in the various trenches on the isthmus by the early hours of 25 July. The outline plan was that the attack should be by two battalions, one to the main breach and one to the more northerly one, with a third battalion in support and with maximum artillery support against the defences. The signal for the assault was to be the blowing of the mine in the drain, and some companies of Portuguese troops were detailed to try to enter the hornwork through the western demi-bastion if possible, although as was always the case with mines, much would have to be left to the local commander after the explosion.

Wellington, having left the direction of the siege to Graham, was clearly anxious not to appear to be interfering with him. This, although understandable, was nevertheless a pity, for, as so often happened when Wellington was not present in person, things went wrong from the start. The most important factor in planning the attack was the time of low tide, which on that particular morning 25 July, occurred at 5am. Unfortunately it was still pitch dark at that time so that the supporting artillery would in fact be quite unable to fire, a point which appears to have escaped the notice of all the planners concerned. When the mine was fired at 5am it did very much more damage than anyone had anticipated, and the French were so astonished by the unexpected explosion that they briefly abandoned the work which the Portuguese might well have captured—except that no one had thought to order them to take ladders with them. The gap in the parallel through which the stormers emerged was very small, so that the leading troops, the right wing of the 3rd/1st Regt, had to straggle out in columns of three, after which they picked their way through the dark across an expanse of slippery rocks and deep sea-water pools left by the receding tide.

Fortunately at this stage the French were not in position in the hornwork, so that the first troops, led by Major Fraser and guided by Lt Harry Jones of the Royal Engineers, were able to reach the breach, up which they scrambled without difficulty. Once on top however the descent was by no means easy, for the stonework battered by the guns had fallen outwards, allowing a practicable ascent but leaving the rear face of the wall almost intact. Thus the stormers were faced by a sheer drop of at least twenty feet, from which the French had cleared any rubble likely to help the descent, and with buildings still burning at its foot. Ladders might have helped, but the ladder party was further back, and having great difficulty in getting its unwieldly burdens forward. By this time the French had opened a heavy fire from their various retrenchments, and the assault therefore came to a stop. Moving with the ladder party was Lt Colin Campbell of the 9th Regt who had under his command the three light companies of the brigade, their task being to get to the top of the breach and clear the high curtain to the west. Campbell forced his way forward and twice mounted the breach with

small parties, but was wounded each time and had to withdraw. Major Fraser was dead by that time and Jones seriously wounded and it was clear that no progress was being made. To make things worse, according to Napier the carronades across the river, charged with the duty of keeping the breaches clear during the hours of darkness, were still firing grape in accordance with their original orders.

By this time too the French had returned to the hornwork, and to the retrenchment between it and the main wall, and were pouring fire into the left wing of the battalion. Many of these, confused in the darkness, thought that the gap between the hornwork and the wall was the breach, but by then all order had inevitably gone and the various rushes of mere handfuls of men were easily repulsed.

The battalion designated to take the northern breach, the 1st/38th, had in the meanwhile also filed out of the parallel and the commanding officer, benefitting from the example before him, halted his troops and formed them into column with a view to moving north. At this

*The 9th Regiment, which provided the reserve for the assault of 25 July, was badly mauled during the first unsuccessful attack on the eastern breaches.*

moment however, the 1st, seeing the position was hopeless and with men falling fast, suddenly retired in a rush and in a few moments both battalions were in a confused mob making for the parallel as best they could. The 9th, in reserve, had also begun to leave the trenches but practically every man of the few who emerged was shot down; the survivors of the two leading battalions then crashed into them and the assault was over. The casualties were high; the 3rd/1st lost 330 men, mostly from its right wing, the 38th lost 53, and the 9th 25, which with Portuguese losses of 138 against the hornwork brought the total up to 571. The French losses were 67, all from small arms fire.

The most frustrated people of all were the members of the Royal Artillery, who having painstakingly identified their principal targets, could do nothing but listen to the combat raging across the river without being in the least able to influence it. Many of them at first believed it to be no more than a feint attack, perhaps intended to induce the defenders to fire their mines, but when daylight revealed the hundreds of red-coated figures littering the breach and the strand, it was all too clear that the affair had been both real and disastrous. As soon as it was daylight the garrison proposed a truce, in the course of which they moved all the wounded into the town to save them from drowning when the tide rose. Napier reports that some wounded were bayoneted, but in general the French seem to have behaved with humanity. Amongst those taken into the place was Lt Jones of the Royal Engineers; thirty-three years later he was to edit the third edition of General Jones's 'Journal of Sieges in Spain' in which he states that he was carried up the breach by four grenadiers with no apparent difficulty, which illustrates the ease of ascent. Unfortunately he seems to have left no record of what the descent into the place was like.

Inevitably the failure gave rise to a great deal of discussion as to its causes. Not surprisingly there were rumours of gross misbehaviour on the part of the troops, which spread and magnified as such gossip always does, and it would be easy enough to dismiss these as emanating in the main from non-combatants and general hangers-on, who always tend to be critical of their betters. It is clear however that even Wellington had misgivings, for he later decided that for the next assault he would use volunteers from the other divisions in order to show the 5th Division 'that they have not been called upon to perform what is impracticable'. Both General Jones and Lt-Col Burgoyne also believed that there had been, if not actual misconduct, at least a

*General Thomas Graham who commanded at the first Siege of San Sebastian. His poor control contributed to the failure of the assault on 25 July 1813.*

*General George Murray, who abandoned the siege of Taragona, leaving behind Dickson's original siege train to fall into French hands.*

marked lack of enthusiasm, although they may have been in some measure trying to excuse their own corps which came in for some criticism which must now be examined. Perhaps the most general comment concerned the timing of the attack, which inevitably led to a complete absence of supporting fire. The artillery had been firing on the place for some days and knew the exact range of every target to a yard, so there is no doubt that they could have given vital help in daylight. Perhaps even more surprising, even in those days of poor communication, was that the time of the attack had never been communicated to the gunners, who were therefore left in the dark, both literally and metaphorically. Wellington had made it clear that he considered that the attack should be made in daylight, and as Graham knew this it is difficult to lay the blame at any lower level.

The second general criticism was the difficulty of getting the troops out of the parallel more than three abreast, which inevitably caused straggling, although even a closely formed body might have found it difficult to hold together in the dark across the strand. Colin Campbell, who led the light companies, was ever

afterwards of the opinion that had the Royals started in what he called 'one big honest lump', and in daylight where officers could have exercised proper control, the thing would have been possible. Lt-Col Gomm of the 9th Regt, who was at that time the Assistant-Quartermaster-General of the 5th Division, laid the blame squarely on the shoulders of the Royal Engineers and Royal Artillery, writing that:

> 'I am afraid that the success on these occasions (here he is referring to Ciudad Rodrigo and Badajos) owing to the almost miraculous efforts of our troops, has checked the progress of science among our engineers, and perhaps done more; for it seems to have inspired them with contempt for as much of it as they had attained. Our soldiers have on all occasions stood fire so well that our artillery have become as summary in their proceedings as our engineers; and, provided they can make a hole in the wall by which we can claw up, they care not about destroying its defences, or facilitating in any degree what is, under the most favourable circumstances, the most desperate of all military enterprises.'

Gomm was a serious professional soldier who later became a field-marshal, and his opinions deserve respect. Even if we discount the slight but inevitable feeling of superiority often exhibited by front line infantry regarding their supporting arms, there must be something in what he says, particularly as regards the engineers, although their earlier complete lack of any proper supporting corps of Sappers and Miners must explain most of their shortcomings in this sphere. Even Gomm, to give him credit, admits in the same letter from which the earlier quotation was taken, that time was often the essence of the matter, and that 'had we attended to all the niceties of the art in the attack of Ciudad Rodrigo, or of Badajos, it is possible we should have taken neither'.

It is also interesting that Gomm does his best to give the lie to the rumours regarding misconduct on the part of the troops engaged, noting that both Graham and Wellington gave them every credit. The former certainly did, but the views of the latter were a good deal more equivocal. Perhaps the criticisms may be summed up by saying that had the assault been launched in daylight by a solid mass of troops, well and closely supported by ample artillery fire and with their ladder parties well to the fore, the plan might have worked. Having regard to the numerous, and often valid, criticisms voiced, one can also sympathise with the soldiers when they felt that they were being made a sacrifice to unintelligent planning. Their courage was undoubted but they were not fools, and they clearly felt that they were entitled to better things from their commanders.

Perhaps the last word should be given to Lt-Col Burgoyne who held firmly that the key to San Sebastian lay in the drain. His plan would have been to have blown the mine, stormed the hornwork, and there established batteries against the body of the place. This in many ways was a more orthodox solution to the one adopted, and having regard to the difficulties of getting at the breaches in the eastern wall, might well have been a better one. It was however offered with hindsight, since nobody was in a position to predict that the mine was going to be so effective.

The failure of the assault on 25 July virtually marked the end of the first phase of the siege of San Sebastian. Wellington rode over to the place from his headquarters at Lesaca as soon as news of the failure reached him

and decided to suspend active operations until fresh supplies of artillery ammunition could be obtained. In making this decision he must have been influenced by reports that were coming in regarding French movements. Soult, who had been briefly recalled from the Peninsula in the spring of 1813, was back in supreme command, and clearly contemplating a resumption of offensive action against the Allied army. The fact that the French were in their own country caused Wellington to have much greater difficulty in obtaining information regarding their movements than had been the case in Spain, and Soult, a considerable strategist, took care to plant some misleading clues regarding his intentions, which indicated that he would certainly try to relieve San Sebastian.

Even as Wellington rode back to his headquarters he received information that heavy fighting was taking place further south. This might be the main thrust, or it might be a feint, and until he knew the truth he was not prepared to take any chances. Far off on the south coast the incompetent Murray had hastily (and quite unnecessarily) abandoned the siege of Tarragona leaving his siege artillery, the same guns which had breached

Ciudad Rodrigo, to fall into the hands of the French, and Wellington had no desire to see the same thing happen at San Sebastian. That day orders were given to Graham to re-embark his heavy guns, leave a small force to blockade the fortress, and concentrate his main body to defend the line of the Bidassoa. These orders were carried out promptly and efficiently, yet not without one final irritating mishap. The withdrawal of the guns could not of course be concealed from the vigilant Rey, who, wishing to test the strength of the opposition on the isthmus, launched a sortie from the hornwork in the early hours of 27 July. This was a complete success. The Portuguese, most of whom must have been asleep, were completely surprised; nearly two hundred of them were captured and the remainder bolted incontinently to the suburb of St Martin in the final humiliating episode of what had been a generally unsatisfactory operation.

*A sketch by Lt Claudius Shaw, Royal Artillery showing San Sebastian looking almost due north. The approach trenches of the Left Attack can be plainly seen on the isthmus. Mount Olla is to the right.*

# CHAPTER TEN

## The Second Siege of San Sebastian

As it turned out, Soult's attack was directed on Pampeluna, but after some initial successes the French were decisively beaten in a period of fierce fighting usually referred to as the Battle of the Pyrenees. As soon as this was over Wellington decided to resume the siege and by 6 August work had begun on unloading the guns from the storeships at Passages.

During the course of the blockade the position on the heights of San Bartholomeo had been greatly strengthened and was considered to be proof against any attempt on the part of the garrison to break out. Rather strangely the blockading troops suspected that attempts were being made by the French to mine under the cask redoubt, which was held as an advanced post. The distance from the enemy works made this very unlikely, but the engineers decided to carry out some counter-mining, not because they were convinced that the rumour was true but because they wished to give some volunteer miners from the line a certain amount of preliminary practice before being called upon to carry out any more serious mining which might become necessary if the projected attacks on the breaches failed. As was expected, no evidence of French mining was found, but the workmen obtained some useful experience, which had, after all, been the main object of the exercise.

After a good deal of discussion it had been decided as early as 7 August that the original plan for the attack should be adhered to, although the extra guns available meant that things could be done on a larger scale. The breaching guns on the Chofres were being increased with a view to making the existing breach very much

*British forces land on Santa Clara Island where their guns could reach both the Castle and the western side of San Sebastian.*

larger, and it was also decided to try to continue the breach round onto the south face of the works. To do this it would be necessary to establish new batteries in the vicinity of St Bartholomeo, so that the eastern demi-bastion, and the curtain behind it, could be destroyed. This plan was not universally popular, for it did nothing to solve the major problem of having to attack on a limited front and within the limited period allowed by the tide, and although the guns might eventually greatly enlarge the breach there was no certainty that this would prove decisive.

The garrison had worked very hard since the raising of the siege to improve their inner defences and would clearly continue to do so as long as possible. The ruins of a street parallel to the east wall, and about 25yds from it, had been filled in with rubble and built up into a solid, loopholed wall some 15ft high. This wall, which ran from the eastern demi-bastion of the high curtain to a point just north of the Tower of Los Hornas, thus provided an intact inner rampart but little inferior to the outer one. All the rubble from the inside of the breach had been painstakingly removed, so that there was still a vertical drop of at least twenty feet into the town itself. Apart from the all important east front, a good deal had also been done to repair the hornwork and provide some protection against shells, while the whole town had been barricaded so as to give the

*A sergeant of the 9th Regiment, armed with a half-pike, during the assault on San Sebastian.*

---

**Distribution of pieces against San Sebastian 26 August 1813**

### THE LEFT ATTACK

| Battery | Pieces | Target |
|---------|--------|--------|
| No5 | 6 × 18 pounders | St Bartholomeo, to breach the east demi-bastion of the high curtain |
| No6 | 7 × 24 pounders | St Bartholomeo, to breach the east demi-bastion of the high curtain |
| | 2 × 8in howitzers | St Bartholomeo, to breach the east demi-bastion of the high curtain |

### THE RIGHT ATTACK

| Battery | Pieces | Target |
|---------|--------|--------|
| No11 | 2 × 8in howitzers | General harassing fire |
| No13 | 1 × 12in mortar (Spanish) | The rear of the breach, the town and castle |
| | 5 × 10in mortars | The rear of the breach, the town and castle |
| No14 | 6 × 24 pounders | The breaches |
| | 5 × 8in howitzers | To enfilade the curtain wall and land front |
| | 4 × 68 pounder carronades | To enfilade the curtain wall and land front |
| No15 | 15 × 24 pounders | The Breaches |
| No16 | 4 × 10in mortars | The land front and castle |
| No17 | 6 × 10in mortars* | The land front, town and castle |

*not yet landed

garrison the chance to make an orderly fighting withdrawal to Mount Orgullo if the besiegers ever succeeded in entering the place.

The French were therefore confident of their ability to hold the place, and on 15 August, Napoleon's birthday, arranged an elaborate illumination on Mount Orgullo, consisting of the words VIVE L'EMPEREUR (or VIVE NAPOLEON LE GRAND according to Lt-Col Frazer RA, who again commanded the guns of the right attack) in flaming letters six feet high.

Wellington although anxious to resume active operations, was reluctant to do so until extra siege guns which had been promised from England, had arrived. Unfortunately the ships carrying them were delayed by adverse winds, and the first convoy did not reach Passages until 19 August. It had on board a second train of twenty-eight pieces, identical in composition to the one provided for the first siege and was followed almost immediately by a second convoy carrying guns originally intended for garrison use in Cuxhaven. These consisted of fifteen 24 pounder guns, eight 18 pounder guns, four 10in mortars, and a small quantity of ammunition, but did not constitute a siege train as such because the guns were on garrison carriages on traversing platforms, excellent in a fortress but relatively useless for battering one. Nevertheless the extra ammunition was useful, and if necessary the pieces themselves could be used to replace some of the original guns with badly enlarged vents. Perhaps more immediately useful was the company of ninety-two of the newly-formed Sappers and Miners which came on the same convoy. The old hands amongst the Engineers were surprised to find that they wore red coats rather than the traditional blue ones of the Corps.

On 23 August yet another convoy arrived with the balance of the promised train, a further twenty-eight pieces identical in composition to the earlier ones. More important than the guns themselves was the fact that all the ammunition indented for also came in with this convoy. A good deal of time had to be spent on unloading all this equipment, since the small harbour at Passages was already full of shipping, and the Royal Naval presence on the coast was so small that very little help could be provided from that source. Much of the work of rowing and unloading the boats was performed by sturdy Basque women who worked untiringly for a dollar a day and their rations. With their help everything was finally got ashore, and by 24 August the siege had been actively resumed. By this time Wellington had more guns than he knew what to do with, so orders were given that those originally destined

for Cuxhaven should be left intact unless absolutely necessary. Extra gunners were also needed, and these were drawn from the various field brigades with the army, although great care had to be taken not to weaken them unduly. The French had been seriously beaten and it would take some time for Soult to re-organise them, but there was no point in taking unnecessary risks.

Work was at once started on the two new batteries on the isthmus, No5 and No6, and some work was also begun on sinking galleries in front of the advanced works there so as to prevent the enemy from driving mines towards them. All this must have been obvious to the Governor, who, disliking what he saw, launched a sortie at midnight. The besiegers however were ready for them and they were quickly driven back, having achieved no more than the capture of a few prisoners.

By 26 August all the extra work on the batteries had been completed. At 9am a signal was given from No11 battery and every piece of ordnance opened fire simultaneously, thus giving ample notice to the garrison that the siege had been resumed. By that evening much damage had been done by the guns of the right attack, although those of the left had made little apparent impression. As may be seen from the map, these latter guns were well placed as far as line was concerned, since low shots struck the east demi-bastion of the hornwork, while high ones took the eastern wall in enfilade. The main problem was that they were too far away from their principal target to be able to batter with much effect, so orders were given to establish a new No7 battery to the north of the ruined suburb of Santa Catalina, and not more than 300yds from the main defences. It was to be armed with six 24 pounders from No6 battery.

On the same night the boats of the naval squadron, together with 200 of the 9th Regt, seized the island of Santa Clara. This was done primarily to prevent the constant coming and going of small French ships which took in ammunition, stores, and reinforcements, and evacuated wounded. A proper naval blockade would have stopped this, but one frigate and a few smaller craft were quite inadequate for this purpose. As the island was a bare 1000yds from the Castle of La Mota it was decided to establish a battery, No10, on its summit, and work was begun accordingly. This clearly perturbed General Rey, who wrote to Soult to say that:

'The enemy, in establishing a battery on this rock, will cause us heavy losses and his fire will prove murderous. If we are forced to shut ourselves up in the Castle we shall suffer greatly because there is not a single shelter there. All the troops will have to bivouac without being able to cover themselves from fire from land and sea. I can only find cover for a hundred sick.'

Fire continued steadily on 27th and did more damage, although this was noticeably greater on the right than on the left attack. That night the enemy launched another sortie on the isthmus, presumably against the new No7 battery which was by then nearing completion, but the trench guards were so alert that in spite of the darkness of the night the French were quickly repulsed. As No7 battery was finished that night an attempt was made to arm it from No6. The original order had been to move six guns, but Sir Richard Fletcher was so convinced of the value of the enfilade fire from the heights of St Bartholomeo that Wellington finally agreed to leave two guns there. Even so the working party was too small and had too little time left after the repulse of the sortie to move even four guns the whole way in the dark. They were therefore left concealed in the approaches until work could be resumed after darkness the next day.

The British fire continued to be heavy on 28th and the breach was by then very extensive. The tower on the north side still stood, although badly knocked about, and was seen to contain a field gun to flank the breach. The guns on the isthmus had by then made a breach in the eastern demi-bastion of the hornwork, but the bastion and curtain behind it still appeared to be intact. The heavy fire of shells from the howitzers, mortars and carronades, also did great damage and many of the besiegers' guns could not be worked. The shrapnel shells were particularly effective, so much so indeed that the French, who did not possess similar projectiles, attempted to improvise them from common shells filled with bullets. These however did not prove to be effective. Shrapnel shells were always to some extent uncertain weapons because their effect depended on their exploding at precisely the right moment, which in its turn made it vital that the fuzes should be accurately cut and the exact range known. This of course was always easier to achieve in a static position than in mobile operations, and may well have accounted for their exceptional efficiency.

On the night of 28 August three of the guns from No6

*The Left and Right Attack during the second Siege of San Sebastian. The British batteries in the Chofre Sand Hills and on Mount Olla, together with battery No7 succeeded in breaching the walls and tower in the south-east corner of the city. Once the hornwork fell, No9 battery was established there.*

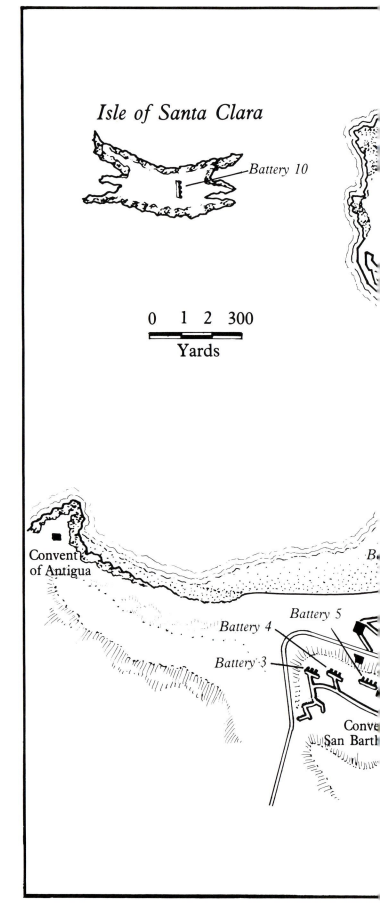

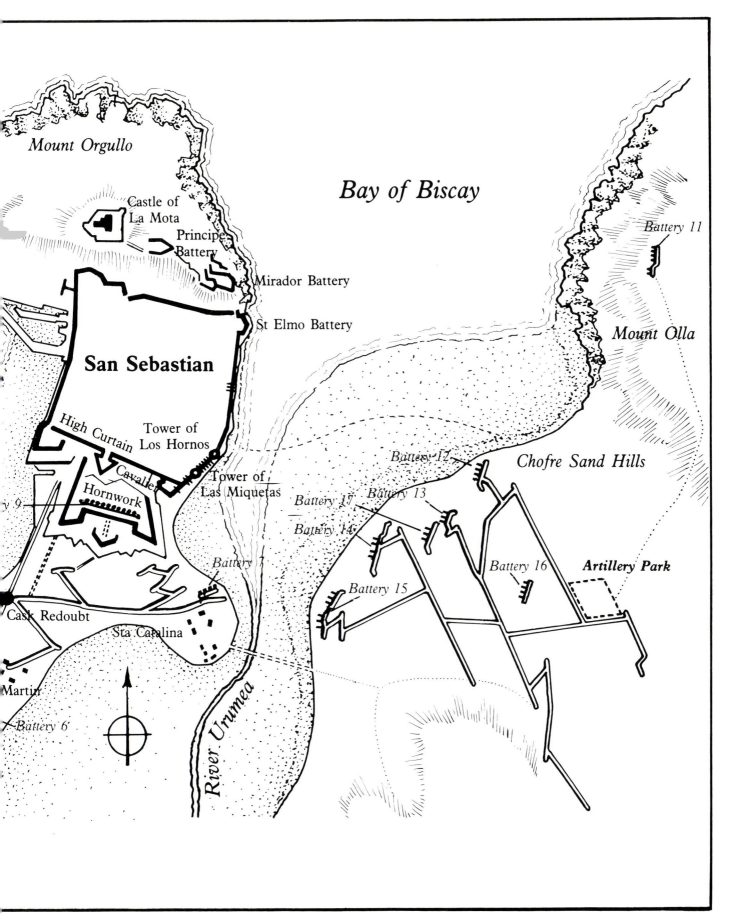

*Mount Orgullo*

*Bay of Biscay*

Castle of
La Mota

Principe
Battery

Mirador Battery

St Elmo Battery

*Battery 11*

*Mount Olla*

**San Sebastian**

High Curtain

Tower of
Los Hornos

Cavalier

Hornwork

*Battery 12*

*Chofre Sand Hills*

Tower of
Las Miquetas

*Battery 17*

*Battery 13*

*Battery 14*

y 9

*Battery 7*

*Battery 16*

**Artillery Park**

Cask Redoubt

Sta Catalina

*Battery 15*

Martin

*Battery 6*

*River Urumea*

battery were finally installed in No7, although the fourth could not be moved because of an accident, presumably damage to the carriage or a wheel. These guns duly opened on the morning of 29th and their extra effect soon became evident. The garrison, always very jealous of fire against their southern front, brought a number of guns to bear on this new battery, and knocked out one of the 24 pounders in it. The 18 pounders in No5 were then turned against the French guns which were soon silenced.

Battery No7 was so close to the works, and the trench guard so small, that there was considerable risk of a French sortie being made at night to spike the guns. Iron plates were therefore chained over the vents at night time to make the operation very difficult to carry out quickly in the dark. At first no similar action was considered necessary for the guns in the right attack, but after several daring Royal Artillery officers had ascertained by personal reconnaissance that the Urumea was easily fordable at low tide, the same precaution was taken there. On 29 August six more 10in mortars were placed in No16 battery. There should have been seven but one dropped out of its slings while being unloaded in the harbour, and the problems of raising almost two tons of iron from a considerable depth of soft mud were so great that it was left there. Work also began in arming No10 battery, on the island of Santa Clara, with five 24 pounders and one 8in howitzer, although in the event only two guns and one howitzer were finally got into position. They were delivered to the island by the Royal Artillery who then handed them over to the Royal Navy who hoisted them up to the top of the hill and manned the battery established there. Some mines having been detected on the scarp of the glacis of the eastern branch of the hornwork, the Chief Engineer requested that some fire might be directed against it in order to shake them loose. As the wall offered some protection to the left flank of the storming parties, care had to be taken not to bring it down, and reduced charges were probably used. The rest of the breaching batteries continued their fire against the eastern face, and by evening both the towers flanking the breach had been destroyed, together with their guns.

On the night of 29 August a false attack was made against the breach in the hope of inducing the garrison to blow their mines. Heavy artillery fire was followed by the advance of a number of small parties with their bugles blowing the Advance, but the garrison were not to be panicked into any premature action.

By mid-morning on 30 August the breach was huge. The new No7 battery had finally ruined the eastern

demi-bastion, whence the breach ran some 300yds further north, resembling in essence a great bank of

*An officer of the 95th Regiment at the time of the Peninsular War. In recognition of its war service, the 95th was removed from numbered line infantry units and became a separate corps, the Rifle Brigade.*

rubble. Although the Engineers pronounced it practicable, much of the wall, which had been well made, had come down in huge slabs which were lying in great jumbles and at all angles, so that many of the more experienced observers, peering through their telescopes from the east bank of the river, must have been somewhat less optimistic. Fire continued all day, that of the mortars, and howitzers being directed at the various castle batteries. Wellington made a careful reconnaissance of the breaches in the afternoon and decided that the assault should take place next day at 11am, at which time the tide would have receded sufficiently to allow it.

Wellington had given much thought to the problem of who should take part in the attack. The obvious people were the 5th Division, but he had not been wholly satisfied with their performance in the earlier assault and was reluctant to expose them to the risk of a second failure. Maj-Gen Oswald and the senior officers of the Division had disliked the plan for the first attack, and when it was virtually re-adopted for the second they made their views very clear to Graham, who himself mistrusted the plan on the grounds, based on hard experience, that at the moment of attack the breach, well retrenched, heavily mined, and with its rear face scarped, might well be the strongest part of the defences.

Wellington's proposal to call for volunteers was understandably not well received by the 5th Division who regarded it as a slur on their reputation. Nevertheless, having come to the conclusion that any failure of morale would be fatal, he called for volunteers from the 1st, 4th, and Light Divisions. The 1st were to find 200 from the Guards and 200 from the Germans; the 4th (which had suffered heavily in the Pyrenees) another 200, and the Light Division 150. When the selection was made on 28 August there was tremendous competition and consequently much disappointment amongst those not selected. Napier, the historian of the war, then a 28 year-old major, later wrote to his wife:

> 'Lord Wellington wrote a letter saying he wanted 100 (sic) men or officers from the Light Division to lead the storm of San Sebastian. Of course I volunteered to command them; I was accepted, and two hours after put in orders to take the command, but lo! when I arrived at the post appointed I found the command had been taken from me and given to Hunt of the 52nd, a colonel by brevet, and nine children dependent on him for bread. I went to Pakenham and Lord Wellington upon the spot with the order in my hand; was told that it was hard, and that I was ill-used, but that it must stand; thus I was cut off from promotion and one of the most splendid opportunities of gaining reputation. Under all these circumstances I wish to quit the Army . . .'

This enthusiasm was confirmed by Rifleman Costello of the 95th, who tells us that soldiers were offering £20 to exchange with their more fortunate comrades who had drawn a place. In the usual course of events few could have afforded this amount of money, but presumably many of them were still flush with their loot from Vittoria. One last task remaining on 30 August was to destroy the sea wall so as to allow the troops to leave their trenches and get onto the beach as quickly as possible and on a wide front. Three mine shafts were thus dug close under it, and each loaded with 540lb of powder. These were exploded at 2am on 31 August and blew down seventy feet of the wall; this gap was then levelled and in order to protect it from fire from the hornwork a traverse of large gabions was hastily erected at the north end.

Command of the assault was given to Lt-Gen Sir James Leith, the permanent commander of the 5th Division, who only rejoined the army on 27 August after spending a year in England to recuperate from a serious wound received at Salamanca. As he was not fully in the picture regarding the situation his predecessor Oswald, deprived of the opportunity to improve on his performance of 25 July, volunteered to remain with him as general adviser, an offer which Leith accepted most gratefully. The new commander made it clear from the start that there was no question of the assault being led by volunteers from the other divisions, and gave that task to Maj-Gen Robinson, whose brigade consisted of 1st/4th, 2nd/47th, and 2nd/59th regiments, the volunteers being placed in support. The latter, sensing that they were not popular, tactfully kept very much to themselves when they arrived on the evening of 30 August, so that no actual clashes occurred.

The French, who naturally realised that an assault was imminent, had done everything in their power to meet it. Most of their guns had been knocked out by the sheer weight of the British artillery fire, but General Rey still had some available. Most of these were in the castle or its adjoining batteries, and were thus too far away to offer support in a close fight, but he also had some concealed much closer to the breaches. The

***Following pages:*** *A view of the second Siege of San Sebastian from No11 battery on Mount Olla, with the batteries in the Chofre Sand Hills to the left.*

numbers vary a little in different accounts, but the Governor himself only mentioned three, two in casemates in the high curtain and one either at, or very near, the east flank of the hornwork.

His main reliance thus had to be on solid retrenchments defended by small arms fire, and reinforced by mines. One of the latter, situated in the middle of the breach, had been charged with twelve hundred-weight of powder, and if it was fired at the right moment Rey might well have calculated on its stopping the assault at once. A mine of that size could kill hundreds of men and demoralise many more, for as we have noted at earlier sieges the British infantry had an understandable dread of weapons of that kind. Although the French had suffered heavily from shell and mortar fire while working on their inner defences, the garrison still consisted of some two thousand five hundred men. The plan was for Robinson's brigade to be formed into two columns, the first to assault the original breach between the towers, and the second to mount the battered, eastern bastion of the high curtain and then the curtain itself. A third column, consisting of volunteers from Bradford's Portuguese, was to ford the river and make straight for the most northerly breach. The assaulting columns were to be preceded by a forlorn hope of the 4th Regt and also by a party of a sergeant and twelve men, the duty of the latter being to locate and cut the fuzes of the mines near the salient angle of the covered way of the eastern demi-bastion of the hornwork. A diversion was also to be created by the boats of the Naval squadron and a few companies of infantry who were to threaten the north side of Mount Orgullo, with a view to pinning down French reserves in the castle. This was to be strictly a demonstration

and no actual landing was to be attempted.

The early morning of 31 August was hot and sultry, with more than a promise of thunder later, and there was so much haze that it was some time before the batteries could see their targets. Once firing became possible the guns opened, upon which the French very sensibly disappeared behind the best cover they could find until it ceased, when they raced out to man their battle positions. Because of this the preliminary bombardment did relatively little damage, although by a supremely fortunate stroke the fuze leading to the great mine in the breach was cut.

It is clear that the assault was regarded as a public spectacle, for soon after daylight the lower slopes of Mount Olla were crowded with spectators, many of whom had taken a day's leave and ridden long distances to be present. The rising layers of rock provided a natural amphitheatre for them and most of them had come with food, drink, cushions and telescopes, in what must have been very much a picnic atmosphere. Many of them were Spaniards from the neighbouring towns, all of whom were wearing their best clothes. General Graham and his staff had taken up their posts in No15 battery, telescopes in hand, and everyone was waiting anxiously for the show to begin at 11am.

They were not kept waiting long, for at 10.55am the forlorn hope of the 4th Regt emerged from the gap blown earlier in the sea wall and made for the central breach. It was led by Lt Francis Maguire, a dashing young Irishman, who to do honour to the occasion was wearing a cocked hat and white feather, a form of head-dress by then largely superseded by the shako. Hundreds of glasses must have been trained on him across the river as he raced on, reached the breach, and

*The breached tower at the eastern end of the curtain wall, made by guns from No7 battery. Though seemingly an easy option it was to prove particularly difficult.*

*The solid French retrenchment constructed in the ruins to the rear of the breaches in the eastern wall caused the British heavy casualties.*

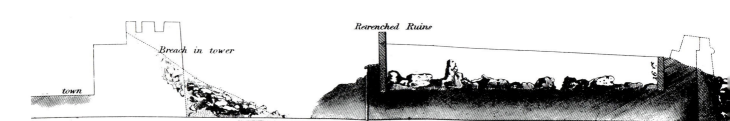

*Lieutenant Francis Maguire, 4th Regiment, who died leading the forlorn hope against the central breach.*

began to scramble up it. Then he was killed, and his men went on over his body, intent only on reaching their objective. By a sad coincidence it was his twenty-first birthday. Just behind the forlorn hope the mine party made for the hornwork, upon which the defenders at once fired the mines and killed them all. Their sacrifice was not completely wasted however for most of the main assaulting party were still too far away to suffer much damage. There was a wide expanse of beach visible and they had been told to keep well clear of the defences until the time came to swing leftwards towards the breaches.

As the more experienced observers had predicted, the main breach turned out to be very difficult indeed. A

fortification on a land face would have consisted of an earth rampart faced with stone, and it was reasonable to assume that enough soil would have come down to afford a reasonable ramp into the stronghold. The eastern rampart was however fundamentally a sea wall, and although much of the front face had been brought down there was no soil anywhere, simply huge jagged masses of stone which were very difficult to climb. There was no question of a concerted rush, only a slow and tedious scramble upwards which ended with the realisation that the rear face was virtually entire and offered a vertical drop of twenty feet or more onto a paved surface strewn with broken carts, old gratings, and similar obstructions. Nor was it possible to scramble down, for the French had painstakingly chipped away all walls, buttresses and anything else offering a foothold on the inner side. All that happened therefore was that as the stormers scrambled up to the summit they were shot down in scores by musketry from a solid, loop-holed wall, less than thirty yards behind the breach. The ruined bastion appeared to offer the best prospects of success, because there the breach was of more usual style. Unfortunately the curtain which rose behind it had been blocked across its whole width by traverses, (solid barriers, often consisting of casks filled with earth) with only a narrow passage through, and as each of these was under musket fire at point blank range from the one further back—one at least in fact was also swept with grape from a light gun—they were impossible to force by frontal attack, especially since the attackers also came under fire from the hornwork to their flank. No progress could therefore be made, and casualties

*Following pages: The breaches at San Sebastian during the assault on 31 August 1813. The fighting was keenly observed from the far bank of the Urumea.*
**Below:** *The breach in the left demi-bastion and the curtain wall permitted access but the vertical drop into the town to the rear, was to present major problems.*

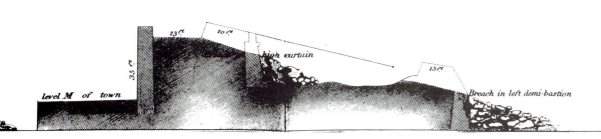

mounted alarmingly.

General Leith, standing in the open on the beach mid-way between the sea wall and the breaches, continued to feed the fight with more troops, although several times the egress from the sea wall was so choked with dead and wounded that he had to order it to be cleared. Very naturally he and his staff, whose rank and role were obvious, attracted heavy fire. Col Fletcher went first, killed instantly by a shot through the neck, and Oswald was carried to the rear with a serious wound soon afterwards. Leith himself was stunned, probably by a blow from a piece of flying debris, but soon recovered and refused to leave his post. Almost miraculously he stayed on his feet practically to the end, when his arm was so badly shattered by a fragment of shell that he was compelled to leave the field. There was no one immediately available to take his place for Robinson was down too, and half his brigade with him.

The volunteers, who had also been fed into the attack on the central breach, had suffered heavily. Being

*The British assault the south-east corner of San Sebastian's defences. Artillery support is evident, as is the explosion of a French mine in the breaches.*

picked men, with the eyes of the army upon them, they made superhuman efforts, and although unsuccessful these did not go unnoticed. A young artillery officer, Lt Claud Shaw, who had watched the attack from the east bank of the river, later recounted with awe to Col Dickson the exploits of one British officer, who:

> 'led a party forward four times along them (ie the ramparts) but his men being killed every time, he went back for more. At the last attempt he was knocked over the wall and fell near forty feet into the ditch. He was conspicuous for having lost his cap, and wearing light facings buttoned back, showing a dark waistcoat.'

This officer, although young Shaw was not to know it, must have been Major Rose of the 20th Regt, whose death is described by Leith-Hay in similar terms. His

Commanding Officer and old friend, Lt-Col Charles Steevens, describes him in his memoirs as a 'fine, high-spirited, brave young Scotsman, the handsomest man in the XX, and of excellent temper'. Rose must have had some presentiment of death because as he and Steevens parted he said 'God bless you, we shall never meet again'.

In spite of all this gallant behaviour it was clear that the attack was making no progress. The survivors were hanging on grimly in the ruins at the foot of the breaches, but could not stay there very much longer, for even if the French could not dislodge them the rising tide certainly would. At this stage the Portuguese, hoping to relieve the pressure, forded the river further north. They advanced rapidly and in good order and suffered a good many casualties from the guns in the northern batteries. One party made for the northern breach, the other for the central one, but once there they too were held up.

General Graham, watching across the river with increasing anxiety now came to a momentous decision, and one in which Dickson must surely have had a hand. Having decided that the high curtain bastion offered the best hope of success, he ordered every available gun to fire at it while the howitzers and mortars deluged the southern end of the town with shells. The guns were accurate, the gunners knew the range (which in most cases was less than 1000yds) and as all the guns (except for those in No7 battery) were firing in enfilade the results were shattering in every sense of the word. The soldiers crouching at the foot of the breaches were briefly startled, but soon realised what was happening and sat back to enjoy the always comforting sound of heavy fire passing safely over their heads but devastating their enemies. Fire was opened at about 12.15 and lasted for some twenty minutes by which time the situation had been transformed. Complete traverses had been swept away, together with their defenders, and after the action whole rows of Frenchmen were found to have been decapitated, apparently by single roundshots, as they fired over the parapet.

When the guns lifted to more distant targets there was a brief pause, then a great surge forward up onto the high curtain. The French troops defending the hornwork, frightened of being cut off from the town, then bolted for the postern while those on the high curtain began to give ground to such an extent that many of the attackers were able to drop down behind the retrenchment covering the eastern wall and take it in reverse. When this happened the Light Division volunteers, relieved of the musketry from the loopholes,

*Lieutenant-Colonel John Steevens, commanding officer of the 20th Regiment who described Major Rose, killed at San Sebastian as 'a brave young Scotsman, the handsomest man in the XX, and of excellent temper'.*

extended northwards until they finally found a place where they could scramble down into the town. Others went on northward to take the smallest breach from the rear, upon which the Portuguese were also able to break into the town.

The French round the *cavalier* bastion continued to resist vigorously until about 1pm when their reserve ammunition suddenly exploded, killing or wounding hundreds of them. The cause of this fortunate accident is not known, for although some of the French attribute it to a British shell, the timing does not support this theory. Gunpowder is, by its nature, notoriously easy to ignite, and a glowing fragment from a cartridge paper, or some similar mishap, may well have been the cause.

Lt-Gen Leith then committed Hay's brigade, his last

reserve. This was almost his final action before he was struck down, and upon the arrival of this fresh surge of attackers the surviving French finally ran down the broad flight of steps from the high curtain into the town and made for the castle, with the British infantry close behind them.

By this time the situation was understandably one of deep confusion. The extensive barricades in the town were still defended but there were insufficient French left to man them all, and it became more and more easy to outflank them. Almost all the general officers were down, and battalion and company commanders were fighting their own little battles in the streets without any sort of overall control or plan. Much of the town was by then on fire as a result of the concentrated shelling, and MajGen Hay, the only surviving officer of his rank, found it quite impossible to make any significant reorganisation with a view to a second-phase attack on the castle. This was inevitable. The troops were scattered round the streets in wild confusion, the town was swathed in smoke from burning buildings, and casualties had been enormous. The 5th Division had lost over half its officers and many battalions were

down to four or five only; Robinson's brigade had lost 57 per cent of its strength, Hay's 35 per cent and the volunteers 30 per cent, and the proportion of dead to wounded was unusually high, due in the main to the grape fire at close range by the guns of the high curtain, which was a worse killer than the musketry.

In these circumstances the fighting had died by 2pm. There were no French left in the town except for dead and wounded and some seven hundred prisoners who were being assembled in the area south of the hornwork, and with the realisation that the battle was over, at least for the moment, a good many of the troops turned their minds to the infinitely more pleasurable prospect of a sack. At this moment a heavy storm, which had been threatening all day, suddenly broke, and under its cover there was a general dispersal to see what could be found.

It is neither necessary, nor possible, to give any coherent account of the disorders which occurred in the town in the two or three days immediately following the capture of the place. Basically they followed the same pattern as those after Badajos, although the situation was made worse by the fact that heavy winds had so fanned the flames that the greater part of the town was burnt to the ground. The British soldiers mainly drank themselves insensible, (although there was some rape and murder), while their wives looted, this also being the main pastime of the Portuguese. The surviving British officers did what they could, but were in so much personal danger from their drunken soldiers that most of them finally abandoned the struggle and left the affair to die of its own accord. Although a good deal of purple prose was later written about it, the statements of officers on the spot suggests that it was largely the work of their usual incorrigibles. There is evidence that the volunteers behaved worst of all, which was probably due to the fact that they were away from their regiments and the influence of officers whom they knew. Many of the worst accusations came from certain official Spanish sources, which stated flatly that Wellington had burnt the town on purpose because of its long commercial associations with France; this, though regrettable, is to some extent understandable in that it came from a proud people who had seen their country fought over and ruined for six years and who only wanted to be left alone.

According to Lt-Col Frazer however, this did not stop the Spanish population from swarming in from miles around to buy looted goods at cut price.

*Major John Werge of the 38th Regiment, one of the many officers and men killed at San Sebastian.*

sle St Clair

On the very day that the British were fighting their way into San Sebastian, Soult made a final desperate effort to redeem his promises to relieve the fortress, but was beaten, mainly by the Spanish army, at the Battle of San Marcial, some miles further east. General Rey, who was in communication with France by sea, heard of this very quickly. He must have realised that his position was hopeless, for he had but thirteen hundred men left, together with four hundred and fifty wounded and almost as many prisoners; he had no bomb-proof shelters in the castle, and only three of its guns could be brought to bear southward, but in spite of this he showed no disposition to surrender. When Wellington returned from the covering army on 1 September he therefore gave orders for the castle to be bombarded and on that and the succeeding two days it was heavily shelled and mortared, doing great damage.

At midday on 3 September firing was stopped and a staff officer sent in with a summons to surrender which General Rey refused, and one cannot but admire him for so doing. He knew that there was no hope of relief and that the best that he and his garrison could expect was to be sent to England as prisoners of war, but presumably felt it his duty to keep as many allied soldiers occupied for as long as possible at whatever the cost in casualties. Amongst these were many of the British prisoners who were kept in the open and not allowed tools with which to dig shelters, Rey's reason

*Massed artillery fire against the hornwork caused the French to flee, opening the way to the town.*

for this being that the British were bombarding his hospital. This information reached Wellington from Lt Jones, the Engineer officer who had been wounded and captured earlier. Graham was greatly perturbed at these losses and suggested an exchange of prisoners but Wellington would have none of it and made it clear, although with regret, that they would have to continue to suffer for a few days longer.

After this, preparations went ahead to pound the castle into ruins and assault it if necessary. It had been difficult to keep many troops in town or to make preparations for a further attack because the place was still burning and houses still coming down, but it was reasonable to expect that the fires would be out very soon. In the meanwhile the north side was held by *picquets* only, with a reserve in the main square, the main body being in the vicinity of the high curtain.

Two new batteries were constructed, No8, for three guns and No9, a very large one, for seventeen guns, the latter being actually on the *terreplein* of the hornwork. No attempt was made by the garrison to hamper the construction of these batteries, and even the guns to arm them were taken across the Urumea fords in broad daylight without any interference. Lt-Col Frazer, who supervised the operation, noted that:

175

'Messieurs the enemy are very civil; though in broad daylight and in the clear view of their batteries, they did not fire a single shot. This was generous enough; had they fired, a confused multitude of six of seven hundred men, and seventy or eighty pairs of bullocks, pulling heavy loads, might have suffered severely.'

One gun was lost in a quicksand, but by the night of 6 September all the remainder were in place and another had also been added to the existing pieces on Santa Clara. At this stage of the siege, according to General Jones, many of the vents were so large that it became necessary to place a piece of stiff paper over the vent with a small hole in it to act as a shoulder for the priming tube, which otherwise tended to slip down into the gun.

A moderate but steady mortar fire was kept up on the castle, during these preparations, and continued until 10am on 8 September when every available gun opened fire simultaneously. There were a total of fifty-six pieces and the fire was so fast and so accurate that only the occasional shot was returned from the castle. As it was only a matter of time before the main magazine was blown up, Rey very sensibly decided to surrender. At about noon therefore a white flag rose slowly up the flagpole, fire was stopped, and the siege was finally over. Reasonable terms were granted in recognition of what had undoubtedly been a gallant defence; the question of the prisoners in the open was discreetly forgotten, although it is of interest to speculate what the reaction of a French commander would have been to a surrendered Spanish governor who had behaved in the same fashion. As it was, the headquarter staff of the garrison became an object of interest; General Rey, although admired for his resolute defence, was generally considered to be a coarse and overbearing man and was not much liked in consequence. According to Col Frazer he was angry about one article in the Capitulation which approved the repatriation to France of the widow and two daughters of a French lieutenant-colonel killed during the siege.

'What!' said he, using an opprobrious and offensive term 'such an article about women in the capitulation of such a garrison and after such a defence.'

It is clear that there was an element in the gallant general of what in modern terms would be classed as male chauvinism; all the same it is difficult not to have some

*The action in the breaches on 31 August 1813. On 8 September the French, anticipating the final assault, hauled down their colours and surrendered.*

sympathy with him, and to feel that one particular article might have been arranged privately.

His Chief-of-Staff, Col Songeon was not much liked either. He was clearly at daggers drawn with his commander and was said to have threatened to shoot him. The commandant of the place on the other hand, Col St Ovary, a veteran of fifty-two years' service, was very much one of the old school and universally popular. He had already served two terms as a prisoner of war in England and efforts were made to allow him to retire to France, but without success. Col Brion, commanding the French artillery, was a plain, sensible kind of man, and well-liked. Having admired the British gunnery, and expressed a wish to see the new battery in the hornwork, his British opposite numbers, with the free-masonry of their kind, at once took him off on a conducted tour.

The British artillery officers also showed a similar interest in the castle and scrambled off up the hill to inspect their handiwork of the previous few days, which was all too evident. The batteries, except for those on the sea side, were all smashed, with their guns dismounted and their carriages wrecked, and the castle itself had been very severely damaged. Even the bakehouse, a natural cavern in the rock, had not escaped entirely for a shell had fallen down the chimney and done considerable damage. The whole area was covered in shallow holes and crevices in the rock, the only cover available to the garrison against the concentrated fire which had been directed upon them, and it was astonishing that they had endured the bombardment for so long.

It is clear now that Major Smith's plan, based on an ancient precedent, was too easily accepted by Wellington and his advisers without enough thought having been given to the changed circumstances. When the Duke of Berwick knocked a technically practicable breach in the eastern wall in 1719 the governor simply surrendered gracefully, (or tamely depending on one's point of view), so that the very grave problems of actually getting an assaulting force to the breach had never had to be solved. Perhaps even more important were the improvements which had been made in siege guns in the previous century, a fact made abundantly clear when we compare the performance of the ancient Portuguese guns at Badajos in 1811 with that of the modern iron ones used the next year. Except to the north, San Sebastian is almost completely dominated by a variety of high ground, from Santa Clara in the west through the heights of Antigua and San Bartholomeo to the Chofre sandhills, and thence to Mount Olla, at ranges varying from six to fifteen hundred yards and although most of these could be disregarded in 1719, they were all now very important in 1813.

Later, when people had had a chance to consider the plan at leisure, there was a fairly general consensus that it was a bad one, and although it is very easy to be wise after the event there would still appear to be much truth in this. Unlike the Duke of Berwick's army, Wellington's troops had to assault over at least two hundred yards of difficult but completely exposed terrain, moving parallel to virtually intact defences, before they could even begin to mount the breach, and they paid a high price accordingly. Wellington, ever in a hurry where sieges were concerned, wanted a quick result, and had the assault of 25 July succeeded by some miracle it would have been hailed as a triumph. As it was, it was proved that even the best troops cannot be expected to enter through impracticable breaches, a fact clearly demonstrated at Badajos in the previous year, and it would have paid him to have thought again. The heights of Bartholomeo remained firmly in his hands throughout and what might be described as orthodox approaches to the hornwork, supported by enfilade fire from the Chofre sandhills, might well have succeeded. It is true that in the first phase only nineteen 24 pounders and six 18 pounders were available, but the effect of some twenty minutes concentrated fire onto the same targets on 31 August made it clear what could have been done. Taken in conjunction with the mine in the drain, an asset which Burgoyne always regretted had not been made proper use of, the hornwork, which was completely without interior defences might well have fallen to an escalade in a matter of days. Such an attack would have had an even better chance of success in the second siege where ample guns were available, and where breaching operations against the east wall could have continued in order to confuse the French as to the actual point of the attack.

It would be ungenerous of any writer on the siege of San Sebastian not to acknowledge the debt that all students of that particular operation owe to Lt-Col Augustus Frazer of the Royal Artillery, to whom various references have already been made. He was an active and highly experienced officer of some twenty years' service who commanded the guns of the right attack throughout the siege, and his almost blow-by-blow account of the final assault on 31 August is invaluable. Battles are confused affairs at best, and it is both unusual and gratifying to find such a precise observer in such a fortunate position. It is not difficult to picture him

*A gunner of the Royal Artillery during the second Siege of San Sebastian. He is holding a hand spike, used for traversing the trail of his cannon.*

in No15 battery, with his watch and notebook on the parapet in front of him and a good glass at his eye, watching keenly and noting events as they occurred, and we must be grateful to him.

Pampeluna finally surrendered on 30 October, after which the British advance northward into France continued. Extensive preparations were made in the early months of 1814 to besiege Bayonne, but Napoleon's abdication, and of course the end of the war, came before it was necessary to put them into effect, so that the siege of San Sebastian turned out to be the last operation of its kind in the campaign. It will thus be seen that all the operations described in this book took place in a period of some twenty-eight months, the main concentration being in 1812 when three major and three minor sieges were undertaken.

If we analyse these strategically, we find that the double siege of Badajos in 1811 was an ill-judged (if understandable) effort to seize a fleeting opportunity without any concept of what such an operation might involve; it thus achieved very little except to give the technical corps some much needed practical experience and the army at large a distaste for the whole business which it never lost. The capture of the frontier fortresses of Ciudad Rodrigo and Badajos in the early months of

1812 was an essential preliminary to Wellington's main incursion into Spain and were thus jointly the most important of all. Burgos was a failure in every respect, for even if it had fallen it is most unlikely that the British Army could have held its ground so far from its bases, so that a retreat would have been inevitable, although conceivably it might have been possible to go into winter quarters in the Salamanca area. The capture of San Sebastian, together with a subsequent fall of Pampeluna, were essential preliminaries to the invasions of the south of France and were thus comparable to those of the fortresses on the Portuguese frontier.

Although Wellington was consistently successful as a field commander, often against considerable odds, it will be clear to the reader that his sieges were not always conducted with the same cool efficiency as his more mobile operations. Many of the reasons for this have been touched on earlier, so that it is not intended here to do much more than summarise them. It is true to say that the British Army of the early 19th century was in no sense geared to undertake military operations of that type. For many years it had been concerned either with remote colonial operations against more or less unsophisticated enemies, or with brief descents upon the coast of Europe in conjunction with the Royal Navy. Neither of these types of activity had any place for the vast and lumbering siege apparatus then essential to reduce any fortified place.

The Royal Engineers consisted of a small body of

officers only, well-trained and professionally competent within their own field but with absolutely no practical experience of the type of siege work which virtually every other European army took for granted. Nor, apart from a small body of military artificers, was there any force of skilled, highly-trained workmen to support them, with the result that they had to rely on infantry working parties with all the accompanying problems of supervision and command of soldiers of another Arm. Quite often too their numbers were so low that they had to borrow infantry officer volunteers as assistant engineers, and although these were brave and did their considerable best they inevitably lacked proper professional training for the task.

The problem of siege artillery was a more local one, for although some would doubt it, it seems certain that suitable guns were usually available in the sense that they were in storeships lying in some convenient harbour. The problem with them, well typified by Dickson's epic move of a train in 1811, was transporting them by land to their final scene of action.

Perhaps the real problem was the essential change in the nature of land warfare which had taken place in the previous twenty years. The traditional mechanics of siege warfare had been evolved in a more leisurely age, when kings and whole courts sometimes moved to the scene of some particularly important one, but these days had gone and warfare had become a very much swifter and more deadly business. The essential constituents, the men, the animals, and the weapons, had themselves changed very little, but improvements in organisation had greatly assisted the speed and flexibility of movement by practically self-contained corps and divisions moving on different axes, although always under the control of a single mind, exercised through the medium of competent staffs.

Everything had speeded up, and this was particularly the case as far as Wellington's Peninsular Army was concerned. It was permanently outnumbered and relied for a successful outcome on good intelligence and good administration, both of which depended to some degree at least on local goodwill. This allowed Wellington to remain concentrated for long periods, move to the right place at the right time, strike suddenly and get away before his opponents, hampered by occupational duties in a bitterly hostile country and chronically short of both

*Wellington in the field in 1813 with his artillery. The Peninsular Campaign changed the art of siege warfare considerably requiring speedy concentration of firepower and the need to achieve rapid victory.*

food and transport, could assemble against him. This system, excellent though it was for mobile operations, made it difficult and dangerous for Wellington to sit down for the sometimes long periods necessary to conduct a siege, and in consequence led to a constant, though never conspicuously successful, search for short cuts which would save time.

Napoleon's orders to his governors of fortresses may perhaps be criticised on purely humanitarian grounds, but on purely military grounds he was right. He of all people knew the value of time, and knew full well that a few days of extra resistance, though it might not save the fortress, could sometimes have incalculable effects on a whole campaign. The older concept of a surrender at discretion when a practicable breach had been made had never been wholly approved by rulers, because it could be too easily used as a cloak to cover either pusillanimity or treachery—so much so indeed that governors often marched their surrendered garrisons out through the breach to demonstrate that it was what it purported to be. Nevertheless as early as 1705, a good hundred years before Napoleon came to the same conclusion, Louis XIV of France had felt constrained to warn his besieged governors that 'It is my intention that you should not surrender until there is a breach in the body of the enceinte, and until you have withstood at least one assault', which clearly gave Napoleon a respectable precedent.

The fact is of course that the practicability of a breach was not so much a question of a negotiable gap in a rampart, as the determination of the garrison to defend it. The breaches at the second siege of Badajos for example were technically 'practicable' by Engineer standards, yet a combination of ingenuity and fierce determination made them probably the strongest points on the perimeter at the time of the assault. It is certain that had not the diversionary attacks succeeded, Badajos would not have fallen to the British on 6 April 1812.

The most successful siege of the series was that of Ciudad Rodrigo in January 1812. It was not in itself a very strong place, but the main breach had been well retrenched and it is probable that it was only the brilliant concept of a second, last minute, breach by which those retrenchments could be turned, that the assault succeeded. Even so there were uncovenanted benefits. Barrie, the Governor, although he seems to have been unduly reviled by his countrymen, was clearly not the most determined of men, and it is interesting to speculate what the result might have been had Phillipon from Badajos, or Dubreton from Burgos, been in command of the place.

# SOURCES and ACKNOWLEDGEMENTS

There are four works, all written by officers who took part in the War, which are essential to the study of British sieges in the Peninsula. The first of these is General Jones's *Journal of Sieges in Spain* in three volumes, first published in 1827, which provides a highly technical account of the various operations, and which is the standard British work on the subject. The author served with the Royal Engineers, and apart from a certain understandable bias in favour of his own corps he is a very fair and very readable authority.

The second is the corresponding French work, *Journal des Sièges dans le Peninsule* by Col Belmas of the French engineers. This appeared ten years after General Jones's book, on which a good deal of it appears to be based, and is a very valuable account from the French point of view. It appeared in four volumes (of which No4 is the one mainly concerned with British sieges) and has never been translated into English.

The *Dickson Papers*, are invaluable for Royal Artillery affairs in general and for siege artillery in particular. Some reference has already been made to the author in the text so that all that we need add here is that he seems to have kept every piece of paper he ever received. His editor wisely included everything, so that amongst highly technical papers on artillery matters one finds the occasional bill for oranges, or fish, or a new waistcoat, which adds a pleasant personal touch to the work.

Lastly there was John Burgoyne, another engineer, who played a major role in the various sieges which he describes. He was clearly an original thinker, and not always disposed to see eye to eye with his superiors. He also eventually became a general and lived to see service in the Crimean War.

There is also a fifth writer of comparable quality, who unfortunately for posterity came late to the Peninsula and thus only served at San Sebastian, of which he has left an invaluable account. This was Col Augustus Frazer to whom reference has already been made in the text.

Apart from despatches, formal histories, and technical works on siege craft and artillery, the remaining books are almost all either by, or at least about, people who actually took part in the operations described. These were mainly infantrymen, whose various accounts show that although sieges started as technical affairs they usually ended up in bloody close-quarter fighting. As usual the writers of the 95th Rifles are well to the fore, but there are many others too whose accounts are well worth reading. As the cavalry played little part in sieges, only one work by a member of that Arm is included. Capt Tomkinson's book is a most valuable and reliable source on the war generally, and which gives us much interesting biographical detail of his friend, hero and erstwhile troop commander, Major Somers-Cocks who died gallantly (as an infantryman) at the ill-fated siege of Burgos.

Chapter 2 would not be complete without some information provided by Maj-Gen Hughes on the puzzling references to the 'drooping' of brass guns contained in it. He refers me to his book *Open Fire* which includes some evidence of post-war tests by the Royal Artillery which tend to prove that the phenomenon was in fact caused chiefly by a combination of badly-worn bores and grossly-undersized projectiles, and that there was no conclusive evidence of 'drooping' in the actual sense of the word. He points out however that Adye's *Bombardier and Pocket Gunner* makes a brief reference to the bores of Portuguese brass guns losing their cylindrical form which suggests at least an element of doubt.

Finally I must also thank General Hughes for much other help. When I was incapacitated by an accident early in 1987 he very kindly agreed to make the preliminary selection of illustrations from Woolwich and I am most grateful both to him and to the staff of The Royal Artillery Institution for all their help.

Military Archive & Research Services would like to thank the many people who supplied illustrations for this book, and in particular Philip Haythornthwaite, the staff of the Royal Engineers Museum, Chatham and last, but not least, the Author.

**Picture credits:**

Apsley House: p128,155
Duke of Cornwall's Light Infantry Museum: p119
Mary Evans Pic Lib: p92,10(B),158
P Haythornthwaite: p21,31,33,44,48,57,64,67,72, 88,104,107,108,112,116,124,140,141,142, 152,154,164,170,173,177
Mansell Collection: p100,182

MARS: p8,10,28,60,70,83,91,109,156
National Army Museum:
p2,22,26,34,36,46,49,51,54,62,69,73,76,78,84,89, 100,101,103,106,110,115,120,122,126,144,148,172, 174,175,180
National Portrait Gallery: p43
Royal Artillery Institution: p16,17,18,19,30,45,83,132
Royal Engineers Museum: p11,13,14

# GLOSSARY

Note: by the early 19th century these terms, many of which are of French origin, tended to be used somewhat less precisely than they had been earlier. This list is mainly based on General Jones's interpretation.

| | |
|---|---|
| **ABATTIS** | a barrier of trees, cut, laid close together, with branches outwards |
| **APPROACHES** | Trenches dug towards a fortress |
| **AUGET** | A wooden trough to hold a saucisson (qv) |
| **BANQUETTE** | A ledge on which soldiers stood to fire over a wall or parapet |
| **EN BARBETTE** | used to describe a gun which fires over a parapet and not through an embrasure |
| **BASTION** | A work with two front faces forming a salient angle, and two flanks, protruding from the curtain wall (qv) so as to allow flanking fire along it |
| **BERM** | a horizontal ledge between two slopes, eg the upper and lower sections of a rampart |
| **BLINDSAP** | A narrow trench, not leading anywhere but used for observation purposes |
| **BOMB-PROOF** | a shelter against shot and shell |
| **BOYAU** | a communication trench |
| **CARCASE** | a type of illuminating shell, fired from a mortar or howitzer |
| **CASEMATE** | a vaulted chamber for guns |
| **CAVALIER** | A work raised on a rampart or bastion to give improved observation and field of fire. Also occasionally constructed by the besiegers for the same purpose |
| **CHEVAL DE FRISE** | a portable barrier equipped with sword blades etc, and used for blocking breaches |
| **COMMUNICATION TRENCH** | a trench linking parallels or offering safe approach for the rear |
| **COUNTER-FORT** | an internal buttress to a curtain wall |
| **COUNTER-GUARD** | an earthwork to protect the base of a curtain wall |
| **COUNTERSCARP** | the vertical face of a ditch on the outer side |
| **COVERED WAY** | a path round the outside of the ditch usually with a banquette and parapet on the outer side. Sometimes used to describe a communication trench |
| **CROWNWORK** | An outwork with a front face consisting of a central salient bastion and two flanking demi-bastions (qv) and thus having in plan some resemblance to a crown |

| | |
|---|---|
| CUNETTE or CUVETTE | A narrow trench dug in the bottom of the ditch and often flooded |
| CURTAIN or CURTAIN WALL | The main wall round a fortress. Often used in a general way in place of a rampart (qv) |
| DEAD GROUND | Ground not visible to an observer because of higher ground intervening |
| DEMI-BASTION | A half bastion used in outworks particularly hornworks (qv) |
| DEMI—LUNE | a term used by the French to describe what the British referred to as a ravelin (qv) |
| EARTHWORKS | see under FIELDWORKS |
| EMBRASURE | A gap in a parapet or battery through which a gun could be fired |
| ENCEINTE | The main perimeter of a fortress |
| ENFILADE | A term usually used as an adjective to describe fire coming from a flank |
| EPAULEMENT | Wings added to batteries and other earthworks to protect the occupants from enfilade fire |
| ESCALADE | Assault on an unbreached wall by means of ladders |
| FASCINE | A tightly-bound bundle of long sticks, used for revetting (qv) |
| FAUSSE-BRAIE | An earth rampart used to protect the base of a curtain wall. Sometimes replaced by the more modern counterguard or tenaille (qv) but still used in the Peninsula. |
| FIELDWORKS | Temporary earthworks, used to strengthen defensive positions in the field |
| FLECHE | A simple earthwork in the shape of a shallow V |
| FLYING SAP | A sap (qv) made as quickly as possible by using a row of gabions (qv) to shelter the workmen |
| FORLORN HOPE | A small party of soldiers, usually under a junior officer, preceding an assault to draw fire and induce the enemy to fire his mines |
| FRAISES | Stout poles set horizontally on a rampart to hinder an assault |
| GABION | A cylindrical wicker basket, about three feet high and two feet in diameter, which was filled with earth to provide rapid cover |
| GLACIS | The open space surrounding a fortress |
| GORGE | The rear of an outwork, usually only protected by palisades and a ditch |
| HORNWORK | An outwork, generally rectangular and having a demi-bastion at each forward angle with a re-entrant angle between them, thus giving a horned effect. There was often also a ravelin in the ditch on the front face. |
| LUNETTE | A small, triangular outwork |
| MINE | a An explosive charge buried in ground over which an attack must pass, b A tunnel dug under the defences and charged with gunpowder |
| MINE CHAMBER | A chamber at the end of the mine gallery into which the powder was packed |

| | |
|---|---|
| **PALISADE** | A fence of stakes used to close the gorge of an outwork or to hinder attackers generally |
| **PARADOS** | The earth bank at the rear of a trench |
| **PARAPET** | An earth or masonry bank at the front of a trench or rampart |
| **RAMPART** | The main defence of a fortress usually consisting of a wide earth bank, revetted on its front face and wide enough for cannon to be mounted on it |
| **RAVELIN** | a triangular outwork, built in the ditch of a fortress so as to protect the curtain<br>See also DEMI-LUNE |
| **REDOUBT** | A small, fully-enclosed outwork |
| **RE-ENTRANT ANGLE** | An angle in a defensive work with the apex facing inwards |
| **RETRENCHMENT** | A defensive work constructed by the besiegers to cut off a breach |
| **REVETTING** | The shoring up of vertical or near-vertical earth banks with timber, turf, fascines (qv) or masonry to prevent their crumbling |
| **SALIENT ANGLE** | An angle in a defensive work with its apex facing forward |
| **SAP** | A narrow trench, designed to make rapid progress forward and usually dug by specially trained workers |
| **SAPPER** | A soldier, trained in siege operations and working under the supervision of engineer officers |
| **SAUCISSON** | A long tube of linen, thin leather, or other suitable material, filled with gunpowder and used as a fuze for firing mines.<br>see also AUGET |
| **SORTIE** | An attack made by the besieged outside their own main defences |
| **STAR FORT** | A small, star-shaped outwork |
| **STORMING PARTY** | A specially selected body of troops to attack a fortress by escalade (qv) or through a breach |
| **TAMBOUR** | A small type of improvised bastion, usually palisaded, and intended to give flanking fire to a stretch of curtain wall |
| **TENAILLE** | An earth bank to protect the base of a curtain wall. See also COUNTER-GUARD and FAUSSE-BRAIE |
| **TERRE PLEIN** | The flat surface of a rampart, usually with a parapet, on which the guns of the place were mounted |
| **TRAVERSE** | A temporary work, usually an earth bank, built to give protection from enfilade fire |
| **WALL-GUN** | A type of large scale musket, usually mounted on a swivel on a rampart, and firing a ball of up to four ounces weight |

# SELECT BIBLIOGRAPHY

| | | | |
|---|---|---|---|
| Aitchison J (Ed Thompson) | An Ensign in the Peninsular War | London | 1981 |
| Anon | A Soldier of the Seventy First | Edinburgh | 1819 |
| Bell G | Rough Notes by an Old Soldier | London | 1867 |
| Belmas J | Journal des Sièges faits ou soutenus par les Français dans le Peninsule de 1807-1814 | Paris | 1839 |
| Blakeney R (Ed Sturgis) | A Boy in the Peninsular War | London | 1899 |
| Blomfield R | Vauban | London | 1938 |
| Boutfleur C | Journal of an Army Surgeon during the Peninsular War | Manchester Privately Printed | 1912 |
| Bruce H A | Life of Sir William Napier | London | 1864 |
| Cooke J H | Memoirs of the Late War | London | 1831 |
| Cooper J | Seven Campaigns | London | 1869 |
| Costello E | Adventures of a Soldier | London | 1852 |
| Donaldson J | Eventful Life of a Soldier | Edinburgh | 1827 |
| Duffy C | Fire and Stone | London | 1975 |
| D'Urban B (Ed Rousseau) | D'Urban's Peninsular Journal | London | 1930 |
| Fletcher I | Craufurd's Light Division | Speldhurst | 1991 |
| | In Hell Before Daylight 2nd ed The Siege & Storming of the fortress of Badajos | Staplehurst | 1994 |
| | Wellington's Regiments | Staplehurst | 1994 |
| Fortescue J | History of the British Army | London | 1910-30 |
| Frazer A (Ed Sabine) | Letters of Colonel Sir Augustus Simon Frazer, written in the Peninsular and Waterloo Campaigns | London | 1859 |
| Gomm W (Ed Carr-Gomm) | Life of Field-Marshal Sir William Gomm | London | 1881 |
| Grattan W (Ed Oman) | Adventures with the Connaught Rangers | London | 1902 |
| Gurwood (Ed) | Wellington Despatches | London | 1837 |
| Hughes B P | British Smoothbore Artillery | London | 1969 |
| Jones J (Ed) | Journal of Sieges in Spain (2nd Edition) | London | 1866 |
| Jourdan J B (Ed Grouchy) | Mémoires Militaires de Jourdan | Paris | ND c 1902 |
| Kincaid J | Adventures in the Rifle Brigade | London | 1929 |
| Larpent F | Private Journal in the Peninsula | London | 1854 |
| Lawrence (Ed Bankes) | Autobiography of Serjeant William Lawrence | London | 1886 |
| Leach J | Rough sketches of the Life of an Old Soldier | London | 1831 |
| Leith-Hay | A Narrative of the Peninsular War | London | 1834 |
| Londonderry, Marquess of | A Narrative of the Peninsular War | London | 1829 |
| Moore-Smith G | Life of John Colborne, Field-Marshal Lord Seaton | London | 1908 |
| Napier G | Life of General Sir George Napier | London | 1884 |
| Napier W | The Peninsular War | London | 1882 |
| Noizet-de-St Paul | Trait Complet de Fortification | Paris | 1818 |
| Oman C | A History of the Peninsular War | London | 1902-30 |
| Oman C | Wellington's Army | London | 1912 |
| Padfield P | Broke and the Shannon | London | 1968 |
| Patterson J | Adventures of Captain John Patterson in the Peninsular War | London | 1837 |

| Ross-Lewin H | With the 32nd in the Peninsula | London | 1904 |
| Robertson D | Journal of Sergeant D. Robinson | London | 1981 |
| Robinson H | Memoirs of Sir Thomas Picton | London | 1836 |
| Sherer M | Recollections of the Peninsula | London | 1825 |
| Simmons G | A British Rifle-Man | London | 1899 |
| Smith H | Autobiography of Sir Harry Smith | London | 1902 |
| Steevens C | Reminiscences of my Military Life | Winchester | 1878 |
| Surtees W | Twenty-five Years in the Rifle Brigade | London | 1833 |
| Tomkinson W | Diary of a Cavalry Officer | London | 1894 |
| Vauban (Ed Rockroth) | A Manual of Siegecraft & Fortification | University of Michigan | 1968 |
| Ward S | Wellington's Headquarters | London | 1957 |
| Warre W | Letters from the Peninsula 1808-1812 | London | 1909 |
| Weller J | Wellington in the Peninsula | London | 1962 |
| Wheeler W (Ed Liddell-Hart) | The Letters of Private Wheeler | London | 1951 |
| Wrottesley G (Ed) | Life and Correspondence of Sir John Fox Burgoyne | London | 1873 |

# INDEX